Aris and Phillips Classical Texts

PLUTARCH

Themistocles

J. L. Marr

Aris & Phillips is an imprint of Oxbow Books

First published in the United Kingdom in 1998. Reprinted 2015 by
OXBOW BOOKS
10 Hythe Bridge Street, Oxford OX1 2EW

and in the United States by
OXBOW BOOKS
908 Darby Road, Havertown, PA 19083

Paperback Edition: ISBN 978-0-85668-677-1

A CIP record for this book is available from the British Library

For a complete list of Aris & Phillips titles, please contact:

UNITED KINGDOM
Oxbow Books
Telephone (01865) 241249
Fax (01865) 794449
Email: oxbow@oxbowbooks.com
www.oxbowbooks.com

UNITED STATES OF AMERICA
Oxbow Books
Telephone (800) 791-9354
Fax (610) 853-9146
Email: queries@casemateacademic.com
www.casemateacademic.com/oxbow

Oxbow Books is part of the Casemate Group

CONTENTS

INTRODUCTION 1

BIBLIOGRAPHY AND ABBREVIATIONS 8

TEXT AND TRANSLATION 11

COMMENTARY 68

INDEX 169

To my mother, Ethel Marr, and in memory of my friend, George Forrest, with everlasting gratitude

Introduction

1. This edition

This edition of Plutarch's *Themistocles* contains a short introduction, a Greek text with facing English translation, and a commentary in the form of explanatory notes headed by a word or words taken from the translation. The introduction, translation, and notes are my own, the text is that of Ziegler (Teubner[4], 1969), with a small number of variant readings which are indicated on p. 7. There have been numerous translations and editions of the *Themistocles*, both in English and in other languages (see Bibliography), but this is the first English language edition which combines an introduction, text, translation, and commentary into a single volume.

The commentary is designed to be of particular use to students of Ancient History and Classical Civilisation, and the emphasis is unashamedly historical (see section 5). In this respect my debt to the comprehensive and scholarly work of Frank Frost (1980) is obvious, and must be fully acknowledged. If, on a number of occasions, I differ from, or take issue with, Frost, that is in fact a testimony to the pervasive influence and overall authority of his work.

The *Themistocles* has been comparatively well served by translators. There is, for example, a readable and reasonably accurate translation by Bernadotte Perrin in the Loeb edition (1948). Most notably, the elegant translation by Ian Scott-Kilvert in a volume in the Penguin Classics series, *Plutarch: The Rise and Fall of Athens* (1960), 77–108, contains many felicitous expressions which can hardly be bettered as translations of the original. My debt to Scott-Kilvert, in particular, is considerable.

In my translation I have attempted to be as literally accurate as possible, consistent with retaining readability. This approach, of course, does not do anything like justice to the richness and variety of Plutarch's prose style, but it does, I think, have two advantages. On the assumption that most readers will be Greekless, or nearly so, I have devoted very little space in the commentary to matters of grammar and syntax. Instead, the translation itself, because it is so literal, will, I hope, serve to indicate to the linguistically interested student exactly how I have construed the Greek. In addition, the Greekless reader can use the translation with some confidence that it does represent what Plutarch actually wrote.

2. Plutarch

Plutarch was born c. A.D.46 into a wealthy, upper class family of Chaeronea, a small town in Boeotia in central Greece. Like his grandfather, Lamprias, and father, Autobulus, he was extremely well educated, first locally, and then for several years as a student at the school of the Platonist Ammonius in Athens (see 32.6 and note).

There Plutarch was a systematic, not to say voracious, reader of a whole range of earlier literature, not just the "classics". This became a habit which stayed with him throughout his life as a philosopher, teacher, and writer. There is no good reason to doubt that he had indeed read all the works of the many scores of authors whose names he cites as his authorities, or from whom he quotes to illustrate his points, in his own substantial body of published works, even though he may not have had a particular source immediately in front of him when he quoted or referred to it. There is an excellent discussion of this question in Frost (1980), 40–59.

In the tradition of such families Plutarch involved himself in public service, and represented his city on embassies abroad. He was made an honorary citizen of Athens (see 32.6 note), and he held a priesthood at Delphi for life from A.D.95. He visited Rome on numerous occasions in both an official and unofficial capacity. There he delivered lectures on philosophy, and, having been given Roman citizenship, became part of a circle of educated members of the imperial administration which included Sosius Senecio, a close friend of the Emperor Trajan. Some late authorities (the Suda, Eusebius) claim that Trajan appointed Plutarch as a consul, and that in his old age he was made governor of Greece by Trajan's successor, Hadrian. Plutarch died during the reign of Hadrian, in c. A.D.120. Detailed accounts of Plutarch's life, circle, and public career can be found in e.g. Barrow (1967), 1–50, and Jones (1971), 3–64.

3. The *Parallel Lives*

The *Lives* were published as a series of twenty-four paired or "parallel" biographies (each pair containing a Greek life, a Roman, and a comparison), written during the last part of Plutarch's life, between the death of Domitian in A.D.96 and c.A.D.120. All but the first pair (Epaminondas / Scipio) survive. Four comparisons (including that for Themistocles / Camillus; see 1.1 note) are now missing. The *Lives* are now normally arranged chronologically, according to the date of the Greek life, though they were not so written (see C.P. Jones, 'Towards a Chronology of Plutarch's Works', *JRS* 56 [1966] 61–74). Thus Themistocles / Camillus comes fourth, after Theseus / Romulus, Lycurgus / Numa, and Solon / Publicola.

Plutarch was not the first to compile biographies of political and military leaders. That had been done some one hundred and fifty years earlier by Cicero's friend, Cornelius Nepos, writing in Latin (see section 7). Furthermore, the sometimes underrated Nepos had written Greek *Lives*, as well as Roman, and had adopted the principle of parallelism. In his *De Viris Illustribus* biographies of famous men were composed and grouped by categories (kings, generals, historians, poets, etc.), and paired (non-Roman with Roman).

Plutarch, however, demonstrated his originality in two ways. He was the first to pair individual lives directly and to make explicit comparisons between them (confining himself to soldiers and statesmen), and, unlike Nepos' brief and factual accounts, he devoted considerable literary effort to the illustration of his subjects' character, *ethos*, and the presentation of them as moral paradigms (see section 5). There is a good discussion of Plutarch and the tradition of literary biography in another volume in this series, by D. Sansone, *Plutarch; Aristeides and Cato* (1989), Introduction, 6–11.

4. The *Lives* and literature

There is, of course, an important literary dimension to the *Lives*, not just in terms of "style", but also in the overall dramatic effect of each work. Plutarch is a distinctive stylist and a fine literary artist, who paid immense attention to the effects, both small scale and overall, which he was deliberately creating as he wrote. This, however, is an aspect of Plutarch's work which can properly be appreciated only by those who can read his Greek with some facility. Most readers of this book will not come into that category. Consequently, it is not an aspect to which I have devoted a great deal of attention in the notes, though I have tried to indicate some of the more obvious literary and dramatic touches, and I have identified and commented on the underlying organisational framework of the *Themistocles*, chapters being grouped into sections to structure the development of the narrative.

In another volume of this series, John Moles' edition of Plutarch's *Cicero* (Moles [1988]), there is a very comprehensive introductory section (1–54), which deals *inter alia* with such typical Plutarchean literary devices as word patterning (12–16). Readers will find much that is valuable for the literary appreciation of any of Plutarch's *Lives* in Moles' *Cicero* Introduction, and I happily refer them to it.

5. The *Lives* and history

It has frequently, and rightly, been pointed out that Plutarch is not, and never regarded himself as, a historian. Chapter 1 of the *Life of Alexander* is an often cited text:– "It is not histories (*historias*) that I am writing but lives (*bious*)...". Plutarch was writing biographies, and his primary focus was on the *character* (*ethos*) of his subjects. Furthermore, his biographies have a *moral purpose*, they illustrate characters which can serve as examples of what should, and should not, be imitated by his readers (and by himself; see *Timoleon* 1.1), and he expected his readers to draw moral lessons from them, as well as reading them for pleasure. Plutarch would have expressed surprise at the notion that anyone should treat his *Lives* as a prime source for the reconstruction of a historical period, or even of a historical career. But that is because *in his day* a large amount of more obviously historical writing was available for such study. For us now most of the authorities available then, and which he himself used in his *Lives*, are lost. We thus have no choice but to make use, for example, of Plutarch's *Life of Themistocles*, however unintended it was for this purpose, if we wish to gain as full and accurate as possible a picture of the historical Themistocles and his times.

Furthermore, there was, perhaps, not such a great gulf between ancient biography and historiography as has sometimes been suggested. For Plutarch, as for most philosophers in antiquity, character revealed itself essentially in *actions* (*praxeis*), in what his subjects publicly did and said (even though these might not have been their best known actions or speeches), and not in their inner complexes and emotions (cf. *Timoleon* 1.1, *Dem.* 11.7). Since his subjects in general, and Themistocles in particular, were highly influential political and military leaders, these "character-indicating" actions and words, as attested by Plutarch, are themselves often of great interest to a historian, even when there is some doubt about their veracity.

Indeed, Plutarch himself did not and could not always maintain a clear distinction between biography and historiography. At *Nicias* 1 he refers to his collected material for that *Life* as "history" (*historia*), albeit "not useless history, but that which contributes to the appreciation of character and temperament". In an important article ("Plutarch's Adaptation of his Source-Material", *JHS* 100 [1980], 127–140, reprinted in Scardigli [1995], 125–154), C.B.R. Pelling has shown (135–39) that Plutarch did not always in practice follow the programmatic theory expounded in *Alex. 1*. There is a great versatility of approach in the *Lives*. The *Caesar*, for example, is not particularly moralistic or personal in approach, but it is historical. The fact is that, as Moles (1988), 33–34, points out, ancient historiography and ancient biography have many similarities, including, often, a shared concern with the accurate recording of things that actually happened.

Thus we should not feel debarred from using the *Lives* for historical purposes, provided that we proceed with due caution. Plutarch is selective; we cannot expect him to tell us everything, or even always the most important things. He highlights and emphasises, or obscures and downplays, often unhistorically, according to his literary or moral purposes (though in the *Themistocles*, at least, he does not seem to invent). He is not meticulous about chronology, which sometimes comes second to dramatic considerations, though he is not completely indifferent to it either (see 2.5 and 27.1–2), and the biographical approach of necessity dictated *some* awareness of chronology. He is sometimes uncritical and naive about the worth of a source (though he is not always uncritical; see 24.6–7, 32.4). Where that source is named we can sometimes take the necessary corrective action; where it is not, we cannot. We have always to be on our guard, and to exercise our own critical faculties, but that does not mean that the historical approach should not be attempted, or cannot be rewarding and worthwhile. In the commentary I hope to demonstrate that it is both.

6. Plutarch's Themistocles

For Plutarch, Themistocles (unlike Aristides) is not a wholly admirable, heroic figure, whose entire life and career could serve as an example of the ideal character in action. Given the nature of the traditions about Themistocles which Plutarch found in his sources, such a picture was not possible, even if he had wanted it. The predominant view of Themistocles, established to a large extent in the literary tradition by Herodotus in book eight of his *Histories* (see e.g. 2.6, 16.2 notes), but which probably went back to the time of his exile, was a hostile one – that

Themistocles was cunning, devious, greedy, unscrupulous and amoral, a political outsider and, ultimately, a traitor. There were certain facts about him which could not be contested even by his bitterest enemies, i.e. his responsibility for building up the Athenian navy in 483/2, for getting Athens and Attica evacuated safely when the Persians invaded in 480, and for the decisive strategic and tactical plans which brought victory at Salamis. Even the hostile tradition could not deny that by these actions Themistocles saved Greece from Persian domination. His character, however, was, according to this tradition, fundamentally flawed, his career was driven by purely self-interested considerations, and his motives and methods were invariably dishonourable ones.

This picture of Themistocles, however, although predominant, and backed by the immense authority of Herodotus, was not universal. There was another, much more favourable, view of him which survived in some of Plutarch's sources, and which went back, probably, to the same period, the time of his exile (see 23.6, 31.5 notes). This view emphasised his intelligence, his foresight, and his good judgement. It can be seen in Thucydides' brief "obituary" of Themistocles (1.138.3), and the more favourable tradition, of Themistocles as a great statesman and loyal Greek, seems to have been the one accepted by the fourth century historian Ephorus, who was, almost certainly, the source of Diodorus' account of Themistocles' career (11.12–19, 27, 39–43, 54–59) – see section 7.

By drawing at different times on these two very different traditions Plutarch was able to create a rich and complex portrait of Themistocles in his *Life* – his Themistocles is thus a far more interesting character than his Aristides or his Cimon. At first we see a (mostly) admirable figure, rising to the top through his ambition, hard work, political nous and popular appeal – then bringing ruin upon himself through his selfishness, greed and arrogance – then employing his intelligence and adaptability to recover his fortunes by securing the favour of the Persian King – and, finally, reasserting his patriotism by a heroic suicide.

This may be, overall, a somewhat unhistorical portrait, but there is no reason to think that Plutarch has *invented* any of the details which have gone into his completed biography. Themistocles was a controversial and attention – attracting figure in his lifetime, and he remained so for many years after his death. Hence there was a large amount of varied material about him, both "historical" and non-historical, accurate and inaccurate, on which Plutarch was able to draw when he came to write this *Life*.

7. Plutarch's sources in the *Themistocles*

Plutarch mentions by name no fewer than twenty eight authors whom, at one time or another, he uses as sources in this *Life*. They are Phanias (1.2, 7.7, 13.5, 27.8, 29.11), Neanthes (1.2, 29.11), Simonides (1.4, 15.4), Stesimbrotus (2.5, 4.5, 24.6–7), Ariston (3.2), Plato (4.4, 32.1), Herodotus (7.6, 17.1, 21.1), Pindar (8.2), Aristotle (10.6), Cleidemus (10.6), Phanodemus (13.1), Acestorides (13.1), Aeschylus (14.1),

Theopompus (19.1, 25.3, 31.3), Aristophanes (19.4), Timocreon (21), Theophrastus (25.1,3), Thucydides (25.2, 27.1), Charon (27.1), Ephorus (27.1), Dinon (27.1), Clitarchus (27.1), Heraclides (27.1), Eratosthenes (27.8), Andocides (32.4), Phylarchus (32.4), Diodorus the topographer (32.5), and Plato the comic poet (32.6). He refers on twenty other occasions to unnamed sources (1.1, 2.6, 2.8, 3.4, 5.1, 6.1, 6.3–4, 6.5, 10.10, 12.1, 13.2, 17.4, 19.1, 19.4, 24.5, 29.9, 29.11, 30.2, 31.6 [twice]). There are also a number of references, direct or indirect, to documentary or monumental source material (5.5, 8.5, 10.4–5, 10.5, 11.1, 15.3, 22.3, 32.4). Of the twenty eight literary sources named, only seven are extant for the passages cited. All the other works are now lost. It is easy to see, therefore, why this *Life* holds such great interest for historians. Although not all the lost works available to, and used by, Plutarch are, strictly speaking, historical, they all would have had some usefulness for anyone seeking to reconstruct as full and accurate as possible a history of Themistocles and his times. Given that, in addition, Themistocles was a supremely significant and controversial historical figure, more so, arguably, than any other Greek whose biography Plutarch wrote, with the exception of Alexander, the justification for taking a primarily historical approach to Plutarch's *Themistocles* is apparent.

It is not just because of the large and varied amount of lost material used in it by Plutarch that his *Themistocles* has a special historical interest. In the case of Themistocles we also have a comparatively large amount of *surviving* historical material, i.e. in the works of the two greatest Greek historians, Herodotus and Thucydides, in Diodorus Siculus, whose *Universal History* was published in, probably, the 30's B.C. (Diodorus' narrative in book eleven is based on the account of the fourth century historian Ephorus), and in the Latin biography of Themistocles by Cornelius Nepos in his *De Viris Illustribus*, written c. 35 B.C. (see Geiger [1985], 84–88). This is a characteristically brief piece of just ten chapters, which was apparently not consulted by Plutarch (though he knew Nepos' work; see e.g. *Lucullus* 43), but whose historical value, despite some inaccuracies, is not negligible. We are thus unusually well equipped, far more so than in the case of e.g. Pericles (see Stadter [1989], Introduction, lii–liii), both to observe Plutarch's techniques of composition at work (noting how at each stage he followed, adapted in various ways, or ignored, existing accounts), and also to mount a comparative historical study – by examining and comparing the various versions which we have we can often reconstruct with some confidence a reasonably accurate picture of Themistocles' controversial life and times.

8. This Text

The text is that of K. Ziegler (Teubner[4], 1969), apart from a small number of divergencies, which are listed below, together with the source of the readings.

This edition			Ziegler	
3.5	ἔτι	S	ἤδη	other MSS
4.1	οὗτος	MSS	οὗτος <τότ’>	Fuhr
4.5	αὖθις	S	καυθεῖσαν αὖθις	Ziegler
5.3	Ἑρμιόνης	other MSS	῾Ερμίονος	S
7.7	παρόντας	S	πολίτας	other MSS
9.5	ἠρία	other MSS	ἡρῷα	S
10.2	διδόντος	MSS	<δια>διδόντος	Reiske
10.4	Ἀθηναίων	MSS	Ἀθηνῶν	Reiske
10.9	πολλοὶ	MSS	πολὺν	Fuhr
12.1	ἄνωθεν	MSS	[ἄνωθεν]	del. Cobet
12.8	Τενεδία	MSS	Τηνία	Reiske
14.1	καὶ	MSS	[καὶ]	del. Coraes
14.1	τραγῳδίᾳ	MSS	[τραγῳδίᾳ]	del. Cobet
14.1	ἦν νεῶν τὸ	other MSS	ἦν ὧν ἦγε	Aeschylus
			(νη-ῶν ἦγε	S)
14.3	τὰς μὲν Ἑλληνικὰς	other MSS	τὰς Ἑλληνικὰς μὲν	S
14.4	Παλληνεὺς	Flacelière	Πελιεὺς	S
16.5	θάλατταν	MSS	[θάλατταν]	del. Blass
18.4	κινδυνεύοντας	S	[κινδυνεύοντας]	del. Blass
19.5	ὅθεν	S	ᾧ	other MSS
21.4	κοβαλικοῖσι	Diehl	κυβαλικοῖσι	Bergk
			(κυμβαλικοῖσι	S)
23.1	Ἀγραυλῆθεν	MSS	Ἀγρυλῆθεν	Cobet
27.2	συνταττομένοις	other MSS	συντεταγμένοις	Ziegler
			(συντεταγμένος	S)
29.9	ἕκαστον	MSS	προς ἕκαστον	Reiske
31.4	κωλύειν	MSS	κολούειν	Blass
32.2	πρεσβυτάτων	MSS	πρεσβυτέρων	Ziegler

The reader is referred to the editions of Ziegler and Flacelière for full reporting of the manuscript evidence, and for a detailed account of the manuscript tradition. The text relies upon the readings of the following three manuscripts almost exclusively:

S = Seitenstettensis 34 (11th or 12th century)
U = Vaticanus Gr. 138 (10th or 11th century)
A = Parisinus 1671 (A.D. 1296).

Bibliography

R.H. Barrow, *Plutarch and his Times* (London, 1967).

A. Blamire, *Plutarch, Life of Cimon* (London, 1989).

A.J. Bowen, *Plutarch, The Malice of Herodotus* (Warminster, 1992).

G. Bowersock, *Cambridge History of Classical Literature* 1 (1985), 665-69 (Plutarch).

W. Burkert, *Greek Religion* (English trans., Oxford, 1985).

A.R. Burn, *Persia and the Greeks* (2nd edition, London, 1984).

W.R. Connor, *Theopompus and Fifth Century Athens* (Washington, 1968).

J.M. Cook, *The Persian Empire* (London, 1983).

M. Crawford and D. Whitehead, *Archaic and Classical Greece* (Cambridge, 1983).

J.K. Davies, *Athenian Propertied Families, 600-300 B.C.* (Oxford, 1971).

R. Develin, *Athenian Officials, 684-321 B.C.* (Cambridge, 1989).

F.J. Frost, *Plutarch's Themistocles: A Historical Commentary* (Princeton, 1980).

J. Geiger, *Cornelius Nepos and Ancient Political Biography* (Stuttgart, 1985).

A.W. Gomme, *A Historical Commentary on Thucydides*, vol. 1 (Oxford, 1945).

W.W. How and J. Wells, *A Commentary on Herodotus*, 2 vols. (Oxford, 1928).

C.P. Jones, *Plutarch and Rome* (Oxford, 1971).

B. Jordan, *The Athenian Navy in the Classical Period* (Berkeley and Los Angeles, 1975).

M. Lang, *The Athenian Agora*, vol. xxv, *Ostraka* (Princeton, 1990).

D. Larmour, "Making Parallels: *Synkrisis* and Plutarch's *Themistocles* and *Camillus*", *Aufstieg und Niedergang der Romischen Welt (=ANRW)* 33.6 (1992), 4155-4200.

R.J. Lenardon, *The Saga of Themistocles* (London, 1978).

D.M. MacDowell, *The Law in Classical Athens* (London, 1978).

R. Meiggs, *The Athenian Empire* (Oxford, 1972).

J.L. Moles, *Plutarch: Lives, Cicero* (Warminster, 1988).

A.J. Podlecki, *The Life of Themistocles* (Montreal and London, 1975).

P.J. Rhodes, *A Commentary on the Aristotelian Athenaion Politeia* (Oxford, 1981).

D.A. Russell, *Plutarch* (London, 1973).

D. Sansone, *Plutarch: Lives, Aristeides and Cato* (Warminster, 1989).

B. Scardigli ed., *Essays on Plutarch's Lives* (Oxford, 1995).

I. Scott-Kilvert, *Plutarch; The Rise and Fall of Athens* (Harmondsworth, 1960).

P. Stadter, *A Commentary on Plutarch's Pericles* (Chapel Hill and London, 1989).

P. Stadter, ed., *Plutarch and the Historical Tradition* (London and New York, 1992).

R. Thomsen, *Eisphora* (Copenhagen, 1964).

R.W. Wallace, *The Areopagus Council, to 307 B.C.* (Baltimore and London, 1985,1989).

A. Wardman, *Plutarch's Lives* (London, 1974).
D. Whitehead, *The Demes of Attica* (Princeton, 1986).

Texts and Editions

C. Sintenis[1], *Plutarchus, Vitae IV* (Leipzig, 1839-46).
C. Sintenis[2], editio minor, *Bibliotheca Teubneriana* (Leipzig, 1852-55).
I. Bekker, *Plutarchus, vitae inter se comparatae* (Leipzig, 1855-57).
H.A. Holden, *Plutarch's Life of Themistocles* (London, 1884).
B. Perrin, *Plutarch's Lives,* vol. 2 (Loeb edition, Cambridge, Mass. and London, 1948).
R. Flacelière, *Plutarque: Vies,* Tome 2 (Budé edition, Paris, 1961).
R. Flacelière, *Plutarque: Vie de Thémistocle* (Paris, 1972).
K. Ziegler, *Plutarchus: Vitae Parallelae,* vol. 1 (Teubner[4] edition, Leipzig, 1969).
C. Carena, M. Manfredini, L. Piccirilli, *Plutarco: Le Vite di Themistocle e di Camillo* (Milan, 1983).

Abbreviations

ATL = B.D. Meritt, H.T. Wade-Gery, M.F. McGregor, *The Athenian Tribute Lists*, 4 vols. (Princeton, 1939-53) .
Fornara = C. Fornara, *Translated Documents of Greece and Rome, 1, Archaic Times to the end of the Peloponnesian War* (Cambridge, 1983) .
FGH = F. Jacoby, *Fragmente der griechischen Historiker* (Berlin, Leiden, 1926-58).
Hill[2] = G.F. Hill, *Sources for Greek History*, new edition by R. Meiggs and A. Andrewes (Oxford, 1951).
IG[2] = *Inscriptiones Graecae*, editio minor (Berlin, 1913-) .
LSJ = H.G. Liddell and R. Scott, *A Greek-English Lexicon*, new edition revised by H.S. Jones (Oxford, 1940).
Malice = Plutarch, *On the Malice of Herodotus, Moralia* 854E-874C.
ML = R. Meiggs and D. Lewis, *A Selection of Greek Historical Inscriptions to the end of the Fifth Century BC.* (Oxford, 1971).
Syll.[3] = H. Dittenberger, *Sylloge Inscriptionum Graecarum* (3rd edition, Leipzig, 1915-24).

References

References to works of Plutarch give the title of the work only, those to other ancient authors use the standard abbreviation as in LSJ. Modern works which appear in the Bibliography are referred to by the Harvard method, i.e. author's name and date of publication, other books and articles are referred to in full.

Plutarch

Themistocles

ΘΕΜΙΣΤΟΚΛΗΣ

1. Θεμιστοκλεῖ δὲ τὰ μὲν ἐκ γένους ἀμαυρότερα πρὸς δόξαν ὑπῆρχε· πατρὸς γὰρ ἦν Νεοκλέους οὐ τῶν ἄγαν ἐπιφανῶν Ἀθήνησι, Φρεαρρίου τῶν δήμων ἐκ τῆς Λεωντίδος φυλῆς, νόθος δὲ πρὸς μητρός, ὡς λέγουσιν·

Ἀβρότονον Θρήισσα γυνὴ γένος· ἀλλὰ τεκέσθαι
τὸν μέγαν Ἕλλησίν φημι Θεμιστοκλέα.

2 Φανίας μέντοι τὴν μητέρα τοῦ Θεμιστοκλέους οὐ Θρᾷτταν, ἀλλὰ Καρίνην, οὐδ' Ἀβρότονον ὄνομα, ἀλλ' Εὐτέρπην ἀναγράφει. Νεάνθης δὲ καὶ πόλιν αὐτῇ τῆς Καρίας Ἁλικαρνασσὸν προστίθησι. 3 διότι καὶ τῶν νόθων εἰς Κυνόσαργες συντελούντων – τοῦτο δ' ἐστὶν ἔξω πυλῶν γυμνάσιον Ἡρακλέους, ἐπεὶ κἀκεῖνος οὐκ ἦν γνήσιος ἐν θεοῖς, ἀλλ' ἐνείχετο νοθείᾳ διὰ τὴν μητέρα θνητὴν οὖσαν – ἔπειθέ τινας ὁ Θεμιστοκλῆς τῶν εὖ γεγονότων νεανίσκων καταβαίνοντας εἰς τὸ Κυνόσαργες ἀλείφεσθαι μετ' αὐτοῦ, καὶ τούτου γενομένου δοκεῖ πανούργως τὸν τῶν νόθων καὶ γνησίων διορισμὸν ἀνελεῖν. 4 ὅτι μέντοι τοῦ Λυκομιδῶν γένους μετεῖχε, δῆλόν ἐστι· τὸ γὰρ Φλυῆσι τελεστήριον, ὅπερ ἦν Λυκομιδῶν κοινόν, ἐμπρησθὲν ὑπὸ τῶν βαρβάρων αὐτὸς ἐπεσκεύασε καὶ γραφαῖς ἐκόσμησεν, ὡς Σιμωνίδης ἱστόρηκεν.

2. Ἔτι δὲ παῖς ὢν ὁμολογεῖται φορᾶς μεστὸς εἶναι, καὶ τῇ μὲν φύσει συνετός, τῇ δὲ προαιρέσει μεγαλοπράγμων καὶ πολιτικός. ἐν γὰρ ταῖς ἀνέσεσι καὶ σχολαῖς ἀπὸ τῶν μαθημάτων γιγνόμενος, οὐκ ἔπαιζεν οὐδ' ἐρρᾳθύμει καθάπερ οἱ πολλοὶ παῖδες, ἀλλ' εὑρίσκετο λόγους τινὰς μελετῶν καὶ συνταττόμενος πρὸς ἑαυτόν. 2 ἦσαν δ' οἱ λόγοι κατηγορία τινὸς ἢ συνηγορία τῶν παίδων. ὅθεν εἰώθει λέγειν πρὸς αὐτὸν ὁ διδάσκαλος ὡς "οὐδὲν ἔσει, παῖ, σὺ μικρόν, ἀλλὰ μέγα πάντως ἀγαθὸν ἢ κακόν". 3 ἐπεὶ καὶ τῶν παιδεύσεων τὰς μὲν ἠθοποιοὺς ἢ πρὸς ἡδονήν τινα καὶ χάριν ἐλευθέριον σπουδαζομένας ὀκνηρῶς καὶ ἀπροθύμως ἐξεμάνθανε, τῶν δ' εἰς σύνεσιν ἢ πρᾶξιν λεγομένων δῆλος ἦν ὑπερερῶν παρ' ἡλικίαν

Themistocles

1. But as for Themistocles, his family circumstances were too humble to endow him with high status from the start. For his father Neocles, who was from the deme Phrearrhioi, and of the tribe Leontis, was not one of the particularly distinguished men at Athens; and through his mother he was illegitimate, so they say:-

"Habrotonon is my name, a Thracian woman by race. But I can state that the child I gave to the Greeks was the great Themistocles."

[2] Phanias, however, writes that the mother of Themistocles was not Thracian but Carian, and called not Habrotonon but Euterpe, while Neanthes even supplies the name of her city in Caria, Halicarnassus [3] For this reason, and because those who were illegitimate used to have their meeting place at Cynosarges (this is an exercise ground outside the city gates, sacred to Heracles, since he too was not a pure-bred member of the society of the gods, but was open to a charge of illegitimacy through his mother being mortal), Themistocles tried to persuade some of the nobly-born youths to go down to Cynosarges and train there together with him; and it is held that, by succeeding in this ploy, he cunningly removed the distinction between the illegitimate and the pure-born Athenians.

[4] However it is clear that he had a connection with the family of the Lycomidae. For when the initiation-shrine of Phlya, which was the property of the Lycomidae, was burned down by the Persians, he restored it at his own expense and had it decorated with paintings, as Simonides has recorded.

2. It is generally agreed that even as a boy he was full of energy, being by nature intelligent, and by choice attracted to a life of action and politics. For in his moments of relaxation and leisure, away from his studies, he did not play or take things easy like the rest of the boys, but was to be found rehearsing or composing speeches all by himself. [2] The speeches would take the form of a prosecution or a defence of one of the other boys. Hence his teacher was accustomed to say to him "You won't turn out to be anything small, my boy, but, whether for good or ill, you will certainly be something great." [3] For he would learn only reluctantly and without enthusiasm those subjects which are character-forming or aim at any pleasant or liberal accomplishment; whereas he manifested a great passion, far beyond his years, for those subjects which are taught with a view to developing intelligence or practical knowledge, since he was someone who put all his

ὡς τῇ φύσει πιστεύων. 4 ὅθεν ὕστερον ἐν ταῖς ἐλευθερίοις καὶ ἀστείαις λεγομέναις διατριβαῖς ὑπὸ τῶν πεπαιδεῦσθαι δοκούντων χλευαζόμενος, ἠναγκάζετο φορτικώτερον ἀμύνεσθαι, λέγων ὅτι λύραν μὲν ἁρμόσασθαι καὶ μεταχειρίσασθαι ψαλτήριον οὐκ ἐπίσταιτο, πόλιν δὲ μικρὰν καὶ ἄδοξον παραλαβὼν ἔνδοξον καὶ μεγάλην ἀπεργάσασθαι. 5 καίτοι Στησίμβροτος Ἀναξαγόρου τε διακοῦσαι τὸν Θεμιστοκλέα φησὶ καὶ περὶ Μέλισσον σπουδάσαι τὸν φυσικόν, οὐκ εὖ τῶν χρόνων ἁπτόμενος· Περικλεῖ γάρ, ὃς πολὺ νεώτερος ἦν Θεμιστοκλέους, Μέλισσος μὲν ἀντεστρατήγει πολιορκοῦντι Σαμίους, Ἀναξαγόρας δὲ συνδιέτριβε. 6 μᾶλλον οὖν ἄν τις προσέχοι τοῖς Μνησιφίλου τὸν Θεμιστοκλέα τοῦ Φρεαρρίου ζηλωτὴν γενέσθαι λέγουσιν, οὔτε ῥήτορος ὄντος οὔτε τῶν φυσικῶν κληθέντων φιλοσόφων, ἀλλὰ τὴν τότε καλουμένην σοφίαν, οὖσαν δὲ δεινότητα πολιτικὴν καὶ δραστήριον σύνεσιν, ἐπιτήδευμα πεποιημένου καὶ διασῴζοντος ὥσπερ αἵρεσιν ἐκ διαδοχῆς ἀπὸ Σόλωνος· ἣν οἱ μετὰ ταῦτα δικανικαῖς μείξαντες τέχναις καὶ μεταγαγόντες ἀπὸ τῶν πράξεων τὴν ἄσκησιν ἐπὶ τοὺς λόγους, σοφισταὶ προσηγορεύθησαν. 7 τούτῳ μὲν οὖν ἤδη πολιτευόμενος ἐπλησίαζεν. ἐν δὲ ταῖς πρώταις τῆς νεότητος ὁρμαῖς ἀνώμαλος ἦν καὶ ἀστάθμητος, ἅτε τῇ φύσει καθ' αὑτὴν χρώμενος, ἄνευ λόγου καὶ παιδείας ἐπ' ἀμφότερα μεγάλας ποιουμένῃ μεταβολὰς τῶν ἐπιτηδευμάτων, καὶ πολλάκις ἐξισταμένῃ πρὸς τὸ χεῖρον, ὡς ὕστερον αὐτὸς ὡμολόγει, καὶ τοὺς τραχυτάτους πώλους ἀρίστους ἵππους γίγνεσθαι φάσκων, ὅταν ἧς προσήκει τύχωσι παιδείας καὶ καταρτύσεως. 8 ἃ δὲ τούτων ἐξαρτῶσιν ἔνιοι διηγήματα πλάττοντες, ἀποκήρυξιν μὲν ὑπὸ τοῦ πατρὸς αὐτοῦ, θάνατον δὲ τῆς μητρὸς ἑκούσιον ἐπὶ τῇ τοῦ παιδὸς ἀτιμίᾳ περιλύπου γενομένης, δοκεῖ κατεψεῦσθαι, καὶ τοὐναντίον εἰσὶν οἱ λέγοντες, ὅτι τοῦ τὰ κοινὰ πράττειν ἀποτρέπων αὐτὸν ὁ πατὴρ ἐπεδείκνυε πρὸς τῇ θαλάττῃ τὰς παλαιὰς τριήρεις ἐρριμμένας καὶ παρορωμένας, ὡς δὴ καὶ πρὸς τοὺς δημαγωγούς, ὅταν ἄχρηστοι γένωνται, τῶν πολλῶν ὁμοίως ἐχόντων.

3. Ταχὺ μέντοι καὶ νεανικῶς ἔοικεν ἅψασθαι τοῦ Θεμιστοκλέους τὰ πολιτικὰ πράγματα καὶ σφόδρα ἡ πρὸς δόξαν ὁρμὴ κρατῆσαι. δι' ἣν εὐθὺς ἐξ ἀρχῆς τοῦ πρωτεύειν

confidence in his natural abilities. [4] Thus it was that, later on in his life, when he was mocked at so-called liberal and refined gatherings by those who regarded themselves as cultured, he was forced to defend himself rather brusquely, saying that he did not know how to tune a lyre or play a harp, but he did know how to take in hand a small and insignificant city and make it famous and mighty. [5] Stesimbrotus says that Themistocles was a pupil of Anaxagoras and studied under Melissus the physicist. However, he is not adhering to correct chronology. For Pericles was much younger than Themistocles, and yet Melissus was the commander opposing Pericles at the siege of Samos, and Anaxagoras was a close friend of Pericles. [6] So one should side rather with those who say that Themistocles was a disciple of Mnesiphilus the Phrearrhian, a man who was neither a rhetorician nor one of the so-called "physical" philosophers, but a professor of what was at that time called *sophia* (wisdom), but which was really just political dexterity combined with practical intelligence. Mnesiphilus preserved this as though it were a distinctive philosophy with a continuous tradition going back to Solon. His successors blended this with forensic skills and transferred its application from the world of action to that of language, acquiring the name "sophists". [7] Anyway, this was the man to whom Themistocles attached himself at the time when he was starting his political career.

However, in his first ventures as a young man he was inconsistent and unstable, since he followed his natural instincts alone, and these, when not directed by reason and training, cause one to veer wildly from one extreme course of action to another, and they often change for the worse. He himself admitted this in later life, when he remarked that even the wildest colts make excellent horses, always provided that they are properly trained and disciplined.

[8] But the stories which some inventive writers attach to this period of his life, involving a public disinheritance by his father and the suicide of his mother out of grief at her son's dishonour, are in my opinion untrue. They are contradicted by those who say that his father was concerned to deter him from a political career, and pointed out to him the old triremes lying abandoned and neglected on the sea-shore, to indicate that the people treat their politicians in the same way when they lose their usefulness.

3. Despite this it does not seem to have been long before Themistocles felt the pull of public affairs and was, while still a young man, completely overcome by the urge to achieve fame. So, right from the beginning, in his

ἐφιέμενος, ἰταμῶς ὑφίστατο τὰς πρὸς τοὺς δυναμένους ἐν τῇ πόλει καὶ πρωτεύοντας ἀπεχθείας, μάλιστα δ' Ἀριστείδην τὸν Λυσιμάχου, τὴν ἐναντίαν αἰεὶ πορευόμενον αὐτῷ. 2 καίτοι δοκεῖ παντάπασιν ἡ πρὸς τοῦτον ἔχθρα μειρακιώδη λαβεῖν ἀρχήν· ἠράσθησαν γὰρ ἀμφότεροι τοῦ καλοῦ Στησίλεω, Κείου τὸ γένος ὄντος, ὡς Ἀρίστων ὁ φιλόσοφος ἱστόρηκεν. ἐκ δὲ τούτου διετέλουν καὶ περὶ τὰ δημόσια στασιάζοντες. 3 οὐ μὴν ἀλλ' ἡ τῶν βίων καὶ τῶν τρόπων ἀνομοιότης ἔοικεν αὐξῆσαι τὴν διαφοράν. πρᾶος γὰρ ὢν φύσει καὶ καλοκἀγαθικὸς τὸν τρόπον ὁ Ἀριστείδης, καὶ πολιτευόμενος οὐ πρὸς χάριν οὐδὲ πρὸς δόξαν, ἀλλ' ἀπὸ τοῦ βελτίστου μετ' ἀσφαλείας καὶ δικαιοσύνης, ἠναγκάζετο τῷ Θεμιστοκλεῖ τὸν δῆμον ἐπὶ πολλὰ κινοῦντι καὶ μεγάλας ἐπιφέροντι καινοτομίας ἐναντιοῦσθαι πολλάκις, ἐνιστάμενος αὐτῷ πρὸς τὴν αὔξησιν.

4 λέγεται γὰρ οὕτω παράφορος πρὸς δόξαν εἶναι καὶ πράξεων μεγάλων ὑπὸ φιλοτιμίας ἐραστής, ὥστε νέος ὢν ἔτι, τῆς ἐν Μαραθῶνι μάχης πρὸς τοὺς βαρβάρους γενομένης καὶ τῆς Μιλτιάδου στρατηγίας διαβοηθείσης, σύννους ὁρᾶσθαι τὰ πολλὰ πρὸς ἑαυτῷ καὶ τὰς νύκτας ἀγρυπνεῖν καὶ τοὺς πότους παραιτεῖσθαι τοὺς συνήθεις, καὶ λέγειν πρὸς τοὺς ἐρωτῶντας καὶ θαυμάζοντας τὴν περὶ τὸν βίον μεταβολήν, ὡς καθεύδειν αὐτὸν οὐκ ἐῴη τὸ Μιλτιάδου τρόπαιον. 5 οἱ μὲν γὰρ ἄλλοι πέρας ᾤοντο τοῦ πολέμου τὴν ἐν Μαραθῶνι τῶν βαρβάρων ἧτταν εἶναι, Θεμιστοκλῆς δ' ἀρχὴν μειζόνων ἀγώνων, ἐφ' οὓς ἑαυτὸν ὑπὲρ τῆς ὅλης Ἑλλάδος ἤλειφε καὶ τὴν πόλιν ἤσκει, πόρρωθεν ἔτι προσδοκῶν τὸ μέλλον.

4. Καὶ πρῶτον μὲν τὴν Λαυρεωτικὴν πρόσοδον ἀπὸ τῶν ἀργυρείων μετάλλων ἔθος ἐχόντων Ἀθηναίων διανέμεσθαι, μόνος εἰπεῖν ἐτόλμησε παρελθὼν εἰς τὸν δῆμον, ὡς χρὴ τὴν διανομὴν ἐάσαντας ἐκ τῶν χρημάτων τούτων κατασκευάσασθαι τριήρεις ἐπὶ τὸν πρὸς Αἰγινήτας πόλεμον. ἤκμαζε γὰρ οὗτος ἐν τῇ Ἑλλάδι μάλιστα, καὶ κατεῖχον οἱ νησιῶται πλήθει νεῶν τὴν θάλατταν. 2 ᾗ καὶ ῥᾷον ὁ Θεμιστοκλῆς συνέπεισεν, οὐ Δαρεῖον οὐδὲ Πέρσας – μακρὰν γὰρ ἦσαν οὗτοι καὶ δέος οὐ

desire to hold the leading position, he boldly took on the enmity of the powerful elite who exercised leadership in the city, especially that of Aristides, son of Lysimachus, who always took the opposite course to him. [2] And yet there is a view that his hostility towards this man had, in its entirety, a juvenile origin. They were both lovers of the beautiful Stesileos, a native of Ceos, according to the account of Ariston the philosopher. Starting from this they continued as bitter rivals in public affairs too. [3] Nevertheless, the dissimilarity of their lives and characters is likely to have increased their mutual hostility. For Aristides was gentle by nature and gentlemanly in character, and he engaged in politics, not to win personal popularity or glory, but to secure what was best for Athens as long as it was consistent with stability and justice. And so, since Themistocles attempted to incite the people to take many radical decisions and tried to introduce major political reforms, Aristides was compelled to oppose him often, and to take a firm stand against the growth of his influence.

[4] Indeed it is said that Themistocles was so carried away by his desire for fame, and had such a passionate ambition to perform great deeds that, though he was still a young man when the battle of Marathon was fought against the barbarians and the generalship of Miltiades received praise from all and sundry, it was observed that he remained wrapped up in his own thoughts and to a great extent kept to himself; and that he lay awake at night, and turned down invitations to his usual drinking parties, and said to those who, in their surprise, queried his change of lifestyle that the triumph of Miltiades would not allow him to sleep. [5] Now the rest of the Athenians thought that the defeat of the barbarians at Marathon marked the end of the war, but Themistocles regarded it as merely the prelude to greater contests, for which he kept himself oiled as an athlete, ready to compete on behalf of the whole of Greece, and, anticipating the threat to come while it was still far off, he put his city into training for it.

4. In the first place, at a time when the customary practice of the Athenians was to distribute among themselves the revenues derived from the silver mines at Laureum, he was the only man brave enough to come before the assembly and propose that they ought to forego the distribution and build triremes from this money for the war against the Aeginetans. This war was at its height, the fiercest conflict in Greece, and it was the islanders who, owing to the number of their ships, controlled the sea. [2] Because of this Themistocles won the day all the more easily, since he did not try to scare them with Darius or the Persians (for they were a long way away and did not

πάνυ βέβαιον ὡς ἀφιξόμενοι παρεῖχον – ἐπισείων, ἀλλὰ τῇ πρὸς Αἰγινήτας ὀργῇ καὶ φιλονικίᾳ τῶν πολιτῶν ἀποχρησάμενος εὐκαίρως ἐπὶ τὴν παρασκευήν. 3 ἑκατὸν γὰρ ἀπὸ τῶν χρημάτων ἐκείνων ἐποιήθησαν τριήρεις, αἷς καὶ πρὸς Ξέρξην ἐναυμάχησαν.

4 Ἐκ δὲ τούτου κατὰ μικρὸν ὑπάγων καὶ καταβιβάζων τὴν πόλιν πρὸς τὴν θάλατταν, ὡς τὰ πεζὰ μὲν οὐδὲ τοῖς ὁμόροις ἀξιομάχους ὄντας, τῇ δ' ἀπὸ τῶν νεῶν ἀλκῇ καὶ τοὺς βαρβάρους ἀμύνασθαι καὶ τῆς Ἑλλάδος ἄρχειν δυναμένους, ἀντὶ μονίμων ὁπλιτῶν, ὥς φησιν ὁ Πλάτων, ναυβάτας καὶ θαλασσίους ἐποίησε, καὶ διαβολὴν καθ' ἑαυτοῦ παρέσχεν, ὡς ἄρα Θεμιστοκλῆς τὸ δόρυ καὶ τὴν ἀσπίδα τῶν πολιτῶν παρελόμενος εἰς ὑπηρέσιον καὶ κώπην συνέστειλε τὸν Ἀθηναίων δῆμον. 5 ἔπραξε δὲ ταῦτα Μιλτιάδου κρατήσας ἀντιλέγοντος, ὡς ἱστορεῖ Στησίμβροτος. εἰ μὲν δὴ τὴν ἀκρίβειαν καὶ τὸ καθαρὸν τοῦ πολιτεύματος ἔβλαψεν ἢ μὴ ταῦτα πράξας, ἔστω φιλοσοφώτερον ἐπισκοπεῖν· ὅτι δ' ἡ τότε σωτηρία τοῖς Ἕλλησιν ἐκ τῆς θαλάττης ὑπῆρξε καὶ τὴν Ἀθηναίων πόλιν αὖθις ἀνέστησαν αἱ τριήρεις ἐκεῖναι, τά τ' ἄλλα καὶ Ξέρξης αὐτὸς ἐμαρτύρησε. 6 τῆς γὰρ πεζικῆς δυνάμεως ἀθραύστου διαμενούσης, ἔφυγε μετὰ τὴν τῶν νεῶν ἧτταν ὡς οὐκ ὢν ἀξιόμαχος, καὶ Μαρδόνιον ἐμποδὼν εἶναι τοῖς Ἕλλησι τῆς διώξεως μᾶλλον ἢ δουλωσόμενον αὐτοὺς ὡς ἐμοὶ δοκεῖ κατέλιπεν.

5. Σύντονον δ' αὐτὸν γεγονέναι χρηματιστὴν οἱ μέν τινές φασι δι' ἐλευθεριότητα· καὶ γὰρ φιλοθύτην ὄντα καὶ λαμπρὸν ἐν ταῖς περὶ τοὺς ξένους δαπάναις, ἀφθόνου δεῖσθαι χορηγίας· οἱ δὲ τοὐναντίον γλισχρότητα πολλὴν καὶ μικρολογίαν κατηγοροῦσιν, ὡς καὶ τὰ πεμπόμενα τῶν ἐδωδίμων πωλοῦντος. 2 ἐπεὶ δὲ Διφιλίδης ὁ ἱπποτρόφος αἰτηθεὶς ὑπ' αὐτοῦ πῶλον οὐκ ἔδωκεν, ἠπείλησε τὴν οἰκίαν αὐτοῦ ταχὺ ποιήσειν δούρειον ἵππον, αἰνιξάμενος ἐγκλήματα συγγενικὰ καὶ δίκας τῷ ἀνθρώπῳ πρὸς οἰκείους τινὰς ταράξειν.

3 Τῇ δὲ φιλοτιμίᾳ πάντας ὑπερέβαλεν, ὥστ' ἔτι μὲν ὢν νέος καὶ ἀφανὴς Ἐπικλέα τὸν ἐξ Ἑρμιόνης κιθαριστὴν σπουδαζόμενον ὑπὸ τῶν Ἀθηναίων ἐκλιπαρῆσαι μελετᾶν παρ' αὐτῷ, φιλοτιμούμενος πολλοὺς τὴν οἰκίαν ζητεῖν καὶ φοιτᾶν

inspire any very serious fear that they were about to arrive), but made timely use of the resentment and jealousy the citizens felt towards the Aeginetans in order to acquire his fleet. [3] Thus one hundred triremes were built with that money, and it was with these that they fought in fact against Xerxes.

[4] After this, by gradually luring the city on and directing its course towards the sea, arguing that with their infantry they were no match even for their nearest neighbours, but with the power they would derive from their ships they could both repel the barbarians and be rulers of all Greece, he turned the Athenians into mariners and seafarers instead of (in Plato's words) "steadfast hoplites". And he brought down upon himself criticism to the effect that "Themistocles robbed his fellow citizens of the spear and the shield and reduced the Athenian people to the use of a rower's cushion and an oar." [5] Moreover, in achieving this, he had to overcome opposition in the assembly from Miltiades, as Stesimbrotus records.

Now whether or not by doing this he damaged the integrity and purity of the citizen body is a question better left to the philosophers to consider. But that the Greeks owed their salvation in the crisis of that time to the sea, and that it was those triremes which established anew the city of Athens are facts, proved more than anything by the actions of Xerxes himself. [6] Although his land forces remained unbroken, he took to flight after the defeat of his ships, in the belief that he was now not a match for the Greeks, and, in my opinion, he left Mardonius behind to serve as an obstacle in the way of their pursuit of him, rather than in the hope of subjugating them.

5. As for his reputation for being a keen money-maker, some say that it was a consequence of his generosity; since he was fond of entertaining, and lavished expenditure on his guests in splendid style, he needed a considerable fortune. Others, on the contrary, accuse him of great stinginess and meanness, alleging that he used to sell even the victuals that people sent to him. [2] When Diphilides the horse-breeder refused to give him a colt he had asked for, he threatened that he would quickly make a wooden horse out of his home, hinting by this that he would provoke complaints against him within his own family, and stir up troublesome lawsuits between him and other members of his household.

[3] He definitely outdid everyone in the desire to be famous; for example, while he was still young and obscure, he prevailed upon Epicles, the lyre-player of Hermione who was much sought after by the Athenians, to practise at his home, because of his ambition that many people should look for his

πρὸς αὐτόν. 4 εἰς δ' Ὀλυμπίαν ἐλθὼν καὶ διαμιλλώμενος τῷ Κίμωνι περὶ δεῖπνα καὶ σκηνὰς καὶ τὴν ἄλλην λαμπρότητα καὶ παρασκευήν, οὐκ ἤρεσκε τοῖς Ἕλλησιν. ἐκείνῳ μὲν γὰρ ὄντι νέῳ καὶ ἀπ' οἰκίας μεγάλης ᾤοντο δεῖν τὰ τοιαῦτα συγχωρεῖν· ὁ δὲ μήπω γνώριμος γεγονώς, ἀλλὰ δοκῶν ἐξ οὐχ ὑπαρχόντων καὶ παρ' ἀξίαν ἐπαίρεσθαι, προσωφλίσκανεν ἀλαζονείαν. 5 ἐνίκησε δὲ καὶ χορηγῶν τραγῳδοῖς, μεγάλην ἤδη τότε σπουδὴν καὶ φιλοτιμίαν τοῦ ἀγῶνος ἔχοντος, καὶ πίνακα τῆς νίκης ἀνέθηκε τοιαύτην ἐπιγραφὴν ἔχοντα· "Θεμιστοκλῆς Φρεάρριος ἐχορήγει, Φρύνιχος ἐδίδασκεν, Ἀδείμαντος ἦρχεν."

6 οὐ μὴν ἀλλὰ τοῖς πολλοῖς ἐνήρμοττε, τοῦτο μὲν ἑκάστου τῶν πολιτῶν τοὔνομα λέγων ἀπὸ στόματος, τοῦτο δὲ κριτὴνἀσφαλῆ περὶ τὰ συμβόλαια παρέχων ἑαυτόν, ὥς που καὶ πρὸς Σιμωνίδην τὸν Κεῖον εἰπεῖν, αἰτούμενόν τι τῶν οὐ μετρίων παρ' αὐτοῦ στρατηγοῦντος, ὡς οὔτ' ἐκεῖνος ἂν γένοιτο ποιητὴς ἀγαθὸς ᾄδων παρὰ μέλος, οὔτ' αὐτὸς ἀστεῖος ἄρχων παρὰ νόμον χαριζόμενος. 7 πάλιν δέ ποτε τὸν Σιμωνίδην ἐπισκώπτων ἔλεγε νοῦν οὐκ ἔχειν, Κορινθίους μὲν λοιδοροῦντα μεγάλην οἰκοῦντας πόλιν, αὑτοῦ δὲ ποιούμενον εἰκόνας οὕτως ὄντος αἰσχροῦ τὴν ὄψιν. αὐξόμενος δὲ καὶ τοῖς πολλοῖς ἀρέσκων, τέλος κατεστασίασε καὶ μετέστησεν ἐξοστρακισθέντα τὸν Ἀριστείδην.

6. Ἤδη δὲ τοῦ Μήδου καταβαίνοντος ἐπὶ τὴν Ἑλλάδα, καὶ τῶν Ἀθηναίων βουλευομένων περὶ στρατηγοῦ, τοὺς μὲν ἄλλους ἑκόντας ἐκστῆναι τῆς στρατηγίας λέγουσιν ἐκπεπληγμένους τὸν κίνδυνον, Ἐπικύδην δὲ τὸν Εὐφημίδου, δημαγωγὸν ὄντα δεινὸν μὲν εἰπεῖν, μαλακὸν δὲ τῇ ψυχῇ καὶ χρημάτων ἥττονα, τῆς ἀρχῆς ἐφίεσθαι καὶ κρατήσειν ἐπίδοξον εἶναι τῇ χειροτονίᾳ. 2 τὸν οὖν Θεμιστοκλέα, δείσαντα μὴ τὰ πράγματα διαφθαρείη παντάπασι τῆς ἡγεμονίας εἰς ἐκεῖνον ἐμπεσούσης, χρήμασι τὴν φιλοτιμίαν ἐξωνήσασθαι παρὰ τοῦ Ἐπικύδους. 3 ἐπαινεῖται δ' αὐτοῦ καὶ τὸ περὶ τὸν δίγλωσσον ἔργον ἐν τοῖς πεμφθεῖσιν ὑπὸ βασιλέως ἐπὶ γῆς καὶ ὕδατος αἴτησιν. 4 ἑρμηνέα γὰρ ὄντα συλλαβὼν διὰ ψηφίσματος ἀπέκτεινεν, ὅτι φωνὴν Ἑλληνίδα βαρβάροις προστάγμασιν

house and come to visit him regularly. [4] Again, on a visit to Olympia he upset the Greeks by trying to rival Cimon in his banquets and fine tents and magnificent furnishings and the like. For people thought that such extravagance was allowable in Cimon, a young man who belonged to a great house, whereas Themistocles had not yet become a person of note, and was thought to be exalting himself beyond his due, without having the background for it, and so he brought upon himself the charge of pretentiousness. [5] Again, when he won a victory as a choregus in the contest for tragedies, which even at that date involved much ambitious rivalry, he set up a votive plaque commemorating his victory, which bore this inscription: "Themistocles of Phrearrhioi was the choregus, Phrynichus was the playwright, Adeimantus was archon".

[6] Despite this trait he enjoyed a good rapport with the common people, partly because he could cite the name of every citizen from memory, partly because he showed himself to be a reliable judge in cases involving contractual disputes. For example, once when he was serving as a general he said to Simonides of Ceos, who was asking him for something he was not entitled to, that, just as Simonides would not be a good poet if he sang counter to the tune, so he himself would not be a good magistrate if he did favours contrary to the law. [7] On another occasion he made fun of Simonides, saying that he was a fool to abuse the Corinthians, when they lived in a powerful city, while at the same time having portraits made of himself, when he was so ugly to look at. Anyway, his power grew and he was popular with the common people, and so eventually he secured a majority against Aristides, and got him banished by ostracism.

6. When the Persian King had actually begun his march on Greece, and the Athenians were debating who should be their general, the other candidates, so they say, terrified by the danger, willingly withdrew their claims to the generalship. But Epicydes, son of Euphemides, a popular leader who was a skilful orator, but a coward at heart and open to bribery, campaigned for the office and seemed likely to win the election. [2] Themistocles was afraid that, if the command fell into his hands, the city's prospects would be completely ruined, and so by means of bribery he bought off the ambitious Epicydes.

[3] He is also to be praised for his action with regard to the bilingual speaker, who was amongst those sent by the King to demand earth and water, and acted as an interpreter. [4] He had him arrested and put to death by a special decree, on the grounds that he had dared to employ the Greek

ἐτόλμησε χρῆσαι. ἔτι δὲ καὶ τὸ περὶ Ἄρθμιον τὸν Ζελείτην· Θεμιστοκλέους γὰρ εἰπόντος καὶ τοῦτον εἰς τοὺς ἀτίμους καὶ παῖδας αὐτοῦ καὶ γένος ἐνέγραψαν, ὅτι τὸν ἐκ Μήδων χρυσὸν εἰς τοὺς Ἕλληνας ἐκόμισε. 5 μέγιστον δὲ πάντων τὸ καταλῦσαι τοὺς Ἑλληνικοὺς πολέμους καὶ διαλλάξαι τὰς πόλεις ἀλλήλαις, πείσαντα τὰς ἔχθρας διὰ τὸν πόλεμον ἀναβαλέσθαι· πρὸς ὃ καὶ Χείλεων τὸν Ἀρκάδα μάλιστα συναγωνίσασθαι λέγουσι.

7. Παραλαβὼν δὲ τὴν ἀρχήν, εὐθὺς μὲν ἐπεχείρει τοὺς πολίτας ἐμβιβάζειν εἰς τὰς τριήρεις, καὶ τὴν πόλιν ἔπειθεν ἐκλιπόντας ὡς προσωτάτω τῆς Ἑλλάδος ἀπαντᾶν τῷ βαρβάρῳ κατὰ θάλατταν. 2 ἐνισταμένων δὲ πολλῶν, ἐξήγαγε πολλὴν στρατιὰν εἰς τὰ Τέμπη μετὰ Λακεδαιμονίων, ὡς αὐτόθι προκινδυνεύσων τῆς Θεσσαλίας, οὔπω τότε μηδίζειν δοκούσης· ἐπεὶ δ' ἀνεχώρησαν ἐκεῖθεν ἄπρακτοι, καὶ Θεσσαλῶν βασιλεῖ προσγενομένων ἐμήδιζε τὰ μέχρι Βοιωτίας, μᾶλλον ἤδη τῷ Θεμιστοκλεῖ προσεῖχον οἱ Ἀθηναῖοι περὶ τῆς θαλάσσης, καὶ πέμπεται μετὰ νεῶν ἐπ' Ἀρτεμίσιον τὰ στενὰ φυλάξων.
3 ἔνθα δὴ τῶν μὲν Ἑλλήνων Εὐρυβιάδην καὶ Λακεδαιμονίους ἡγεῖσθαι κελευόντων, τῶν δ' Ἀθηναίων, ὅτι πλήθει τῶν νεῶν σύμπαντας ὁμοῦ τι τοὺς ἄλλους ὑπερέβαλλον, οὐκ ἀξιούντων ἑτέροις ἕπεσθαι, συνιδὼν τὸν κίνδυνον ὁ Θεμιστοκλῆς αὐτός τε τὴν ἀρχὴν τῷ Εὐρυβιάδῃ παρῆκε, καὶ κατεπράυνε τοὺς Ἀθηναίους, ὑπισχνούμενος, ἂν ἄνδρες ἀγαθοὶ γένωνται πρὸς τὸν πόλεμον, ἑκόντας αὐτοῖς παρέξειν εἰς τὰ λοιπὰ πειθομένους τοὺς Ἕλληνας. 4 διὸ καὶ δοκεῖ τῆς σωτηρίας αἰτιώτατος γενέσθαι τῇ Ἑλλάδι, καὶ μάλιστα τοὺς Ἀθηναίους προαγαγεῖν εἰς δόξαν, ὡς ἀνδρείᾳ μὲν τῶν πολεμίων, εὐγνωμοσύνῃ δὲ τῶν συμμάχων περιγενομένους.
5 Ἐπεὶ δὲ ταῖς Ἀφεταῖς τοῦ βαρβαρικοῦ στόλου προσμείξαντος, ἐκπλαγεὶς ὁ Εὐρυβιάδης τῶν κατὰ στόμα νεῶν τὸ πλῆθος, ἄλλας δὲ πυνθανόμενος διακοσίας ὑπὲρ Σκιάθου κύκλῳ περιπλεῖν, ἐβούλετο τὴν ταχίστην εἴσω τῆς Ἑλλάδος κομισθεὶς ἅψασθαι Πελοποννήσου καὶ τὸν πεζὸν στρατὸν ταῖς

language to transmit barbarian commands. Praiseworthy too was his treatment of Arthmius of Zeleia. For it was on Themistocles' proposal that the Athenians inscribed the names of this man, his children and his family, on the list of those outlawed, on the grounds that he had brought gold from the Persians and offered it to the Greeks. [5] But the greatest of all his achievements was to put a stop to the wars of Greeks against Greeks, and to reconcile the cities with one another, persuading them to suspend their mutual hatreds in view of the war against Persia. They say that Cheileos the Arcadian also played an important role in helping him to secure this objective.

7. Immediately on assuming the command he attempted to get the citizens to embark on their triremes, and he tried to persuade them to leave their city and face the barbarians at sea as far away from Greece as possible. [2] But many people opposed this plan, so he took a large infantry force out to the vale of Tempe, marching together with the Spartans, with the intention of making a forward stand there in defence of Thessaly, which at that time was not yet thought to be taking the Persian side. But they withdrew from that position without accomplishing anything, and then the Thessalians went over to the side of the King, and all Greece as far as Boeotia medised; and then at last the Athenians started to pay more attention to Themistocles' advice to use the sea, and he was sent with a fleet to guard the straits at Artemisium.

[3] It was here that the rest of the Greeks urged Eurybiades and the Spartans to take the overall command. But, since the number of ships the Athenians supplied just about exceeded that of all the rest put together, they did not think it was right for them to have to follow the orders of others. Realising the danger of this, Themistocles voluntarily surrendered his own command to Eurybiades, and mollified the Athenians by promising them that, if they proved themselves brave men in this conflict, he would guarantee that the Greeks would willingly follow their lead in the future. [4] Because of this action he is regarded as the man who was most responsible for Greece's salvation, and who more than anyone promoted the Athenians' reputation as men who outdid their enemies in courage and their allies in good sense.

[5] But when the Persian fleet arrived at Aphetae Eurybiades was terrified by the number of ships that faced him, and, when he got news that another two hundred were sailing around to his rear beyond Sciathos, he wanted to take the quickest route back into the interior of Greece, and land in the Peloponnese, where he could surround his fleet with his infantry forces for

ναυσὶ προσπεριβαλέσθαι, παντάπασιν ἀπρόσμαχον ἡγούμενος τὴν κατὰ θάλατταν ἀλκὴν βασιλέως, δείσαντες οἱ Εὐβοεῖς μὴ σφᾶς οἱ Ἕλληνες πρόωνται, κρύφα τῷ Θεμιστοκλεῖ διελέγοντο, Πελάγοντα μετὰ χρημάτων πολλῶν πέμψαντες. 6 ἃ λαβὼν ἐκεῖνος, ὡς Ἡρόδοτος ἱστόρηκε, τοῖς περὶ τὸν Εὐρυβιάδην ἔδωκεν. ἐναντιουμένου δ' αὐτῷ μάλιστα τῶν πολιτῶν Ἀρχιτέλους, ὃς ἦν μὲν ἐπὶ τῆς ἱερᾶς νεὼς τριήραρχος, οὐκ ἔχων δὲ χρήματα τοῖς ναύταις χορηγεῖν ἔσπευδεν ἀποπλεῦσαι, παρώξυνεν ἔτι μᾶλλον ὁ Θεμιστοκλῆς τοὺς τριηρίτας ἐπ' αὐτόν, ὥστε τὸ δεῖπνον ἁρπάσαι συνδραμόντας. 7 τοῦ δ' Ἀρχιτέλους ἀθυμοῦντος ἐπὶ τούτῳ καὶ βαρέως φέροντος, εἰσέπεμψεν ὁ Θεμιστοκλῆς πρὸς αὐτὸν ἐν κίστῃ δεῖπνον ἄρτων καὶ κρεῶν, ὑποθεὶς κάτω τάλαντον ἀργυρίου καὶ κελεύσας αὐτόν τε δειπνεῖν ἐν τῷ παρόντι καὶ μεθ' ἡμέραν ἐπιμεληθῆναι τῶν τριηριτῶν· εἰ δὲ μή, καταβοήσειν αὐτοῦ πρὸς τοὺς παρόντας ὡς ἔχοντος ἀργύριον παρὰ τῶν πολεμίων. ταῦτα μὲν οὖν Φανίας ὁ Λέσβιος εἴρηκεν.

8. Αἱ δὲ γενόμεναι τότε πρὸς τὰς τῶν βαρβάρων ναῦς περὶ τὰ στενὰ μάχαι κρίσιν μὲν εἰς τὰ ὅλα μεγάλην οὐκ ἐποίησαν, τῇ δὲ πείρᾳ μέγιστα τοὺς Ἕλληνας ὤνησαν, ὑπὸ τῶν ἔργων παρὰ τοὺς κινδύνους διδαχθέντας, ὡς οὔτε πλήθη νεῶν οὔτε κόσμοι καὶ λαμπρότητες ἐπισήμων οὔτε κραυγαὶ κομπώδεις ἢ βάρβαροι παιᾶνες ἔχουσί τι δεινὸν ἀνδράσιν ἐπισταμένοις εἰς χεῖρας ἰέναι καὶ μάχεσθαι τολμῶσιν, ἀλλὰ δεῖ τῶν τοιούτων καταφρονοῦντας ἐπ' αὐτὰ τὰ σώματα φέρεσθαι καὶ πρὸς ἐκεῖνα διαγωνίζεσθαι συμπλακέντας. 2 ὃ δὴ καὶ Πίνδαρος οὐ κακῶς ἔοικε συνιδὼν ἐπὶ τῆς ἐν Ἀρτεμισίῳ μάχης εἰπεῖν·

ὅθι παῖδες Ἀθαναίων ἐβάλοντο φαεννὰν
κρηπῖδ' ἐλευθερίας·

ἀρχὴ γὰρ ὄντως τοῦ νικᾶν τὸ θαρρεῖν. 3 ἔστι δὲ τῆς Εὐβοίας τὸ Ἀρτεμίσιον ὑπὲρ τὴν Ἑστίαιαν αἰγιαλὸς εἰς βορέαν ἀναπεπταμένος, ἀνταίρει δ' αὐτῷ μάλιστα τῆς ὑπὸ Φιλοκτήτῃ γενομένης χώρας Ὀλιζών. 4 ἔχει δὲ ναὸν οὐ μέγαν Ἀρτέμιδος ἐπίκλησιν Προσηῴας, καὶ δένδρα περὶ αὐτὸν πέφυκε καὶ στῆλαι κύκλῳ λίθου λευκοῦ πεπήγασιν· ὁ δὲ λίθος τῇ χειρὶ τριβόμενος καὶ χρόαν καὶ ὀσμὴν κροκίζουσαν

extra protection, since he considered the sea-power of the King to be absolutely invincible. At this the Euboeans, fearing that the Greeks would abandon them, held secret negotiations with Themistocles, sending Pelagon to him with a considerable amount of money. [6] This he accepted, and he was the one who gave it to Eurybiades, as Herodotus has recorded.

Among his fellow citizens the fiercest opposition he encountered came from Architeles, who was captain of the sacred ship, but was eager to sail off home since he did not have money to pay the sailors. So Themistocles stirred up his crew even more against him, with the result that they got together, made a rush at him, and snatched away his meal. [7] Then, while Architeles was still feeling despondent and aggrieved at this, Themistocles sent him a meal of bread and meat in a box, and put a talent of silver at the bottom of it. He told him to eat his dinner at once, and take care of his crew next day. Otherwise, he said, he would loudly denounce him to all and sundry, as a receiver of money from the enemy. That at any rate is what Phanias of Lesbos has said.

8. The battles which were now fought against the fleet of the barbarians in the straits did not produce a decisive result for the war as a whole, it is true. But they did benefit the Greeks a great deal in terms of the experience they gained in them, since they learnt from their efforts in the face of danger that neither masses of ships, nor brilliantly decorated figure-heads, nor boastful shouts, nor wild battle-cries hold any terror for men who know how to come to close quarters and have the courage to fight there; what they must do is despise such superficialities, attack the actual persons of the enemy, and fight it out to the end in hand to hand combat. [2] This is something which Pindar seems to have understood well in saying of the battle of Artemisium:-

"It was there that Athens' brave sons planted the gleaming corner-stone of liberty." For confidence is truly the beginning of victory.

[3] Artemisium is a part of Euboea, a beach stretching northwards beyond Hestiaea, and just about opposite to it lies Olizon, in the territory that was once ruled by Philoctetes. [4] It has a small temple of Artemis, with the title Proseoea ("facing the east"), which has trees growing round it and a ring of upright slabs of white stone. This stone, if you rub it with your hand, gives

ἀναδίδωσιν. 5 ἐν μιᾷ δὲ τῶν στηλῶν ἐλεγεῖον ἦν τόδε γεγραμμένον·

παντοδαπῶν ἀνδρῶν γενεὰς Ἀσίας ἀπὸ χώρας
 παῖδες Ἀθηναίων τῷδέ ποτ' ἐν πελάγει
ναυμαχίᾳ δαμάσαντες, ἐπεὶ στρατὸς ὤλετο Μήδων,
 σήματα ταῦτ' ἔθεσαν παρθένῳ Ἀρτέμιδι.

6 δείκνυται δὲ τῆς ἀκτῆς τόπος ἐν πολλῇ τῇ πέριξ θινὶ κόνιν τεφρώδη καὶ μέλαιναν ἐκ βάθους ἀναδιδούς, ὥσπερ πυρίκαυστον, ἐν ᾧ τὰ ναυάγια καὶ ‹τοὺς› νεκροὺς καῦσαι δοκοῦσι.

9. Τῶν μέντοι ‹τὰ› περὶ Θερμοπύλας εἰς τὸ Ἀρτεμίσιον ἀπαγγελλόντων πυθόμενοι Λεωνίδαν τε κεῖσθαι καὶ κρατεῖν Ξέρξην τῶν κατὰ γῆν παρόδων, εἴσω τῆς Ἑλλάδος ἀνεκομίζοντο, τῶν Ἀθηναίων ἐπὶ πᾶσι τεταγμένων δι' ἀρετὴν καὶ μέγα τοῖς πεπραγμένοις φρονούντων. 2 παραπλέων δὲ τὴν χώραν ὁ Θεμιστοκλῆς, ᾗπερ κατάρσεις ἀναγκαίας καὶ καταφυγὰς ἑώρα τοῖς πολεμίοις, ἐνεχάραττε κατὰ τῶν λίθων ἐπιφανῆ γράμματα, τοὺς μὲν εὑρίσκων ἀπὸ τύχης, τοὺς δ' αὐτὸς ἱστὰς περὶ τὰ ναυλόχια καὶ τὰς ὑδρείας, ἐπισκήπτων Ἴωσι διὰ τῶν γραμμάτων, εἰ μὲν οἷόν τε, μετατάξασθαι πρὸς αὐτούς, πατέρας ὄντας καὶ προκινδυνεύοντας ὑπὲρ τῆς ἐκείνων ἐλευθερίας, εἰ δὲ μή, κακοῦν τὸ βαρβαρικὸν ἐν ταῖς μάχαις καὶ συνταράττειν. ταῦτα δ' ἤλπιζεν ἢ μεταστήσειν τοὺς Ἴωνας ἢ ταράξειν ὑποπτοτέρους τοὺς βαρβάρους γενομένους.

3 Ξέρξου δὲ διὰ τῆς Δωρίδος ἄνωθεν ἐμβαλόντος εἰς τὴν Φωκίδα καὶ τὰ τῶν Φωκέων ἄστη πυρπολοῦντος, οὐ προσήμυναν οἱ Ἕλληνες, καίπερ τῶν Ἀθηναίων δεομένων εἰς τὴν Βοιωτίαν ἀπαντῆσαι πρὸ τῆς Ἀττικῆς, ὥσπερ αὐτοὶ κατὰ θάλατταν ἐπ' Ἀρτεμίσιον ἐβοήθησαν. 4 μηδενὸς δ' ὑπακούοντος αὐτοῖς, ἀλλὰ τῆς Πελοποννήσου περιεχομένων καὶ πᾶσαν ἐντὸς Ἰσθμοῦ τὴν δύναμιν ὡρμημένων συνάγειν, καὶ διατειχιζόντων τὸν Ἰσθμὸν εἰς θάλατταν ἐκ θαλάττης, ἅμα μὲν ὀργὴ τῆς προδοσίας εἶχε τοὺς Ἀθηναίους, ἅμα δὲ δυσθυμία καὶ κατήφεια μεμονωμένους. 5 μάχεσθαι μὲν γὰρ οὐ διενοοῦντο μυριάσι στρατοῦ τοσαύταις· ὃ δ' ἦν μόνον ἀναγκαῖον ἐν τῷ παρόντι, τὴν πόλιν ἀφέντας ἐμφῦναι ταῖς

off the colour and odour of saffron. [5] On one of the slabs the following elegiac poem has been inscribed:-

"Athens' brave sons once crushed in battle on this stretch of sea
the diverse nations of men who came from the land of Asia,
and, when the army of the Medes was destroyed,
they dedicated these tokens to Artemis the virgin."

[6] One can be shown a place on the shore in the middle of a long stretch of sand where there comes up from deep down a dark ashy powder, apparently the product of fire; and it is believed that they burned their wrecks and dead bodies here.

9. However, when they learned from the messengers who brought the news of Thermopylae to Artemisium that Leonidas lay dead and that Xerxes was in control of the mountain passes, they withdrew further back into Greece, with the Athenians bringing up the rear in recognition of their bravery, full of pride as they were at their achievements. [2] As Themistocles sailed along the coast, whenever he spotted places where the enemy would have to land for supplies and shelter he had conspicuous messages engraved on stones, some of which he found conveniently to hand, while others he had deliberately set up near the anchorages and watering places. In the messages he entreated the Ionians to come over, if they could, to the side of the Athenians, who were their ancestors and were risking everything for *their* freedom, or, if they could not, to damage the barbarian cause in the battles and create confusion in their ranks. By these means he hoped he might either bring the Ionians over, or cause the enemy problems by making the barbarians more suspicious of them.

[3] Meanwhile, although Xerxes had marched through Doris and descended on Phocis and was now burning the towns of the Phocians, the other Greeks failed to send them any help. The Athenians too begged them to take a stand in Boeotia in defence of Attica, just as they themselves had gone by sea to Artemisium to help others. [4] But no one would listen to them. Clinging fast to the Peloponnese they were all eager to concentrate all their forces south of the Isthmus, and were building a wall across the Isthmus from sea to sea. So the Athenians were, at one and the same time, enraged by this betrayal, and disheartened and dejected at being left in an isolated position. [5] They could not imagine that they could continue fighting against an army of such immense numbers; but as for the only thing left open to them in the crisis, namely, to abandon their city and transplant

ναυσίν, οἱ πολλοὶ χαλεπῶς ἤκουον, ὡς μήτε νίκης δεόμενοι μήτε σωτηρίαν ἐπιστάμενοι θεῶν ἱερὰ καὶ πατέρων ἠρία προϊεμένων.

10. Ἔνθα δὴ Θεμιστοκλῆς, ἀπορῶν τοῖς ἀνθρωπίνοις λογισμοῖς προσάγεσθαι τὸ πλῆθος, ὥσπερ ἐν τραγῳδίᾳ μηχανὴν ἄρας, σημεῖα δαιμόνια καὶ χρησμοὺς ἐπῆγεν αὐτοῖς, σημεῖον μὲν λαμβάνων τὸ τοῦ δράκοντος, ὃς ἀφανὴς ταῖς ἡμέραις ἐκείναις ἐκ τοῦ σηκοῦ δοκεῖ γενέσθαι, 2 καὶ τὰς καθ' ἡμέραν αὐτῷ προτιθεμένας ἀπαρχὰς εὑρίσκοντες ἀψαύστους, οἱ ἱερεῖς ἐξήγγελλον εἰς τοὺς πολλούς, τοῦ Θεμιστοκλέους λόγον διδόντος ὡς ἀπολέλοιπε τὴν πόλιν ἡ θεὸς ὑφηγουμένη πρὸς τὴν θάλασσαν αὐτοῖς· 3 τῷ δὲ χρησμῷ πάλιν ἐδημαγώγει, λέγων μηδὲν ἄλλο δηλοῦσθαι ξύλινον τεῖχος ἢ τὰς ναῦς· διὸ καὶ τὴν Σαλαμῖνα θείαν, οὐχὶ δεινὴν οὐδὲ σχετλίαν καλεῖν τὸν θεόν, ὡς εὐτυχήματος μεγάλου τοῖς Ἕλλησιν ἐπώνυμον ἐσομένην. 4 κρατήσας δὲ τῇ γνώμῃ ψήφισμα γράφει, τὴν μὲν πόλιν παρακαταθέσθαι τῇ Ἀθηνᾷ τῇ Ἀθηναίων μεδεούσῃ, τοὺς δ' ἐν ἡλικίᾳ πάντας ἐμβαίνειν εἰς τὰς τριήρεις, παῖδας δὲ καὶ γυναῖκας καὶ ἀνδράποδα σῴζειν ἕκαστον ὡς ἂν δύνηται. 5 κυρωθέντος δὲ τοῦ ψηφίσματος οἱ πλεῖστοι τῶν Ἀθηναίων ὑπεξέθεντο γενεὰς καὶ γυναῖκας εἰς Τροιζῆνα, φιλοτίμως πάνυ τῶν Τροιζηνίων ὑποδεχομένων· καὶ γὰρ τρέφειν ἐψηφίσαντο δημοσίᾳ, δύο ὀβολοὺς ἑκάστῳ διδόντες, καὶ τῆς ὀπώρας λαμβάνειν ἐξεῖναι τοὺς παῖδας πανταχόθεν, ἔτι δ' ὑπὲρ αὐτῶν διδασκάλοις τελεῖν μισθούς. τὸ δὲ ψήφισμα Νικαγόρας ἔγραψεν.

6 Οὐκ ὄντων δὲ δημοσίων χρημάτων τοῖς Ἀθηναίοις, Ἀριστοτέλης μέν φησι τὴν ἐξ Ἀρείου πάγου βουλὴν πορίσασαν ὀκτὼ δραχμὰς ἑκάστῳ τῶν στρατευομένων αἰτιωτάτην γενέσθαι τοῦ πληρωθῆναι τὰς τριήρεις, Κλείδημος δὲ καὶ τοῦτο τοῦ Θεμιστοκλέους ποιεῖται στρατήγημα. 7 καταβαινόντων γὰρ εἰς Πειραιᾶ τῶν Ἀθηναίων φησὶν ἀπολέσθαι τὸ Γοργόνειον ἀπὸ τῆς θεοῦ τοῦ ἀγάλματος· τὸν οὖν Θεμιστοκλέα προσποιούμενον ζητεῖν καὶ διερευνώμενον ἅπαντα, χρημάτων ἀνευρίσκειν πλῆθος ἐν ταῖς ἀποσκευαῖς ἀποκεκρυμμένον, ὧν εἰς μέσον κομισθέντων εὐπορῆσαι τοὺς ἐμβαίνοντας εἰς τὰς ναῦς ἐφοδίων. 8 Ἐκπλεούσης δὲ τῆς πόλεως τοῖς μὲν οἶκτον τὸ θέαμα, τοῖς δὲ θαῦμα τῆς τόλμης

themselves into their ships, this was a distressing idea for the majority of them. They said they neither wanted "victory" nor understood what "salvation" could mean, if it involved abandoning to the enemy the temples of their gods and the tombs of their forefathers.

10. At this point Themistocles, at a loss how to win over the populace by rational arguments, proceeded to bring divine portents and oracles to bear on them, like a playwright deploying machinery in a tragedy. As a portent he took the incident of the snake, which, it is believed, disappeared from its sacred enclosure during that period. [2] When the priests discovered that the choice offerings, which were set out for it each day, remained untouched they announced to the people - a story supplied by Themistocles - that the goddess had abandoned her city and was guiding them to the sea.

[3] He also tried to sway the people with the oracle, saying that a wooden wall could indicate nothing other than their fleet. Thus (he said) the god had called Salamis "divine", not "terrible" or "cruel", precisely because its name would be associated with a great blessing for the Greeks. [4] His view prevailed, and he proposed a decree to the effect that the city itself should be entrusted to the safe keeping of Athena "who guards the Athenians", but that all the men of military age should embark on the triremes, with each man providing as best he could for the safety of his children, wife, and slaves. [5] When the decree had been ratified most of the Athenians evacuated their children and wives to Troezen, where the Troezenians welcomed them very enthusiastically. They actually voted to maintain them at public expense, with each refugee being given two obols a day, and to allow the children to pick the ripe fruit in anyone's field, and, further, to pay teachers' fees on their behalf. A man called Nicagoras proposed the decree.

[6] Since the Athenians did not have public funds at their disposal the council of the Areopagus, according to Aristotle, provided each combatant with eight drachmas, and so was most responsible for getting the triremes manned. But Cleidemus portrays this too as a stratagem on the part of Themistocles. [7] He says that, when the Athenians were going down to the Piraeus, the Gorgon's head was lost from the statue of the goddess. So Themistocles pretended to look for it, and, through a comprehensive search, discovered a large amount of money hidden away in the baggage. This was confiscated, and from it the crews embarking on the ships were provided with substantial expenses.

[8] When the whole city was putting out to sea the spectacle induced in some people sorrow, and in others astonishment at their boldness, as they

παρεῖχε, γενεὰς μὲν ἄλλῃ προπεμπόντων, αὐτῶν δ' ἀκάμπτων πρὸς οἰμωγὰς καὶ δάκρυα γονέων καὶ περιβολὰς διαπερώντων εἰς τὴν νῆσον. 9 καίτοι πολλοὶ μὲν οἱ διὰ γῆρας ὑπολειπόμενοι τῶν πολιτῶν ἔλεον εἶχον, ἦν δέ τις καὶ ἀπὸ τῶν ἡμέρων καὶ συντρόφων ζῴων ἐπικλῶσα γλυκυθυμία, μετ' ὠρυγῆς καὶ πόθου συμπαραθεόντων ἐμβαίνουσι τοῖς ἑαυτῶν τροφεῦσιν. 10 ἐν οἷς ἱστορεῖται κύων Ξανθίππου τοῦ Περικλέους πατρός, οὐκ ἀνασχόμενος τὴν ἀπ' αὐτοῦ μόνωσιν, ἐναλέσθαι τῇ θαλάττῃ καὶ τῇ τριήρει παρανηχόμενος ἐκπεσεῖν εἰς τὴν Σαλαμῖνα, καὶ λιποθυμήσας ἀποθανεῖν εὐθύς· οὗ καὶ τὸ δεικνύμενον ἄχρι νῦν καὶ καλούμενον Κυνὸς σῆμα τάφον εἶναι λέγουσι.

11. Ταῦτά τε δὴ μεγάλα τοῦ Θεμιστοκλέους, καὶ τοὺς πολίτας αἰσθόμενος ποθοῦντας Ἀριστείδην καὶ δεδιότας μὴ δι' ὀργὴν τῷ βαρβάρῳ προσθεὶς ἑαυτὸν ἀνατρέψῃ τὰ πράγματα τῆς Ἑλλάδος – ἐξωστράκιστο γὰρ πρὸ τοῦ πολέμου καταστασιασθεὶς ὑπὸ Θεμιστοκλέους -, γράφει ψήφισμα, τοῖς ἐπὶ χρόνῳ μεθεστῶσιν ἐξεῖναι κατελθοῦσι πράττειν καὶ λέγειν τὰ βέλτιστα τῇ Ἑλλάδι μετὰ τῶν ἄλλων πολιτῶν.
2 Εὐρυβιάδου δὲ τὴν μὲν ἡγεμονίαν τῶν νεῶν ἔχοντος διὰ τὸ τῆς Σπάρτης ἀξίωμα, μαλακοῦ δὲ παρὰ τὸν κίνδυνον ὄντος, αἴρειν δὲ βουλομένου καὶ πλεῖν ἐπὶ τὸν Ἰσθμόν, ὅπου καὶ τὸ πεζὸν ἤθροιστο τῶν Πελοποννησίων, ὁ Θεμιστοκλῆς ἀντέλεγεν. ὅτε καὶ τὰ μνημονευόμενα λεχθῆναί φασι· 3 τοῦ γὰρ Εὐρυβιάδου πρὸς αὐτὸν εἰπόντος· "ὦ Θεμιστόκλεις, ἐν τοῖς ἀγῶσι τοὺς προεξανισταμένους ῥαπίζουσι", "ναί" εἶπεν ὁ Θεμιστοκλῆς, "ἀλλὰ τοὺς ἀπολειφθέντας οὐ στεφανοῦσιν". ἐπαραμένου δὲ τὴν βακτηρίαν ὡς πατάξοντος, ὁ Θεμιστοκλῆς ἔφη· "πάταξον μέν, ἄκουσον δέ." 4 θαυμάσαντος δὲ τὴνπρᾳότητα τοῦ Εὐρυβιάδου καὶ λέγειν κελεύσαντος, ὁ μὲν Θεμιστοκλῆς ἀνῆγεν αὐτὸν ἐπὶ τὸν λόγον· 5 εἰπόντος δέ τινος ὡς ἀνὴρ ἄπολις οὐκ ὀρθῶς διδάσκοι τοὺς ἔχοντας ἐγκαταλιπεῖν καὶ προέσθαι τὰς πατρίδας, ὁ Θεμιστοκλῆς ἐπιστρέψας τὸν λόγον "ἡμεῖς τοι" εἶπεν "ὦ μοχθηρέ, τὰς μὲν οἰκίας καὶ τὰ τείχη καταλελοίπαμεν, οὐκ ἀξιοῦντες ἀψύχων ἕνεκα δουλεύειν· πόλις δ' ἡμῖν ἔστι μεγίστη τῶν Ἑλληνίδων, αἱ διακόσιαι τριήρεις, αἳ νῦν μὲν ὑμῖν παρεστᾶσι βοηθοὶ

sent off their families in one direction while they themselves crossed over to the island, unmoved by the cries and tears and embraces of their parents. [9] A pitiful sight also were the many citizens who were being left behind because of their old age. There was some heartbreaking affection too shown by the tame domestic animals, who ran along by the side of their masters, and howled with longing as they embarked. [10] There is a story that one of these animals, a dog belonging to Xanthippus, the father of Pericles, could not bear to be separated from him, and so it jumped into the sea and swam alongside his trireme, and, on being washed ashore at Salamis, it collapsed and died on the spot. They say that the place which one can still be shown to this day, called Dog's Mound, is its tomb.

11. These were certainly fine achievements on Themistocles' part, but, in addition, he saw that the citizens missed Aristides, and were afraid that, out of resentment, he might join the barbarians' side and so wreck the Greek cause (he had been ostracised before the war, after being politically defeated by Themistocles). He therefore proposed a decree that those who had been removed from Athens for a specific period should be allowed to return home and to act and speak in the best interests of Greece, in the company of their fellow-citizens.

[2] Eurybiades held the overall command of the fleet because of the prestige of Sparta, but he was a coward in the face of danger and wanted to hoist sail and make for the Isthmus, which was where the infantry forces of the Peloponnesians had been mustered. But this was opposed by Themistocles, and it was at this juncture, so they say, that he came out with some memorable remarks. [3] When Eurybiades said to him "Themistocles, at the games they thrash those athletes who start before the signal", "Yes," replied Themistocles, "but they give no crowns of victory to those who get left at the post." And when Eurybiades lifted up his stick as if to strike him Themistocles said "Strike me if you wish, but you must listen to me." [4] Eurybiades was impressed by his mild response and told him to speak out, so Themistocles tried to bring him round to his point of view. [5] But someone objected that a man who did not have a city was not qualified to instruct those who did to leave in the lurch and abandon their native lands. At this Themistocles turned fiercely on him, and said "It is true, you rascal, that we have left behind us our homes and our walls, since our honour did not permit us to endure slavery just for the sake of such lifeless things, but we do have the greatest city of all in Greece, our two hundred triremes, which now stand

σῴζεσθαι δι' αὐτῶν βουλομένοις, εἰ δ' ἄπιτε δεύτερον ἡμᾶς προδόντες, αὐτίκα πεύσεταί τις Ἑλλήνων Ἀθηναίους καὶ πόλιν ἐλευθέραν καὶ χώραν οὐ χείρονα κεκτημένους ἧς ἀπέβαλον." ταῦτα τοῦ Θεμιστοκλέους εἰπόντος, ἔννοια καὶ δέος ἔσχε τὸν Εὐρυβιάδην τῶν Ἀθηναίων, μὴ σφᾶς ἀπολείποντες οἴχωνται. 6 τοῦ δ' Ἐρετριέως πειρωμένου τι λέγειν πρὸς αὐτόν, "ἦ γάρ" ἔφη "καὶ ὑμῖν περὶ πολέμου τίς ἐστι λόγος, οἳ καθάπερ αἱ τευθίδες μάχαιραν μὲν ἔχετε, καρδίαν δ' οὐκ ἔχετε;"

12. Λέγεται δ' ὑπό τινων τὸν μὲν Θεμιστοκλέα περὶ τούτων ἀπὸ τοῦ καταστρώματος ἄνωθεν τῆς νεὼς διαλέγεσθαι, γλαῦκα δ' ὀφθῆναι διαπετομένην ἐπὶ δεξιᾶς τῶν νεῶν καὶ τοῖς καρχησίοις ἐπικαθίζουσαν· διὸ δὴ καὶ μάλιστα προσέθεντο τῇ γνώμῃ καὶ παρεσκευάζοντο ναυμαχήσοντες. 2 ἀλλ' ἐπεὶ τῶν πολεμίων ὅ τε στόλος τῇ Ἀττικῇ κατὰ τὸ Φαληρικὸν προσφερόμενος τοὺς πέριξ ἀπέκρυψεν αἰγιαλούς, αὐτός τε βασιλεὺς μετὰ τοῦ πεζοῦ στρατοῦ καταβὰς ἐπὶ τὴν θάλατταν ἄθρους ὤφθη, τῶν δυνάμεων ὁμοῦ γενομένων, ἐξερρύησαν οἱ τοῦ Θεμιστοκλέους λόγοι τῶν Ἑλλήνων, καὶ πάλιν ἐπάπταινον οἱ Πελοποννήσιοι πρὸς τὸν Ἰσθμόν, εἴ τις ἄλλο τι λέγοι χαλεπαίνοντες. ἐδόκει δὴ τῆς νυκτὸς ἀποχωρεῖν, καὶ παρηγγέλλετο πλοῦς τοῖς κυβερνήταις. 3 ἔνθα δὴ βαρέως φέρων ὁ Θεμιστοκλῆς εἰ τὴν ἀπὸ τοῦ τόπου καὶ τῶν στενῶν προέμενοι βοήθειαν οἱ Ἕλληνες διαλυθήσονται κατὰ πόλεις, ἐβουλεύετο καὶ συνετίθει τὴν περὶ τὸν Σίκιννονπραγματείαν. 4 ἦν δὲ τῷ μὲν γένει Πέρσης ὁ Σίκιννος αἰχμάλωτος, εὔνους δὲ τῷ Θεμιστοκλεῖ καὶ τῶν τέκνων αὐτοῦ παιδαγωγός. ὃν ἐκπέμπει πρὸς τὸν Ξέρξην κρύφα, κελεύσας λέγειν ὅτι Θεμιστοκλῆς ὁ τῶν Ἀθηναίων στρατηγὸς αἱρούμενος τὰ βασιλέως ἐξαγγέλλει πρῶτος αὐτῷ τοὺς Ἕλληνας ἀποδιδράσκοντας, καὶ διακελεύεται μὴ παρεῖναι φυγεῖν αὐτοῖς, ἀλλ' ἐν ᾧ ταράττονται τῶν πεζῶν χωρὶς ὄντες ἐπιθέσθαι καὶ διαφθεῖραι τὴν ναυτικὴν δύναμιν. 5 ταῦτα δ' ὁ Ξέρξης ὡς ἀπ' εὐνοίας λελεγμένα δεξάμενος, ἥσθη καὶ εὐθὺς ἐξέφερε πρὸς τοὺς ἡγεμόνας τῶν νεῶν, τὰς μὲν ἄλλας πληροῦν καθ' ἡσυχίαν, διακοσίαις δ' ἀναχθέντας ἤδη περιβαλέσθαι τὸν πόρον ἐν κύκλῳ πάντα καὶ διαζῶσαι τὰς νήσους, ὅπως ἐκφύγοι μηδεὶς τῶν πολεμίων. 6 τούτων δὲ πραττομένων

ready to help you, if you want to be saved by them. But if you retreat and betray us for a second time, the Greek world will soon hear that the Athenians have acquired an independent city and a territory that is certainly not inferior to the one they have given up." On hearing Themistocles say this, Eurybiades was struck by the frightening thought that the Athenians might sail off and abandon them. [6] Again, when the Eretrian commander attempted to make some point against him, Themistocles exclaimed, "Really! And what comment are you Eretrians entitled to make on the subject of war, when, like the cuttlefish, you have a sword, but no heart?"

12. Some writers relate that, while Themistocles was engaged in this discussion, speaking from the upper deck of his ship, an owl was observed to fly through the fleet from the right and perch on his masthead. It was for this reason in particular that they accepted his view, and began to make preparations for a naval battle. [2] But when the great armada of the enemy occupied the coast of Attica down to the bay of Phalerum and actually hid from view the surrounding coastline, and the King himself came down to the sea shore in person with his infantry and could be seen amid the vast throng, the arguments of Themistocles drained out of the minds of the Greeks at the sight of this concentration of forces. The Peloponnesians once again began to look with longing towards the Isthmus, and they got angry at anyone who suggested anything else. They resolved to withdraw during the night, and the order to sail was passed down to the helmsmen. [3] It was at this point that Themistocles, disturbed by the thought that the Greeks were going to throw away the advantage of their position in the narrow straits and split up and go back to their various cities, planned and organised the Sicinnus affair.

[4] Sicinnus was by nationality a Persian, a prisoner of war, but a man devoted to Themistocles and tutor of his children. He sent him to Xerxes secretly with orders to say this: "Themistocles the Athenian general has opted to join the King's side, and is the first to inform him that the Greeks are trying to slip away, and he urges him not to allow them to escape but to attack and destroy their naval force while they are in disarray and separated from their infantry." [5] Xerxes took this as a message sent in good faith and was delighted. He immediately issued an order for action to his naval commanders, telling them to man the main body of the fleet at their leisure, but to put to sea at once with two hundred ships, taking them round to block the straits completely, encircling the islands, so that none of the enemy could escape.

[6] While this was being done Aristides, the son of Lysimachus, who was

Ἀριστείδης ὁ Λυσιμάχου πρῶτος αἰσθόμενος ἧκεν ἐπὶ τὴν
σκηνὴν τοῦ Θεμιστοκλέους, οὐκ ὢν φίλος, ἀλλὰ καὶ δι' ἐκεῖνον
ἐξωστρακισμένος ὥσπερ εἴρηται· προελθόντι δὲ τῷ
Θεμιστοκλεῖ φράζει τὴν κύκλωσιν. 7 ὁ δὲ τήν τ' ἄλλην
καλοκἀγαθίαν τοῦ ἀνδρὸς εἰδὼς καὶ τῆς τότε παρουσίας
ἀγάμενος λέγει τὰ περὶ τὸν Σίκιννον αὐτῷ καὶ παρεκάλει τῶν
Ἑλλήνων συνεπιλαμβάνεσθαι καὶ συμπροθυμεῖσθαι πίστιν
ἔχοντα μᾶλλον, ὅπως ἐν τοῖς στενοῖς ναυμαχήσωσιν. 8 ὁ μὲν
οὖν Ἀριστείδης ἐπαινέσας τὸν Θεμιστοκλέα τοὺς ἄλλους
ἐπῄει στρατηγοὺς καὶ τριηράρχους, ἐπὶ τὴν μάχην παροξύνων.
ἔτι δ' ὅμως ἀπιστούντων, ἐφάνη Τενεδία τριήρης αὐτόμολος,
ἧς ἐναυάρχει Παναίτιος, ἀπαγγέλλουσα τὴν κύκλωσιν, ὥστε
καὶ θυμῷ τοὺς Ἕλληνας ὁρμῆσαι μετὰ τῆς ἀνάγκης πρὸς τὸν
κίνδυνον.

13. Ἅμα δ' ἡμέρᾳ Ξέρξης μὲν ἄνω καθῆστο, τὸν στόλον
ἐποπτεύων καὶ τὴν παράταξιν, ὡς μὲν Φανόδημός φησιν ὑπὲρ
τὸ Ἡράκλειον, ᾗ βραχεῖ πόρῳ διείργεται τῆς Ἀττικῆς ἡ
νῆσος, ὡς δ' Ἀκεστόδωρος ἐν μεθορίᾳ τῆς Μεγαρίδος ὑπὲρ
τῶν καλουμένων Κεράτων, χρυσοῦν δίφρον θέμενος καὶ
γραμματεῖς πολλοὺς παραστησάμενος, ὧν ἔργον ἦν
ἀπογράφεσθαι τὰ κατὰ τὴν μάχην πραττόμενα.
2 Θεμιστοκλεῖ δὲ παρὰ τὴν ναυαρχίδα τριήρη σφαγιαζομένῳ
τρεῖς προσήχθησαν αἰχμάλωτοι, κάλλιστοι μὲν ἰδέσθαι τὴν
ὄψιν, ἐσθῆτι δὲ καὶ χρυσῷ κεκοσμημένοι διαπρεπῶς. ἐλέγοντο
δὲ Σανδαύκης παῖδες εἶναι τῆς βασιλέως ἀδελφῆς καὶ
Ἀρταΰκτου.
3 τούτους ἰδὼν Εὐφραντίδης ὁ μάντις, ὡς ἅμα μὲν ἀνέλαμψεν
ἐκ τῶν ἱερῶν μέγα καὶ περιφανὲς πῦρ, ἅμα δὲ πταρμὸς ἐκ
δεξιῶν ἐσήμηνε, τὸν Θεμιστοκλέα δεξιωσάμενος ἐκέλευσε τῶν
νεανίσκων κατάρξασθαι καὶ καθιερεῦσαι πάντας ὠμηστῇ
Διονύσῳ προσευξάμενον· οὕτω γὰρ ἅμα σωτηρίαν καὶ νίκην
ἔσεσθαι τοῖς Ἕλλησιν. 4 ἐκπλαγέντος δὲ τοῦ Θεμιστοκλέους
ὡς μέγα τὸ μάντευμα καὶ δεινόν, οἷον εἴωθεν ἐν μεγάλοις
ἀγῶσι καὶ πράγμασι χαλεποῖς, μᾶλλον ἐκ τῶν παραλόγων ἢ
τῶν εὐλόγων τὴν σωτηρίαν ἐλπίζοντες οἱ πολλοὶ τὸν θεὸν
ἅμα κοινῇ κατεκαλοῦντο φωνῇ, καὶ τοὺς αἰχμαλώτους τῷ
βωμῷ προσαγαγόντες ἠνάγκασαν, ὡς ὁ μάντις ἐκέλευσε, τὴν

the first to be aware of it, came to the tent of Themistocles, a man to whom he was no friend. Indeed it was at Themistocles' doing that he had been ostracised, as I have stated. But when Themistocles came to the entrance he informed him about the encirclement. [7] Themistocles appreciated that he was a man of noble character at all times, but he particularly admired his coming to him at that moment, and so he told him about the Sicinnus stratagem and urged him, as one who had greater credit with the Greeks than himself, to help him to win them over and make them eager to fight a naval battle within the straits. [8] Aristides, for his part, praised Themistocles, and went the rounds of the other generals and captains, trying to rouse their spirits for the fight. Even so they were still unconvinced. But then a trireme of Tenedos appeared, a deserter, commanded by Panaetius, which confirmed that they were encircled. So the Greeks set out to face their danger with a courage which came from necessity.

13. At daybreak Xerxes took his seat on high ground, where he could overlook his force and its order of battle. According to Phanodemus this was above the Heracleum, where the island of Salamis is separated by only a narrow channel from Attica, but according to Acestorides it was where Attica borders on the territory of Megara, above the so-called "Horns". He had a golden seat placed there for him, and several secretaries were in attendance, whose task was to record the events of the battle as they happened.

[2] Meanwhile Themistocles was conducting a sacrifice by the side of the admiral's trireme, and three prisoners of war were brought before him. They were of handsome appearance, and were strikingly dressed in fine clothes and gold ornaments. They were said to be the sons of Sandauce, the King's sister, and Artayctes. [3] Just as Euphrantides the seer caught sight of them a big bright flame shot up from the sacrificial animals, and, at the same moment, a sneeze was heard on the right hand side. At this he grasped Themistocles' right hand, and urged him to consecrate the young men and sacrifice them all to Dionysus the Flesh Eater, with a prayer of supplication. For this, he said, would bring the Greeks salvation and victory. [4] Themistocles was stunned by the seer's utterance, monstrous and terrible as it was. But the rank and file, as is often the case at times of great danger and severe crisis, put their hopes of salvation in irrational rather than rational actions, and, invoking the god by name with a united voice, they dragged the prisoners to the altar, and forced the sacrifice to be performed as the seer had

θυσίαν συντελεσθῆναι. 5 ταῦτα μὲν οὖν ἀνὴρ φιλόσοφος καὶ γραμμάτων οὐκ ἄπειρος ἱστορικῶν Φανίας ὁ Λέσβιος εἴρηκε.

14. Περὶ δὲ τοῦ πλήθους τῶν βαρβαρικῶν νεῶν Αἰσχύλος ὁ ποιητὴς ὡς ἂν εἰδὼς καὶ διαβεβαιούμενος ἐν τραγῳδίᾳ Πέρσαις λέγει ταῦτα·

Ξέρξῃ δέ, καὶ γὰρ οἶδα, χιλιὰς μὲν ἦν
νεῶν τὸ πλῆθος· αἱ δ' ὑπέρκοποι τάχει
ἑκατὸν δὶς ἦσαν ἑπτά θ'· ὧδ' ἔχει λόγος.

2 τῶν δ' Ἀττικῶν ἑκατὸν ὀγδοήκοντα τὸ πλῆθος οὐσῶν ἑκάστη τοὺς ἀπὸ καταστρώματος μαχομένους ὀκτωκαίδεκα εἶχεν, ὧν τοξόται τέσσαρες ἦσαν, οἱ λοιποὶ δ' ὁπλῖται.
3 Δοκεῖ δ' οὐχ ἧττον εὖ τὸν καιρὸν ὁ Θεμιστοκλῆς ἢ τὸν τόπον συνιδὼν καὶ φυλάξας, μὴ πρότερον ἀντιπρῴρους καταστῆσαι ταῖς βαρβαρικαῖς τὰς τριήρεις, ἢ τὴν εἰωθυῖαν ὥραν παραγενέσθαι, τὸ πνεῦμα λαμπρὸν ἐκ πελάγους αἰεὶ καὶ κῦμα διὰ τῶν στενῶν κατάγουσαν· ὃ τὰς μὲν Ἑλληνικὰς οὐκ ἔβλαπτε ναῦς, ἁλιτενεῖς οὔσας καὶ ταπεινοτέρας, τὰς δὲ βαρβαρικὰς ταῖς τε πρύμναις ἀνεστώσας καὶ τοῖς καταστρώμασιν ὑψορόφους καὶ βαρείας ἐπιφερομένας ἔσφαλλε προσπῖπτον καὶ παρεδίδου πλαγίας τοῖς Ἕλλησιν ὀξέως προσφερομένοις καὶ τῷ Θεμιστοκλεῖ προσέχουσιν ὡς ὁρῶντι μάλιστα τὸ συμφέρον· ὅθεν κατ' ἐκεῖνον ὁ Ξέρξου ναύαρχος Ἀριαμένης ναῦν ἔχων μεγάλην ὥσπερ ἀπὸ τείχους ἐτόξευε καὶ ἠκόντιζεν, ἀνὴρ ἀγαθὸς ὢν καὶ τῶν βασιλέως ἀδελφῶν πολὺ κράτιστος καὶ δικαιότατος. 4 τοῦτον μὲν οὖν Ἀμεινίας ὁ Δεκελεὺς καὶ Σωκλῆς ὁ Παλληνεύς ὁμοῦ πλέοντες, ὡς αἱ νῆες ἀντίπρῳροι προσπεσοῦσαι καὶ συνερείσασαι τοῖς χαλκώμασιν ἐνεσχέθησαν, ἐπιβαίνοντα τῆς αὐτῶν τριήρους ὑποστάντες καὶ τοῖς δόρασι τύπτοντες εἰς τὴν θάλασσαν ἐξέβαλον, καὶ τὸ σῶμα μετὰ τῶν ἄλλων διαφερόμενον ναυαγίων Ἀρτεμισία γνωρίσασα πρὸς Ξέρξην ἀνήνεγκεν.

15. Εν δὲ τούτῳ τοῦ ἀγῶνος ὄντος φῶς μὲν ἐκλάμψαι μέγα λέγουσιν Ἐλευσινόθεν, ἦχον δὲ καὶ φωνὴν τὸ Θριάσιον κατέχειν πεδίον ἄχρι θαλάττης, ὡς ἀνθρώπων ὁμοῦ πολλῶν τὸν μυστικὸν ἐξαγόντων Ἴακχον. ἐκ δὲ τοῦ πλήθους τῶν φθεγγομένων κατὰ μικρὸν ἀπὸ γῆς ἀναφερόμενον νέφος ἔδοξεν αὖθις ὑπονοστεῖν καὶ κατασκήπτειν εἰς τὰς τριήρεις.

urged. [5] This at any rate is the story told by Phanias of Lesbos, who was a learned man, and well acquainted with works of history.

14. With regard to the number of the barbarian ships, the playwright Aeschylus writes as follows in his tragedy *The Persians*, as one who knew and could have been certain about it:-

"But Xerxes, and I do know this, had a thousand ships in total, and there were two hundred and seven especially fast ones. Such is the count."

[2] The Athenian contingent numbered one hundred and eighty, each ship having eighteen marines to fight on the deck, of whom four were archers and the rest hoplites.

[3] Themistocles appears to have judged the best time for the battle as skilfully as he did the best place, and to have been careful not to send the triremes bow on against the barbarian ships until that particular time of day when the breeze always blows fresh from the sea, and a swell rolls through the straits. This did no harm to the Greek ships, which were of shallow draught and lay quite low in the water, but when it caught the barbarian ships, with their raised sterns and high decks and sluggish manoeuvrability, it caused havoc, and swung them round broadside to the Greeks, who attacked them keenly. They kept their eyes on Themistocles, in the belief that he saw better than anyone what were the best tactics. For this reason, ranged against him on board a great ship, Xerxes' admiral Ariamenes kept shooting arrows and javelins at him as though from the top of a city wall. He was a brave man, and by far the strongest and most principled of the King's brothers. [4] Now Ameinias of the deme Deceleia and Socles of Pallene were sailing together in the same trireme, and, when the two ships struck each other bow to bow and were then pressed together and impaled on each other by their bronze beaks, Ariamenes tried to board their trireme. But they stood up to him and, striking him with their spears, they pitched him overboard into the sea. His body was recognised by Artemisia as it floated about amidst all the wreckage, and she had it brought back to Xerxes.

15. When the battle was at this stage it is said that a great light flashed out from Eleusis, and a reverberating sound filled the Thriasian plain right down to the sea, as though coming from a large body of men escorting Iacchus, god of the Mysteries, in a procession. Then, out of the shouting throng, a cloud seemed slowly to rise up from the land, and then to come down and

2 ἕτεροι δὲ φάσματα καὶ εἴδωλα καθορᾶν ἔδοξαν ἐνόπλων ἀνδρῶν ἀπ' Αἰγίνης τὰς χεῖρας ἀνεχόντων πρὸ τῶν Ἑλληνικῶν τριήρων, οὓς εἴκαζον Αἰακίδας εἶναι παρακεκλημένους εὐχαῖς πρὸ τῆς μάχης ἐπὶ τὴν βοήθειαν.
3 πρῶτος μὲν οὖν λαμβάνει ναῦν Λυκομήδης, ἀνὴρ Ἀθηναῖος τριηραρχῶν, ἧς τὰ παράσημα περικόψας ἀνέθηκεν Ἀπόλλωνι δαφνηφόρῳ Φλυῆσιν. 4 οἱ δ' ἄλλοι τοῖς βαρβάροις ἐξισούμενοι τὸ πλῆθος ἐν στενῷ κατὰ μέρος προσφερομένους καὶ περιπίπτοντας ἀλλήλοις ἐτρέψαντο μέχρι δείλης ἀντισχόντας, ὥσπερ εἴρηκε Σιμωνίδης, τὴν καλὴν ἐκείνην καὶ περιβόητον ἀράμενοι νίκην, ἧς οὔθ' Ἕλλησιν οὔτε βαρβάροις ἐνάλιον ἔργον εἴργασται λαμπρότερον, ἀνδρείᾳ μὲν καὶ προθυμίᾳ κοινῇ τῶν ναυμαχησάντων, γνώμῃ δὲ καὶ δεινότητι τῇ Θεμιστοκλέους.

16. Μετὰ δὲ τὴν ναυμαχίαν Ξέρξης μὲν ἔτι θυμομαχῶν πρὸς τὴν ἀπότευξιν ἐπεχείρει διὰ χωμάτων ἐπάγειν τὸ πεζὸν εἰς Σαλαμῖνα τοῖς Ἕλλησιν, ἐμφράξας τὸν διὰ μέσου πόρον· 2 Θεμιστοκλῆς δ' ἀποπειρώμενος Ἀριστείδου λόγῳ γνώμην ἐποιεῖτο λύειν τὸ ζεῦγμα ταῖς ναυσὶν ἐπιπλεύσαντας εἰς Ἑλλήσποντον, "ὅπως ἔφη "τὴν Ἀσίαν ἐν τῇ Εὐρώπῃ λάβωμεν." 3 δυσχεραίνοντος δὲ τοῦ Ἀριστείδου καὶ λέγοντος ὅτι "νῦν μὲν τρυφῶντι τῷ βαρβάρῳ πεπολεμήκαμεν· ἐὰν δὲ κατακλείσωμεν εἰς τὴν Ἑλλάδα καὶ καταστήσωμεν εἰς ἀνάγκην ὑπὸ δέους ἄνδρα τηλικούτων δυνάμεων κύριον, οὐκέτι καθήμενος ὑπὸ σκιάδι χρυσῇ θεάσεται τὴν μάχην ἐφ' ἡσυχίας, ἀλλὰ πάντα τολμῶν καὶ πᾶσιν αὐτὸς παρὼν διὰ τὸν κίνδυνον ἐπανορθώσεται τὰ παρειμένα καὶ βουλεύσεται βέλτιον ὑπὲρ τῶν ὅλων. 4 οὐ τὴν οὖσαν οὖν" ἔφη "δεῖ γέφυραν ὦ Θεμιστόκλεις ἡμᾶς ἀναιρεῖν, ἀλλ' ἑτέραν εἴπερ οἷόν τε προσκατασκευάσαντας ἐκβαλεῖν διὰ τάχους τὸν ἄνθρωπον ἐκ τῆς Εὐρώπης", "οὐκοῦν" εἶπεν ὁ Θεμιστοκλῆς "εἰ δοκεῖ ταῦτα συμφέρειν, ὥρα σκοπεῖν καὶ μηχανᾶσθαι πάντας ἡμᾶς, ὅπως ἀπαλλαγήσεται τὴν ταχίστην ἐκ τῆς Ἑλλάδος."
5 Ἐπεὶ δὲ ταῦτ' ἔδοξεν, ἔπεμπέ τινα τῶν βασιλικῶν εὐνούχων ἐν τοῖς αἰχμαλώτοις ἀνευρὼν Ἀρνάκην ὄνομα, φράζειν βασιλεῖ κελεύσας ὅτι τοῖς μὲν Ἕλλησι δέδοκται τῷ ναυτικῷ

settle over the triremes. [2] Others thought they saw phantoms and images of armed men coming from Aegina, with their hands stretched out to protect the Greek triremes. They imagined that these were the sons of Aeacus, whom they had invoked in prayers before the battle to come to their aid.

[3] The first man to capture an enemy ship was Lycomedes, an Athenian trireme-captain. He cut off its figure-head, and dedicated it to Apollo the Laurel-wearer at Phlya. [4] Then the rest, finding themselves on equal terms numerically with the barbarians, because the narrow straits only allowed the enemy to bring to bear one detachment at a time and caused their ships to keep colliding with one another, put them to flight, though their resistance lasted till evening. Thus, as Simonides has said, they won that fine and famous victory - and no more brilliant exploit has ever been performed at sea either by Greeks or barbarians - thanks to the courage and enthusiasm of all who fought in the battle, but particularly thanks to the good judgement and cleverness of Themistocles.

16. After the sea-battle Xerxes, who was still spoiling for a fight despite his failure, started to build moles, over which he could transport his infantry to attack the Greeks at Salamis by blocking up the intervening straits. [2] Then Themistocles, by way of drawing out Aristides' view, made an apparently serious proposal that they should take the fleet and sail to the Hellespont and destroy the bridge of boats there, "In order", he said, "that we may capture Asia while still remaining in Europe." [3] But Aristides was unhappy with the idea, and replied, "Up to now the barbarian whom we have been fighting has been complacent, but if we shut him up in Greece, and frighten into desperate necessity a man who commands such large forces, he will no longer stay sitting under a golden parasol, just quietly watching the hostilities. Instead he will steel himself for anything, and involve himself personally in every action because of the danger he is in, and as a result he will compensate for his previous negligence and make better plans for securing his overall objectives. [4] So we ought not to think of destroying the existing bridge, Themistocles, but should rather build another one next to it, if that is possible, so as to get the man out of Europe as quickly as we can." "Very well then," said Themistocles, "if you think that that is where our interest lies, it is time for all of us to take thought and come up with a plan to get him out of Greece by the fastest route possible."

[5] When this policy had been agreed, he sent one of the royal eunuchs whom he had found among the prisoners of war, a man called Arnaces, with instructions to tell the King that the Greeks had decided, now that their fleet

κεκρατηκότας ἀναπλεῖν εἰς τὸν Ἑλλήσποντον ἐπὶ τὸ ζεῦγμα καὶ λύειν τὴν γέφυραν, Θεμιστοκλῆς δὲ κηδόμενος βασιλέως παραινεῖ σπεύδειν ἐπὶ τὴν αὐτοῦ θάλατταν καὶ περαιοῦσθαι, μέχρις αὐτὸς ἐμποιεῖ τινας διατριβὰς τοῖς συμμάχοις καὶ μελλήσεις πρὸς τὴν δίωξιν. 6 ταῦθ' ὁ βάρβαρος ἀκούσας καὶ γενόμενος περίφοβος, διὰ τάχους ἐποιεῖτο τὴν ἀναχώρησιν, καὶ πεῖραν ἡ Θεμιστοκλέους καὶ 'Αριστείδου φρόνησις ἐν Μαρδονίῳ παρέσχεν, εἴγε πολλοστημορίῳ τῆς Ξέρξου δυνάμεως διαγωνισάμενοι Πλαταιᾶσιν εἰς τὸν περὶ τῶν ὅλων κίνδυνον κατέστησαν.

17. Πόλεων μὲν οὖν τὴν Αἰγινητῶν ἀριστεῦσαί φησιν Ἡρόδοτος, Θεμιστοκλεῖ δὲ καίπερ ἄκοντες ὑπὸ φθόνου τὸ πρωτεῖον ἀπέδοσαν ἅπαντες. 2 ἐπεὶ γὰρ ἀναχωρήσαντες εἰς τὸν Ἰσθμὸν ἀπὸ τοῦ βωμοῦ τὴν ψῆφον ἔφερον οἱ στρατηγοί, πρῶτον μὲν ἕκαστος αὑτὸν ἀπέφαινεν ἀρετῇ, δεύτερον δὲ μεθ' αὑτὸν Θεμιστοκλέα. 3 Λακεδαιμόνιοι δ' εἰς τὴν Σπάρτην αὐτὸν καταγαγόντες, Εὐρυβιάδῃ μὲν ἀνδρείας, ἐκείνῳ δὲ σοφίας ἀριστεῖον ἔδοσαν θαλλοῦ στέφανον, καὶ τῶν κατὰ τὴν πόλιν ἁρμάτων τὸ πρωτεῦον ἐδωρήσαντο καὶ τριακοσίους τῶν νέων πομποὺς ἄχρι τῶν ὅρων συνεξέπεμψαν. 4 λέγεται δ' 'Ολυμπίων τῶν ἑξῆς ἀγομένων, καὶ παρελθόντος εἰς τὸ στάδιον τοῦ Θεμιστοκλέους, ἀμελήσαντας τῶν ἀγωνιστῶν τοὺς παρόντας ὅλην τὴν ἡμέραν ἐκεῖνον θεᾶσθαι καὶ τοῖς ξένοις ἐπιδεικνύειν ἅμα θαυμάζοντας καὶ κροτοῦντας, ὥστε καὶ αὐτὸν ἡσθέντα πρὸς τοὺς φίλους ὁμολογῆσαι τὸν καρπὸν ἀπέχειν τῶν ὑπὲρ τῆς Ἑλλάδος αὐτῷ πονηθέντων.

18. Καὶ γὰρ ἦν τῇ φύσει φιλοτιμότατος, εἰ δεῖ τεκμαίρεσθαι διὰ τῶν ἀπομνημονευομένων. αἱρεθεὶς γὰρ ναύαρχος ὑπὸ τῆς πόλεως, οὐδὲν οὔτε τῶν ἰδίων οὔτε τῶν κοινῶν κατὰ μέρος ἐχρημάτιζεν, ἀλλὰ πᾶν ἀνεβάλλετο τὸ προσπῖπτον εἰς τὴν ἡμέραν ἐκείνην καθ' ἣν ἐκπλεῖν ἔμελλεν, ἵν' ὁμοῦ πολλὰ πράττων πράγματα καὶ παντοδαποῖς ἀνθρώποις ὁμιλῶν μέγας εἶναι δοκῇ καὶ πλεῖστον δύνασθαι.

2 Τῶν δὲ νεκρῶν τοὺς ἐκπεσόντας ἐπισκοπῶν παρὰ τὴν θάλατταν, ὡς εἶδε περικειμένους ψέλια χρυσᾶ καὶ στρεπτούς,

had given them control of the sea, to sail north to the Hellespont to attack the pontoon bridge of boats and destroy it, but that Themistocles, out of his regard for the King, advised him to hurry back towards his home waters and cross over to Asia, while he himself would engineer various delays and postponements of the allies' pursuit. [6] On hearing this the barbarian leader was extremely alarmed and quickly began to organise his retreat. The wisdom shown here by Themistocles and Aristides was demonstrated in the campaign against Mardonius, when, although the Greeks at Plataea had to fight against only a small fraction of Xerxes' army, they still found themselves in danger of losing everything.

17. Herodotus tells us that of all the Greek states the Aeginetans proved themselves the bravest, and that everyone awarded the first prize for individuals to Themistocles, albeit unintentionally because of their jealousy. [2] For when the generals had withdrawn to the Isthmus and proceeded to cast their votes, taken from the altar there, each one of them declared himself first in valour, with Themistocles second after himself. [3] And the Lacedaemonians invited him down to Sparta, where they gave Eurybiades a prize for valour and Themistocles one for wisdom - an olive crown each - and they presented him with the finest chariot in the city, and sent him off with an escort of three hundred young men to accompany him as far as the frontier. [4] It is said that, when the next Olympic games were being celebrated and Themistocles entered the stadium, the spectators lost interest in the competitors and spent the whole day watching him, pointing him out to foreigners with words of admiration and applause. Themistocles was delighted by this, and agreed with his friends that he was reaping in full measure the reward for his great efforts on Greece's behalf.

18. Certainly he was by nature very eager to be famous, if one may judge from the well-known stories told about him. For example, having been elected admiral by the city, he would refuse to transact any part of his private or public business as it occurred, but would postpone everything that came up until the day on which he was to set sail, in order that, by dealing with a great deal of business all at once, and having meetings with all sorts of people, he would give the appearance of being an important and very powerful figure.

[2] Again, when he was looking at some Persian corpses which had been washed up along the seashore, and noticed that they were adorned with gold bracelets and necklaces, he himself passed them by, but pointed them out to

αὐτὸς μὲν παρῆλθε, τῷ δ' ἑπομένῳ φίλῳ δείξας εἶπεν· "ἀνελοῦ σαυτῷ· σὺ γὰρ οὐκ εἶ Θεμιστοκλῆς." 3 Πρὸς δέ τινα τῶν καλῶν γεγονότων 'Αντιφάτην, ὑπερηφάνως αὐτῷ κεχρημένον πρότερον, ὕστερον δὲ θεραπεύοντα διὰ τὴν δόξαν "ὦ μειράκιον" εἶπεν, "ὀψὲ μέν, ἀμφότεροι δ' ὁμοῦ νοῦν ἐσχήκαμεν." 4 Ἔλεγε δὲ τοὺς 'Αθηναίους οὐ τιμᾶν αὐτὸν οὐδὲ θαυμάζειν, ἀλλ' ὥσπερ πλατάνῳ χειμαζομένους μὲν ὑποτρέχειν κινδυνεύοντας, εὐδίας δὲ περὶ αὐτοὺς γενομένης τίλλειν καὶ κολούειν. 5 Τοῦ δὲ Σεριφίου πρὸς αὐτὸν εἰπόντος ὡς οὐ δι' αὐτὸν ἔσχηκε δόξαν, ἀλλὰ διὰ τὴν πόλιν, "ἀληθῆ λέγεις" εἶπεν· "ἀλλ' οὔτ' ἂν ἐγὼ Σερίφιος ὢν ἐγενόμην ἔνδοξος, οὔτε σὺ 'Αθηναῖος." 6 Ἑτέρου δέ τινος τῶν στρατηγῶν, ὡς ἔδοξέ τι χρήσιμον διαπεπρᾶχθαι τῇ πόλει, θρασυνομένου πρὸς τὸν Θεμιστοκλέα καὶ τὰς ἑαυτοῦ ταῖς ἐκείνου πράξεσιν ἀντιπαραβάλλοντος, ἔφη τῇ ἑορτῇ τὴν ὑστεραίαν ἐρίσαι, λέγουσαν ὡς ἐκείνη μὲν ἀσχολιῶν τε μεστὴ καὶ κοπώδης ἐστίν, ἐν αὐτῇ δὲ πάντες ἀπολαύουσι τῶν παρεσκευασμένων σχολάζοντες· τὴν δ' ἑορτὴν πρὸς ταῦτ' εἰπεῖν· "ἀληθῆ λέγεις· ἀλλ' ἐμοῦ μὴ γενομένης σὺ οὐκ ἂν ἦσθα·" "κἀμοῦ τοίνυν" ἔφη "τότε μὴ γενομένου, ποῦ ἂν ἦτε νῦν ὑμεῖς;" 7 Τὸν δ' υἱὸν ἐντρυφῶντα τῇ μητρὶ καὶ δι' ἐκείνην ἑαυτῷ σκώπτων ἔλεγε πλεῖστον τῶν Ἑλλήνων δύνασθαι· τοῖς μὲν γὰρ Ἕλλησιν ἐπιτάσσειν 'Αθηναίους, 'Αθηναίοις δ' ἑαυτόν, αὑτῷ δὲ τὴν ἐκείνου μητέρα, τῇ μητρὶ δ' ἐκεῖνον. 8 Ἴδιος δέ τις ἐν πᾶσι βουλόμενος εἶναι, χωρίον μὲν πιπράσκων ἐκέλευε κηρύττειν ὅτι καὶ γείτονα χρηστὸν ἔχει· 9 τῶν δὲ μνωμένων αὐτοῦ τὴν θυγατέρα τὸν ἐπιεικῆ τοῦ πλουσίου προκρίνας, ἔφη ζητεῖν ἄνδρα χρημάτων δεόμενον μᾶλλον ἢ χρήματα ἀνδρός. ἐν μὲν οὖν τοῖς ἀποφθέγμασι τοιοῦτός τις ἦν.

19. Γενόμενος δ' ἀπὸ τῶν πράξεων ἐκείνων, εὐθὺς ἐπεχείρει τὴν πόλιν ἀνοικοδομεῖν καὶ τειχίζειν, ὡς μὲν ἱστορεῖ

a friend who was following and said "Help yourself; you are not Themistocles." [3] A certain Antiphates had been one of the attractive young men at Athens, and in those days had treated Themistocles with disdain, but later he started to court him, because of his subsequent fame. To him he said "My boy, it's late in the day, but now we have both recovered our senses."

[4] He used to say that the Athenians did not honour or admire him for himself, but treated him like a plane tree. They ran beneath his branches when there was a storm and they were in danger of getting drenched, but, when they had a period of fine weather, they plucked and pruned him.

[5] Again, when the man from Seriphos said to him that he had not acquired his great reputation because of his own merits, but because of the city he came from, he replied "That is true, I would not have become famous if I had been a Seriphian. But neither would you, even if you had been an Athenian."

[6] When another member of the board of generals, who thought he had done some useful service to the state, began to attack Themistocles by boldly comparing his own achievements with his, he answered "The day called After the Festival once began a quarrel with the Festival Day saying `You are taken up with tasks and tiresome work, but on my day everyone enjoys at their leisure what has been prepared beforehand.' To this the Festival Day replied, `That is true, but if I had not come first you would not have come at all.' So in my case too, if I had not come then, where would the rest of you be now?"

[7] He once said jokingly of his son, who was spoiled by his mother and, through her, by himself, that he was the most powerful person in Greece, since the Athenians gave orders to the Greeks, he gave orders to the Athenians, the boy's mother gave orders to him, and the boy gave orders to his mother.

[8] He wished to be rather special in everything he did, and so, when he was putting an estate up for sale, he ordered a proclamation to be made that it had an excellent neighbour to go with it. [9] Again, of the two suitors for his daughter's hand, he chose the one who was able in preference to the one who was rich, saying that he was looking for a man without money rather than money without a man.

So he showed in his sayings the sort of man he was.

19. Fresh from these great achievements he at once set to work to to rebuild and fortify the city. He bribed the ephors not to oppose it, or so

Θεόπομπος χρήμασι πείσας μὴ ἐναντιωθῆναι τοὺς ἐφόρους, ὡς δ' οἱ πλεῖστοι, παρακρουσάμενος. 2 ἧκε μὲν γὰρ εἰς Σπάρτην ὄνομα πρεσβείας ἐπιγραψάμενος· ἐγκαλούντων δὲ τῶν Σπαρτιατῶν ὅτι τειχίζουσι τὸ ἄστυ, καὶ Πολυάρχου κατηγοροῦντος ἐπίτηδες ἐξ Αἰγίνης ἀποσταλέντος, ἠρνεῖτο καὶ πέμπειν ἐκέλευεν εἰς Ἀθήνας τοὺς κατοψομένους, ἅμα μὲν ἐμβάλλων τῷ τειχισμῷ χρόνον ἐκ τῆς διατριβῆς, ἅμα δὲ βουλόμενος ἀνθ' αὑτοῦ τοὺς πεμπομένους ὑπάρχειν τοῖς Ἀθηναίοις. 3 ὃ καὶ συνέβη· γνόντες γὰρ οἱ Λακεδαιμόνιοι τὸ ἀληθὲς οὐκ ἠδίκησαν αὐτόν, ἀλλ' ἀδήλως χαλεπαίνοντες ἀπέπεμψαν.

ἐκ δὲ τούτου τὸν Πειραιᾶ κατεσκεύαζε, τὴν τῶν λιμένων εὐφυΐαν κατανοήσας καὶ τὴν πόλιν ὅλην ἁρμοττόμενος πρὸς τὴν θάλατταν, καὶ τρόπον τινὰ τοῖς παλαιοῖς βασιλεῦσι τῶν Ἀθηναίων ἀντιπολιτευόμενος. 4 ἐκεῖνοι μὲν γὰρ ὡς λέγεται πραγματευόμενοι τοὺς πολίτας ἀποσπάσαι τῆς θαλάττης, καὶ συνεθίσαι ζῆν μὴ πλέοντας, ἀλλὰ τὴν χώραν φυτεύοντας, τὸν περὶ τῆς Ἀθηνᾶς διέδοσαν λόγον, ὡς ἐρίσαντα περὶ τῆς χώρας Ποσειδῶνα δείξασα τὴν μορίαν τοῖς δικασταῖς ἐνίκησεν. Θεμιστοκλῆς δ' οὐχ, ὥσπερ Ἀριστοφάνης ὁ κωμικός φησι, τῇ πόλει "τὸν Πειραιᾶ προσέμαξεν", ἀλλὰ τὴν πόλιν ἐξῆψε τοῦ Πειραιῶς καὶ τὴν γῆν τῆς θαλάττης· 5 ὅθεν καὶ τὸν δῆμον ηὔξησε κατὰ τῶν ἀρίστων καὶ θράσους ἐνέπλησεν, εἰς ναύτας καὶ κελευστὰς καὶ κυβερνήτας τῆς δυνάμεως ἀφικομένης. 6 διὸ καὶ τὸ βῆμα τὸ ἐν Πυκνὶ πεποιημένον ὥστ' ἀποβλέπειν πρὸς τὴν θάλατταν ὕστερον οἱ τριάκοντα πρὸς τὴν χώραν ἀπέστρεψαν, οἰόμενοι τὴν μὲν κατὰ θάλατταν ἀρχὴν γένεσιν εἶναι δημοκρατίας, ὀλιγαρχίᾳ δ' ἧττον δυσχεραίνειν τοὺς γεωργοῦντας.

20. Θεμιστοκλῆς δὲ καὶ μεῖζόν τι περὶ τῆς ναυτικῆς διενοήθη δυνάμεως. ἐπεὶ γὰρ ὁ τῶν Ἑλλήνων στόλος ἀπηλλαγμένου Ξέρξου κατῆρεν εἰς Παγασὰς καὶ διεχείμαζε, δημηγορῶν ἐν τοῖς Ἀθηναίοις ἔφη τινα πρᾶξιν ἔχειν ὠφέλιμον μὲν αὐτοῖς καὶ σωτήριον, ἀπόρρητον δὲ πρὸς τοὺς πολλούς. 2 τῶν δ' Ἀθηναίων Ἀριστείδῃ φράσαι μόνῳ κελευόντων, κἂν ἐκεῖνος δοκιμάσῃ, περαίνειν, ὁ μὲν Θεμιστοκλῆς ἔφρασε τῷ Ἀριστείδῃ τὸ νεώριον ἐμπρῆσαι διανοεῖσθαι τῶν Ἑλλήνων· ὁ δ'

Theopompus records; though in the accounts of most authorities he employed deception. [2] He came to Sparta as an envoy, having ensured that his name was put down for the embassy. Then, when the Spartans complained that the Athenians were continuing to build the city wall, and Polyarchus was dispatched from Aegina specifically to make the same accusation, Themistocles kept denying it, and told them to send people to Athens to see for themselves. His motive was to gain time from the delay for the completion of the fortification, and, at the same time, to put the envoys into the Athenians' hands as a safeguard for his own security. [3] It did turn out just as he had planned. For when the Spartans discovered the truth, they did not harm him, but, instead, concealed their anger and sent him away.

After this he started to develop the Piraeus, because he had noticed the favourable shape of its harbours, and wished to join the entire city to the sea. Thus in a way he adopted the opposite policy to that of the ancient kings of Athens. [4] For they, it is said, in their efforts to draw the citizens away from the sea, and accustom them to make a living not by seafaring but by cultivating the land, disseminated the story about Athena. This was to the effect that, when Poseidon was contending with her for authority over the country, she won the judges' verdict by revealing to them the sacred olive tree. Themistocles did not "knead the Piraeus onto the city", as Aristophanes the comic poet puts it, but, rather, he fastened the city on to the Piraeus, and the land on to the sea. [5] As a result he increased the strength of the common people as against the nobility, and filled them with boldness, as political power fell into the hands of oarsmen and boatswains and helmsmen. [6] This was also the reason why the speaker's platform on the Pnyx, which had been constructed so as to look out towards the sea, was later turned round by the Thirty to face inland, because they took the view that Athens' maritime empire had been the begetter of democracy, and that those who worked on the land were less hostile to an oligarchy.

20. Next Themistocles thought up an even more ambitious plan for securing naval supremacy. When the Greek fleet, after Xerxes' retreat, had put in at Pagasae and was laid up there for the winter, he made a speech before the Athenian assembly, in which he said he had in mind a certain course of action which would bring them advantages and security, but which could not be publicly divulged. [2] The Athenians told him to reveal it to Aristides alone, and, if he approved it, to put it into effect. So Themistocles explained to Aristides that his plan was to burn the Greek fleet in its dockyard.

Ἀριστείδης εἰς τὸν δῆμον προελθὼν ἔφη τῆς πράξεως ἣν διανοεῖται πράττειν ὁ Θεμιστοκλῆς μηδεμίαν εἶναι μήτε λυσιτελεστέραν μήτ' ἀδικωτέραν. οἱ μὲν οὖν Ἀθηναῖοι διὰ ταῦτα παύσασθαι τῷ Θεμιστοκλεῖ προσέταξαν.

3 Ἐν δὲ τοῖς Ἀμφικτυονικοῖς συνεδρίοις τῶν Λακεδαιμονίων εἰσηγουμένων ὅπως ἀπείργωνται τῆς Ἀμφικτυονίας αἱ μὴ συμμαχήσασαι κατὰ τοῦ Μήδου πόλεις, φοβηθεὶς μὴ Θετταλοὺς καὶ Ἀργείους, ἔτι δὲ Θηβαίους ἐκβαλόντες τοῦ συνεδρίου παντελῶς ἐπικρατήσωσι τῶν ψήφων καὶ γένηται τὸ δοκοῦν ἐκείνοις, συνεῖπε ταῖς πόλεσι καὶ μετέθηκε τὰς γνώμας τῶν πυλαγόρων, διδάξας ὡς τριάκοντα καὶ μία μόναι πόλεις εἰσὶν αἱ τοῦ πολέμου μετασχοῦσαι, καὶ τούτων αἱ πλείους παντάπασι μικραί· 4 δεινὸν οὖν εἰ τῆς ἄλλης Ἑλλάδος ἐκσπόνδου γενομένης ἐπὶ ταῖς μεγίσταις δυσὶν ἢ τρισὶ πόλεσιν ἔσται τὸ συνέδριον. ἐκ τούτου μὲν οὖν μάλιστα τοῖς Λακεδαιμονίοις προσέκρουσε· διὸ καὶ τὸν Κίμωνα προῆγον ταῖς τιμαῖς, ἀντίπαλον ἐν τῇ πολιτείᾳ τῷ Θεμιστοκλεῖ καθιστάντες.

21. Ἦν δὲ καὶ τοῖς συμμάχοις ἐπαχθὴς περιπλέων τε τὰς νήσους καὶ χρηματιζόμενος ἀπ' αὐτῶν· οἷα καὶ πρὸς Ἀνδρίους ἀργύριον αἰτοῦντά φησιν αὐτὸν Ἡρόδοτος εἰπεῖν τε καὶ ἀκοῦσαι. 2 δύο γὰρ ἥκειν ἔφη θεοὺς κομίζων, Πειθὼ καὶ Βίαν· οἱ δ' ἔφασαν εἶναι καὶ παρ' αὐτοῖς θεοὺς μεγάλους δύο, Πενίαν καὶ Ἀπορίαν, ὑφ' ὧν κωλύεσθαι δοῦναι χρήματα ἐκείνῳ.

3 Τιμοκρέων δ' ὁ Ῥόδιος μελοποιὸς ἐν ᾄσματι καθάπτεται πικρότερον τοῦ Θεμιστοκλέους, ὡς ἄλλους μὲν ἐπὶ χρήμασι φυγάδας διαπραξαμένου κατελθεῖν, αὐτὸν δὲ ξένον ὄντα καὶ φίλον προεμένου δι' ἀργύριον. 4 λέγει δ' οὕτως·

ἀλλ' εἰ τύ γα Παυσανίαν ἢ καὶ τύ γα Ξάνθιππον αἰνεῖς
ἢ τύ γα Λευτυχίδαν, ἐγὼ δ' Ἀριστείδαν ἐπαινέω
ἄνδρ' ἱερᾶν ἀπ' Ἀθανᾶν
ἐλθεῖν ἕνα λῷστον· ἐπεὶ Θεμιστοκλέα γ' ἤχθαρε Λατώ,
ψεύσταν, ἄδικον, προδόταν, ὃς Τιμοκρέοντα ξεῖνον ἐόντα
ἀργυρίοισι κοβαλικοῖσι πεισθεὶς οὐ κατᾶγεν
εἰς πατρίδα Ἰάλυσον,
λαβὼν δὲ τρί' ἀργυρίου τάλαντ' ἔβα πλέων εἰς ὄλεθρον,
τοὺς μὲν κατάγων ἀδίκως, τοὺς δ' ἐκδιώκων, τοὺς δὲ καίνων.

Thereupon Aristides came forward to speak, and told the people that no scheme could be more advantageous than that of Themistocles – and none more unjust. As a result the Athenians ordered Themistocles to abandon it.

[3] At a meeting of the Amphictyonic delegates the Spartans put forward a proposal that all those states which had not fought in the alliance against the Persians should be debarred from the Amphictyonic Council. But Themistocles was afraid that, if they succeeded in expelling from the council the Thessalians and the Argives, and the Thebans as well, they would completely control the votes, and so be able to do anything they wanted. [4] So he spoke on behalf of these states, and changed the views of the delegates by pointing out that the cities which had taken part in the war were only thirty-one in number, and of these the majority were extremely small. So it would be intolerable, he argued, if the rest of Greece should be excluded, and the Council be at the mercy of the two or three biggest cities. It was through this intervention, in particular, that he upset the Spartans. As a result they started to promote the career of Cimon by bestowing their favours on him, thus setting him up as a political rival to Themistocles.

21. He became obnoxious to the allies as well, by sailing round the islands trying to extort money from them. As an example of this, Herodotus tells us of his remark and the reply he got when he demanded money from the Andrians. [2] He said he had come bringing with him two gods, Persuasion and Force; but they replied that they also had two important gods, Poverty and Scarcity, and by these they were prevented from giving him any money.

[3] Timocreon, the lyric poet of Rhodes, attacks Themistocles rather bitterly in a song, where he says that, in return for a bribe, Themistocles secured the restoration home of other exiles, but abandoned him, though he was his host and a friend, all because of money. [4] He speaks as follows:-

> "You may praise Pausanias, you may praise Xanthippus, you may praise Leotychidas, but I give my praise to Aristides, who is by far the best man to come from holy Athens; for Leto hates Themistocles, that liar, criminal and traitor, who, though Timocreon was his host, for a dirty bribe refused to restore him to his native city Ialysus. Instead he pocketed three silver talents and then sailed off (to Hell I hope), restoring men without justification, banishing men, killing men, while he stuffed

ἀργυρίου δ' ὑπόπλεως, Ἰσθμοῖ γελοίως πανδόκευε ψυχρὰ κρέα
παρέχων·
οἱ δ' ἤσθιον κηὔχοντο μὴ ὥραν Θεμιστοκλέος γενέσθαι.

5 πολὺ δ' ἀσελγεστέρᾳ καὶ ἀναπεπταμένῃ μᾶλλον εἰς τὸν Θεμιστοκλέα βλασφημίᾳ κέχρηται μετὰ τὴν φυγὴν αὐτοῦ καὶ τὴν καταδίκην ὁ Τιμοκρέων, ᾆσμα ποιήσας οὗ ἐστιν ἀρχή·

6 Μοῦσα τοῦδε τοῦ μέλεος
κλέος ἀν' Ἕλλανας τίθει,
ὡς ἐοικὸς καὶ δίκαιον.

7 λέγεται δ' ὁ Τιμοκρέων ἐπὶ μηδισμῷ φυγεῖν συγκαταψηφισαμένου τοῦ Θεμιστοκλέους. ὡς οὖν ὁ Θεμιστοκλῆς αἰτίαν ἔσχε μηδίζειν, ταῦτ' ἐποίησεν εἰς αὐτόν·

οὐκ ἄρα Τιμοκρέων μόνος
Μήδοισιν ὁρκιατομεῖ,
ἀλλ' ἐντὶ κἆλλοι δὴ πονηροί·
οὐκ ἐγὼ μόνα κόλουρις·
ἐντὶ κἆλλαι ἀλώπεκες.

22. Ἤδη δὲ καὶ τῶν πολιτῶν διὰ τὸ φθονεῖν ἡδέως τὰς διαβολὰς προσιεμένων, ἠναγκάζετο λυπηρὸς εἶναι τῶν αὐτοῦ πράξεων πολλάκις ἐν τῷ δήμῳ μνημονεύων, καὶ πρὸς τοὺς δυσχεραίνοντας "τί κοπιᾶτε" εἶπεν "ὑπὸ τῶν αὐτῶν πολλάκις εὖ πάσχοντες;" 2 ἠνίασε δὲ τοὺς πολλοὺς καὶ τὸ τῆς Ἀρτέμιδος ἱερὸν εἰσάμενος, ἣν Ἀριστοβούλην μὲν προσηγόρευσεν ὡς ἄριστα τῇ πόλει καὶ τοῖς Ἕλλησι βουλευσάμενος, πλησίον δὲ τῆς οἰκίας κατεσκεύασεν ἐν Μελίτῃ τὸ ἱερόν, οὗ νῦν τὰ σώματα τῶν θανατουμένων οἱ δήμιοι προβάλλουσι καὶ τὰ ἱμάτια καὶ τοὺς βρόχους τῶν ἀπαγχομένων καὶ καθαιρεθέντων ἐκφέρουσιν. 3 ἔκειτο δὲ καὶ τοῦ Θεμιστοκλέους εἰκόνιον ἐν τῷ ναῷ τῆς Ἀριστοβούλης ἔτι καθ' ἡμᾶς, καὶ φαίνεταί τις οὐ τὴν ψυχὴν μόνον, ἀλλὰ καὶ τὴν ὄψιν ἡρωικὸς γενόμενος.

4 Τὸν μὲν οὖν ἐξοστρακισμὸν ἐποιήσαντο κατ' αὐτοῦ, κολούοντες τὸ ἀξίωμα καὶ τὴν ὑπεροχήν, ὥσπερ εἰώθεσαν ἐπὶ πάντων οὓς ᾤοντο τῇ δυνάμει βαρεῖς καὶ πρὸς ἰσότητα δημοκρατικὴν ἀσυμμέτρους εἶναι. 5 κόλασις γὰρ οὐκ ἦν ὁ ἐξοστρακισμός, ἀλλὰ παραμυθία φθόνου καὶ κουφισμός, ἡδομένου τῷ ταπεινοῦν τοὺς ὑπερέχοντας καὶ τὴν δυσμένειαν εἰς ταύτην τὴν ἀτιμίαν ἀποπνέοντος.

himself full of cash; yet, when he gave a banquet at the Isthmus, he brought scorn on himself by serving up only cold meat. So the guests, while eating this, prayed to the gods that there should be no happy returns for Themistocles."

[5] But after Themistocles' flight and condemnation Timocreon indulged in much more vulgar and explicit abuse against him, composing the poem which begins [6] "Muse, make this song well known throughout Greece, as is only fair and right." [7] It is said that Timocreon was exiled on a charge of collaborating with the Persians, and that Themistocles participated in the vote of condemnation. So, when Themistocles in turn was charged with Medising, Timocreon composed these lines about him:

"So Timocreon was not the only one to cut a deal with the Persians. To be sure, there are other villains too. I am not the only one with a docked tail. There are other foxes like me."

22. Eventually even his fellow citizens were happy, because of their jealousy of him, to accept such slanders, and, since he then felt the need frequently to remind the assembly of his achievements, he became annoying. He once said to those who were complaining "How can you grow tired of receiving benefits so often from the same men?"

[2] He upset the common people also when he built the temple of the goddess Artemis, because he gave her the epithet "Best Counsellor", implying that it was he who had given the best advice to the city and to the Greeks, and because he sited it near his own house in Melite. This is the place where nowadays the public executioners throw out the bodies of those who have been put to death, and where they leave the clothes and nooses used by those who have committed suicide by hanging themselves. [3] Indeed, a bust of Themistocles stood in the temple of Artemis Best Counsellor right down to my time, and it shows that he was a man of heroic features, as well as one who had a heroic spirit.

[4] So in the end they employed the procedure of ostracism against him, thus curtailing his reputation and pre-eminence, as was their custom in the case of all those whose power they considered to be oppressive or incommensurate with the equality characteristic of democracy. [5] For ostracism was not a punishment, but a means of appeasing and alleviating an envy which delights in humbling the eminent and in venting its malice through this form of disfranchisement.

23. Ἐκπεσόντος δὲ τῆς πόλεως αὐτοῦ καὶ διατρίβοντος ἐν Ἄργει, τὰ περὶ Παυσανίαν συμπεσόντα κατ' ἐκείνου παρέσχε τοῖς ἐχθροῖς ἀφορμάς. ὁ δὲ γραψάμενος αὐτὸν προδοσίας Λεωβώτης ἦν ὁ Ἀλκμαίωνος Ἀγραυλῆθεν, ἅμα συνεπαιτιωμένων τῶν Σπαρτιατῶν. 2 ὁ γὰρ Παυσανίας πράττων ἐκεῖνα δὴ τὰ περὶ τὴν προδοσίαν, πρότερον μὲν ἀπεκρύπτετο τὸν Θεμιστοκλέα καίπερ ὄντα φίλον· ὡς δ' εἶδεν ἐκπεπτωκότα τῆς πολιτείας καὶ φέροντα χαλεπῶς, ἐθάρρησεν ἐπὶ τὴν κοινωνίαν τῶν πρασσομένων παρακαλεῖν, γράμματα τοῦ βασιλέως ἐπιδεικνύμενος αὐτῷ καὶ παροξύνων ἐπὶ τοὺς Ἕλληνας ὡς πονηροὺς καὶ ἀχαρίστους. 3 ὁ δὲ τὴν μὲν δέησιν ἀπετρίψατο τοῦ Παυσανίου καὶ τὴν κοινωνίαν ὅλως ἀπείπατο, πρὸς οὐδένα δὲ τοὺς λόγους ἐξήνεγκεν οὐδὲ κατεμήνυσε τὴν πρᾶξιν, εἴτε παύσεσθαι προσδοκῶν αὐτόν, εἴτ' ἄλλως καταφανῆ γενήσεσθαι σὺν οὐδενὶ λογισμῷ πραγμάτων ἀτόπων καὶ παραβόλων ὀρεγόμενον. 4 οὕτω δὲ τοῦ Παυσανίου θανατωθέντος, ἐπιστολαί τινες ἀνευρεθεῖσαι καὶ γράμματα περὶ τούτων εἰς ὑποψίαν ἐνέβαλον τὸν Θεμιστοκλέα, καὶ κατεβόων μὲν αὐτοῦ Λακεδαιμόνιοι, κατηγόρουν δ' οἱ φθονοῦντες τῶν πολιτῶν, οὐ παρόντος, ἀλλὰ διὰ γραμμάτων ἀπολογουμένου μάλιστα ταῖς προτέραις κατηγορίαις· 5 διαβαλλόμενος γὰρ ὑπὸ τῶν ἐχθρῶν πρὸς τοὺς πολίτας ὡς ἄρχειν μὲν αἰεὶ ζητῶν, ἄρχεσθαι δὲ μὴ πεφυκὼς μηδὲ βουλόμενος, οὐκ ἄν ποτε βαρβάροις αὐτὸν οὐδὲ πολεμίοις ἀποδόσθαι μετὰ τῆς Ἑλλάδος. 6 οὐ μὴν ἀλλὰ συμπεισθεὶς ὑπὸ τῶν κατηγορούντων ὁ δῆμος ἔπεμψεν ἄνδρας οἷς εἴρητο συλλαμβάνειν καὶ ἀνάγειν αὐτὸν κριθησόμενον ἐν τοῖς Ἕλλησιν.

24. Προαισθόμενος δ' ἐκεῖνος εἰς Κέρκυραν διεπέρασεν, οὔσης αὐτῷ πρὸς τὴν πόλιν εὐεργεσίας. γενόμενος γὰρ αὐτῶν κριτὴς πρὸς Κορινθίους ἐχόντων διαφοράν, ἔλυσε τὴν ἔχθραν εἴκοσι τάλαντα κρίνας τοὺς Κορινθίους καταβαλεῖν καὶ Λευκάδα κοινῇ νέμειν ἀμφοτέρων ἄποικον. 2 ἐκεῖθεν δ' εἰς Ἤπειρον ἔφυγε, καὶ διωκόμενος ὑπὸ τῶν Ἀθηναίων καὶ τῶν Λακεδαιμονίων, ἔρριψεν ἑαυτὸν εἰς ἐλπίδας χαλεπὰς καὶ ἀπόρους, καταφυγὼν πρὸς Ἄδμητον, ὃς βασιλεὺς μὲν ἦν Μολοσσῶν, δεηθεὶς δέ τι τῶν Ἀθηναίων καὶ προπηλακισθεὶς

23. After he had been banished from his city and was living in Argos, the Pausanias affair provided his enemies with ammunition to use against him. The man who brought the indictment for treason against him was Leobotes, the son of Alcmaeon, of the deme Agraule, but the Spartans were involved in the accusation as well. [2] When Pausanias was conducting those treasonable negotiations of his he at first kept them concealed from Themistocles, even though he was his friend. But when he saw that Themistocles had been banished from his state, and felt resentful about it, he plucked up courage and invited him to become a partner in his activities, showing him a letter sent from the King, and urging him to turn against the Greeks as a worthless and ungrateful people. [3] Themistocles rebuffed Pausanias' approach and totally rejected the suggested partnership, but he did not disclose the proposals to anyone, or denounce the scheme, because he expected that Pausanias would either give it up of his own accord, or be found out by others, since he was pursuing such shocking and risky objectives so recklessly.

[4] The result was that certain letters and documents concerning these matters were discovered, after Pausanias had been put to death, which cast suspicion on Themistocles. The Spartans loudly denounced him, and, at the same time, those citizens who were jealous of him pressed their attacks. Although he was not there in person he defended himself in a letter, making particular use of the allegations which had been levelled against him previously. [5] He wrote that he had been denounced publicly by his enemies as a man who always sought to rule, but who had no inclination or desire to be ruled; that being so, he argued, he could never have sold himself and Greece to the rule of barbarians, still less to those who had waged war against them. [6] Despite his arguments the people were convinced by his accusers, and sent officers with orders to arrest him and bring him back to stand trial before a Panhellenic court.

24. But he got word of this in advance, and went across to Corcyra, where he was honoured as a public benefactor of that city. For he had been accepted as an arbitrator when they were involved in a dispute with the Corinthians, and he had settled the quarrel by his judgment that the Corinthians should pay an indemnity of twenty talents, and that Leucas should be administered as a joint colony of both states. [2] From there he fled to Epirus, and, as he was still being pursued by the Athenians and Spartans, he resorted to a dangerous and desperate gamble on escape by taking refuge with Admetus. He was king of the Molossians, but once, when he had asked the Athenians for some favour, he had been humiliatingly

ὑπὸ τοῦ Θεμιστοκλέους, ὅτ' ἤκμαζεν ἐν τῇ πολιτείᾳ, δι' ὀργῆς εἶχεν αὐτὸν αἰεί, καὶ δῆλος ἦν εἰ λάβοι τιμωρησόμενος. 3 ἐν δὲ τῇ τότε τύχῃ μᾶλλον ὁ Θεμιστοκλῆς φοβηθεὶς συγγενῆ καὶ πρόσφατον φθόνον ὀργῆς παλαιᾶς καὶ βασιλικῆς, ταύτῃ φέρων ὑπέθηκεν ἑαυτόν, ἱκέτης τοῦ Ἀδμήτου καταστὰς ἴδιόν τινα καὶ παρηλλαγμένον τρόπον. 4 ἔχων γὰρ αὐτοῦ τὸν υἱὸν ὄντα παῖδα πρὸς τὴν ἑστίαν προσέπεσε, ταύτην μεγίστην καὶ μόνην σχεδὸν ἀναντίρρητον ἡγουμένων ἱκεσίαν τῶν Μολοσσῶν. 5 ἔνιοι μὲν οὖν Φθίαν τὴν γυναῖκα τοῦ βασιλέως λέγουσιν ὑποθέσθαι τῷ Θεμιστοκλεῖ τὸ ἱκέτευμα τοῦτο καὶ τὸν υἱὸν ἐπὶ τὴν ἑστίαν καθίσαι μετ' αὐτοῦ· τινὲς δ' αὐτὸν τὸν Ἄδμητον, ὡς ἀφοσιώσαιτο πρὸς τοὺς διώκοντας τὴν ἀνάγκην δι' ἣν οὐκ ἐκδίδωσι τὸν ἄνδρα, διαθεῖναι καὶ συντραγῳδῆσαι τὴν ἱκεσίαν. 6 ἐκεῖ δ' αὐτῷ τὴν γυναῖκα καὶ τοὺς παῖδας ἐκκλέψας ἐκ τῶν Ἀθηνῶν Ἐπικράτης ὁ Ἀχαρνεὺς ἀπέστειλεν· ὃν ἐπὶ τούτῳ Κίμων ὕστερον κρίνας ἐθανάτωσεν, ὡς ἱστορεῖ Στησίμβροτος. 7 εἶτ' οὐκ οἶδ' ὅπως ἐπιλαθόμενος τούτων, ἢ τὸν Θεμιστοκλέα ποιῶν ἐπιλαθόμενον, πλεῦσαί φησιν εἰς Σικελίαν καὶ παρ' Ἱέρωνος αἰτεῖν τοῦ τυράννου τὴν θυγατέρα πρὸς γάμον, ὑπισχνούμενον αὐτῷ τοὺς Ἕλληνας ὑπηκόους ποιήσειν· ἀποτριψαμένου δὲ τοῦ Ἱέρωνος, οὕτως εἰς τὴν Ἀσίαν ἀπᾶραι.

25. Ταῦτα δ' οὐκ εἰκός ἐστιν οὕτω γενέσθαι. Θεόφραστος γὰρ ἐν τοῖς Περὶ βασιλείας ἱστορεῖ τὸν Θεμιστοκλέα, πέμψαντος εἰς Ὀλυμπίαν Ἱέρωνος ἵππους ἀγωνιστὰς καὶ σκηνήν τινα κατεσκευασμένην πολυτελῶς στήσαντος, εἰπεῖν ἐν τοῖς Ἕλλησι λόγον, ὡς χρὴ τὴν σκηνὴν διαρπάσαι τοῦ τυράννου καὶ κωλῦσαι τοὺς ἵππους ἀγωνίσασθαι. 2 Θουκυδίδης δ' ἐκπλεῦσαί φησιν αὐτὸν ἐπὶ τὴν ἑτέραν καταβάντα θάλατταν ἀπὸ Πύδνης, οὐδενὸς εἰδότος ὅστις εἴη τῶν πλεόντων, μέχρι οὗ πνεύματι τῆς ὁλκάδος εἰς Νάξον καταφερομένης ὑπ' Ἀθηναίων πολιορκουμένην τότε, φοβηθεὶς ἀναδείξειεν ἑαυτὸν τῷ τε ναυκλήρῳ καὶ τῷ κυβερνήτῃ, καὶ τὰ μὲν δεόμενος, τὰ δ' ἀπειλῶν καὶ λέγων ὅτι κατηγορήσοι καὶ καταψεύσοιτο πρὸς τοὺς Ἀθηναίους, ὡς οὐκ ἀγνοοῦντες, ἀλλὰ

rebuffed by Themistocles, then in his political prime. As a result, Admetus felt undying anger towards him, and had made it clear that he would take his revenge on him, if he ever got hold of him. [3] However, in his present plight, Themistocles was more afraid of the freshly aroused spite of his fellow citizens than the long-standing wrath of a foreign king. So he resolutely threw himself upon Admetus' mercy and made himself his suppliant in a peculiar and extraordinary fashion. [4] He took Admetus' infant son in his arms and fell on his knees before the household hearth - this being considered by the Molossians to be the most powerful form of supplication, and the only one that is virtually impossible to refuse. [5] Some say that it was Phthia, the king's wife, who suggested this particular act of supplication to Themistocles, and that she seated her son down on the hearth together with him; others that Admetus himself arranged the supplication scene and acted his part in it, in order to furnish himself with a religious sanction which obliged him to refuse to surrender the man to his pursuers.

[6] His wife and children were smuggled out of Athens and sent to join him in Epirus by Epicrates of the deme Acharnae. He was subsequently prosecuted for this by Cimon, and put to death, as Stesimbrotus records. [7] But then somehow or other he forgets this, or makes Themistocles forget it, when he says that he sailed to Sicily and asked the tyrant Hieron for the hand of his daughter in marriage, promising him that he would make the Greeks subject to him; but that he was given the brush-off by Hieron, and so he then set sail for Asia.

25. But that is an unlikely version of events. For Theophrastus in his work *On Kingship* records that, when Hieron sent a team of horses to Olympia to race there and erected a lavishly decorated tent, Themistocles delivered a speech before the assembled Greeks, urging them to tear the tyrant's tent to pieces and prevent his horses from competing. [2] Furthermore, Thucydides says that he in fact set sail from Pydna, having travelled across country to the sea on the other side of Greece, and that none of his fellow passengers knew who he was, until the vessel was driven by a storm to Naxos, which at that time was being besieged by the Athenians. Then he became alarmed, and revealed his identity to the captain and the helmsman. Then, partly by entreaties, partly by threats to the effect that he would denounce them to the Athenians and falsely allege that they had been well aware who he was right

χρήμασι πεισθέντες ἐξ ἀρχῆς ἀναλάβοιεν αὐτόν, οὕτως ἀναγκάσειε παραπλεῦσαι καὶ λαβέσθαι τῆς 'Ασίας. 3 τῶν δὲ χρημάτων αὐτῷ πολλὰ μὲν ὑπεκκλαπέντα διὰ τῶν φίλων εἰς 'Ασίαν ἔπλει, τῶν δὲ φανερῶν γενομένων καὶ συναχθέντων εἰς τὸ δημόσιον Θεόπομπος μὲν ἑκατὸν τάλαντα, Θεόφραστος δ' ὀγδοήκοντά φησι γενέσθαι τὸ πλῆθος, οὐδὲ τριῶν ἄξια ταλάντων κεκτημένου τοῦ Θεμιστοκλέους πρὶν ἅπτεσθαι τῆς πολιτείας.

26. Ἐπεὶ δὲ κατέπλευσεν εἰς Κύμην καὶ πολλοὺς ᾔσθετο τῶν ἐπὶ θαλάττῃ παραφυλάττοντας αὐτὸν λαβεῖν, μάλιστα δὲ τοὺς περὶ Ἐργοτέλη καὶ Πυθόδωρον - ἦν γὰρ ἡ θήρα λυσιτελὴς τοῖς γε τὸ κερδαίνειν ἀπὸ παντὸς ἀγαπῶσι, διακοσίων ἐπικεκηρυγμένων αὐτῷ ταλάντων ὑπὸ τοῦ βασιλέως - ἔφυγεν εἰς Αἰγάς, Αἰολικὸν πολισμάτιον, ὑπὸ πάντων ἀγνοούμενος πλὴν τοῦ ξένου Νικογένους, ὃς Αἰολέων πλείστην οὐσίαν ἐκέκτητο καὶ τοῖς ἄνω δυνατοῖς γνώριμος ὑπῆρχε. 2 παρὰ τούτῳ κρυπτόμενος ἡμέρας ὀλίγας διέτριψεν· εἶτα μετὰ τὸ δεῖπνον ἐκ θυσίας τινὸς "Ολβιος ὁ τῶν τέκνων τοῦ Νικογένους παιδαγωγὸς ἔκφρων γενόμενος καὶ θεοφόρητος ἀνεφώνησεν ἐν μέτρῳ ταυτί· "Νυκτὶ φωνήν, νυκτὶ βουλήν, νυκτὶ τὴν νίκην δίδου," 3 καὶ μετὰ ταῦτα κατακοιμηθεὶς ὁ Θεμιστοκλῆς ὄναρ ἔδοξεν ἰδεῖν δράκοντα κατὰ τῆς γαστρὸς αὐτοῦ περιελιττόμενον καὶ προσανέρποντα τῷ τραχήλῳ· γενόμενον δ' ἀετόν, ὡς ἥψατο τοῦ προσώπου, περιβαλόντα τὰς πτέρυγας ἐξᾶραι καὶ κομίζειν πολλὴν ὁδόν, εἶτα χρυσοῦ τινος κηρυκείου φανέντος, ἐπὶ τούτῳ στῆσαι βεβαίως αὐτόν, ἀμηχάνου δείματος καὶ ταραχῆς ἀπαλλαγέντα. 4 Πέμπεται δ' οὖν ὑπὸ τοῦ Νικογένους μηχανησαμένου τι τοιόνδε. τοῦ βαρβαρικοῦ γένους τὸ πολὺ καὶ μάλιστα τὸ Περσικὸν εἰς ζηλοτυπίαν τὴν περὶ τὰς γυναῖκας ἄγριον φύσει καὶ χαλεπόν ἐστιν. 5 οὐ γὰρ μόνον τὰς γαμετάς, ἀλλὰ καὶ τὰς ἀργυρωνήτους καὶ παλλακευομένας ἰσχυρῶς παραφυλάττουσιν, ὡς ὑπὸ μηδενὸς ὁρᾶσθαι τῶν ἐκτός, ἀλλ' οἴκοι μὲν διαιτᾶσθαι κατακεκλειμένας, ἐν δὲ ταῖς ὁδοιπορίαις ὑπὸ σκηναῖς κύκλῳ περιπεφραγμένας ἐπὶ τῶν ἁρμαμαξῶν ὀχεῖσθαι. 6 τοιαύτης τῷ Θεμιστοκλεῖ κατασκευασθείσης ἀπήνης, καταδὺς ἐκομίζετο, τῶν περὶ αὐτὸν ἀεὶ τοῖς ἐντυγχάνουσι καὶ πυνθανομένοις

from the beginning, but had taken him on board in return for a bribe, he forced them to sail by the island and make the coast of Asia.

[3] Much of his property was spirited away for him by his friends, and sent by ship to Asia. Even so, the total value of that which was openly declared and confiscated by the Athenian treasury was one hundred talents, according to Theopompus, while Theophrastus says eighty. Yet Themistocles did not possess even three talents worth of property before he started his political career.

26. When he landed at Cyme he learned that many people along the coast were on the look out for a chance to capture him, especially Ergoteles and Pythodorus and their associates. The hunt for him offered lucrative prospects to those happy to make money from any and every activity, as a price of two hundred talents had been publicly set on his head by the King. So he fled to Aegae, a small town in Aeolis, where he was unknown to anyone except his host Nicogenes, who was the wealthiest man in Aeolis and a person well-known to the authorities to the east. [2] With him he spent a few days in hiding. Then, after the dinner which followed some sacrifice, Olbius, the tutor of Nicogenes' children, fell into a divinely inspired trance, and uttered this line of verse:

"To night entrust voice, good counsel, and victory".

[3] Later, as he lay in bed asleep, Themistocles dreamt that he saw a snake winding itself over his stomach and creeping up to his neck. But as soon as it touched his face, it turned into an eagle, which wrapped its wings around him, lifted him from the ground, and carried him a long way off. Then a sort of herald's staff made of gold appeared, and the eagle set him safely down on this, relieving him from his state of desperate terror and panic.

[4] At any rate he was sent on his way by Nicogenes, who had devised the following plan. The majority of barbarian nations, and the Persians in particular, show a cruel and harsh side to their natures in their jealous attitude towards their women. [5] They keep under close guard not only their wives but also their female slaves and concubines, so that they are not seen by any outsiders. At home they live shut up in their own quarters, and, when they go on journeys, they travel within tents, which enclose them on all sides and are mounted on wheeled wagons. [6] A vehicle of this sort was prepared for Themistocles, and he started on his journey ensconced within it, while his attendants told anyone who met them and enquired about it that

λεγόντων, ὅτι γύναιον Ἑλληνικὸν ἄγουσιν ἀπ' Ἰωνίας πρός τινα τῶν ἐπὶ θύραις βασιλέως.

27. Θουκυδίδης μὲν οὖν καὶ Χάρων ὁ Λαμψακηνὸς ἱστοροῦσι τεθνηκότος Ξέρξου πρὸς τὸν υἱὸν αὐτοῦ τῷ Θεμιστοκλεῖ γενέσθαι τὴν ἔντευξιν· Ἔφορος δὲ καὶ Δείνων καὶ Κλείταρχος καὶ Ἡρακλείδης, ἔτι δ' ἄλλοι πλείονες πρὸς αὐτὸν ἀφικέσθαι τὸν Ξέρξην. 2 τοῖς δὲ χρονικοῖς δοκεῖ μᾶλλον ὁ Θουκυδίδης συμφέρεσθαι, καίπερ οὐδ' αὐτοῖς ἀτρέμα συνταττομένοις. ὁ δ' οὖν Θεμιστοκλῆς γενόμενος παρ' αὐτὸ τὸ δεινόν, ἐντυγχάνει πρῶτον Ἀρταβάνῳ τῷ χιλιάρχῳ, λέγων Ἕλλην μὲν εἶναι, βούλεσθαι δ' ἐντυχεῖν βασιλεῖ περὶ πραγμάτων μεγάλων καὶ πρὸς ἃ τυγχάνοι μάλιστα σπουδάζων ἐκεῖνος. 3 ὁ δέ φησιν· "ὦ ξένε, νόμοι διαφέρουσιν ἀνθρώπων· ἄλλα δ' ἄλλοις καλά· καλὸν δὲ πᾶσι τὰ οἰκεῖα κοσμεῖν καὶ σῴζειν. 4 ὑμᾶς μὲν οὖν ἐλευθερίαν μάλιστα θαυμάζειν καὶ ἰσότητα λόγος· ἡμῖν δὲ πολλῶν νόμων καὶ καλῶν ὄντων κάλλιστος οὗτός ἐστι, τιμᾶν βασιλέα καὶ προσκυνεῖν ὡς εἰκόνα θεοῦ τοῦ τὰ πάντα σῴζοντος. 5 εἰ μὲν οὖν ἐπαινῶν τὰ ἡμέτερα προσκυνήσεις, ἔστι σοι καὶ θεάσασθαι βασιλέα καὶ προσειπεῖν· εἰ δ' ἄλλο τι φρονεῖς, ἀγγέλοις ἑτέροις χρήσῃ πρὸς αὐτόν. βασιλεῖ γὰρ οὐ πάτριον ἀνδρὸς ἀκροᾶσθαι μὴ προσκυνήσαντος." 6 ταῦθ' ὁ Θεμιστοκλῆς ἀκούσας, λέγει πρὸς αὐτόν· "ἀλλ' ἐγὼ τὴν βασιλέως ὦ Ἀρτάβανε φήμην καὶ δύναμιν αὐξήσων ἀφῖγμαι, καὶ αὐτός τε πείσομαι τοῖς ὑμετέροις νόμοις, ἐπεὶ θεῷ τῷ μεγαλύνοντι Πέρσας οὕτω δοκεῖ, καὶ δι' ἐμὲ πλείονες τῶν νῦν βασιλέα προσκυνήσουσιν. 7 ὥστε τοῦτο μηδὲν ἐμποδὼν ἔστω τοῖς λόγοις οὓς βούλομαι πρὸς ἐκεῖνον εἰπεῖν." "τίνα δέ" εἶπεν ὁ Ἀρτάβανος "Ἑλλήνων ἀφῖχθαι φῶμεν; οὐ γὰρ ἰδιώτῃ τὴν γνώμην ἔοικας." καὶ ὁ Θεμιστοκλῆς· "τοῦτ' οὐκ ἄν" ἔφη "πύθοιτό τις Ἀρτάβανε πρότερος βασιλέως."
8 οὕτω μὲν ὁ Φανίας φησίν· ὁ δ' Ἐρατοσθένης ἐν τοῖς Περὶ πλούτου προσιστόρησε, διὰ γυναικὸς Ἐρετρικῆς ἣν ὁ χιλίαρχος εἶχε τῷ Θεμιστοκλεῖ τὴν πρὸς αὐτὸν ἔντευξιν γενέσθαι καὶ σύστασιν.

28. Ἐπεὶ δ' οὖν εἰσήχθη πρὸς βασιλέα καὶ προσκυνήσας ἔστη σιωπῇ, προστάξαντος τῷ ἑρμηνεῖ τοῦ βασιλέως ἐρωτῆσαι

they were conveying a young Greek woman from Ionia to one of the King's courtiers.

27. Now Thucydides and Charon of Lampsacus record that Xerxes was dead, and that Themistocles had his meeting with Xerxes' son. On the other hand Ephorus, Dinon, Clitarchus, Heraclides, and many others too, say that it was Xerxes himself whom he came before. [2] It seems to me that Thucydides' version corresponds better with the chronological data, though even these are not firmly in accordance with one another. Anyway Themistocles, having reached his moment of crisis, first of all had a meeting with Artabanus the Chiliarch, and told him that he was a Greek, but that he wished to have an audience with the King on matters which were of the highest importance, and in which the King was particularly interested.

[3] Artabanus replied "Stranger, men's customs differ. Different nations have different views about what is good conduct. But all agree it is a good thing to honour and uphold the customs of one's own country. [4] Now you Greeks are said to admire liberty and equality above all else. For us, on the other hand, out of our many noble customs the noblest of all is this, to honour the King, and prostrate oneself before him as an image of the god who preserves the whole world. [5] So, if you approve our customs and will prostrate yourself, you have permission to see the King and speak to him. But if you take a different view you will need to use messengers instead to communicate with him. For it is not the custom of our country for the King to give an audience to someone who has not prostrated himself."

[6] When Themistocles heard this he said "Artabanus, I have come here to increase his fame and power, and so not only will I observe your customs myself, since that is what pleases the god who makes the Persians great, but through my efforts more men than do so now will prostrate themselves before the King. [7] Hence this matter must not be allowed to stand in the way of my saying the things I want to say to him." "Which of the Greeks", asked Artabanus, "am I to say has arrived? For your intelligence does not seem to be that of merely an ordinary person." Themistocles replied, "That is something, Artabanus, which no one may learn before the King."

[8] This is the story as told by Phanias. Eratosthenes, in his book *On Wealth*, adds the detail that it was through a woman of Eretria, to whom the Chiliarch was married, that Themistocles secured his interview with him and his introduction to the King.

28. At any rate, when he had been brought before the King he did prostrate himself, and then stood in silence. The King ordered the interpreter to ask

τίς ἐστι, καὶ τοῦ ἑρμηνέως ἐρωτήσαντος εἶπεν· 2 "ἥκω σοι βασιλεῦ Θεμιστοκλῆς ὁ Ἀθηναῖος ἐγὼ φυγάς, ὑφ' Ἑλλήνων διωχθείς, ᾧ πολλὰ μὲν ὀφείλουσι Πέρσαι κακά, πλείω δ' ἀγαθὰ κωλύσαντι τὴν δίωξιν, ὅτε τῆς Ἑλλάδος ἐν ἀσφαλεῖ γεγενημένης παρέσχε τὰ οἰκεῖα σῳζόμενα χαρίσασθαί τι καὶ ὑμῖν. 3 ἐμοὶ μὲν οὖν πάντα πρέποντα ταῖς παρούσαις συμφοραῖς ἐστι, καὶ παρεσκευασμένος ἀφῖγμαι δέξασθαί τε χάριν εὐμενῶς διαλλαττομένου καὶ παραιτεῖσθαι μνησικακοῦντος ὀργήν· 4 σὺ δὲ τοὺς ἐμοὺς ἐχθροὺς μάρτυρας θέμενος ὧν εὐεργέτησα Πέρσας, νῦν ἀπόχρησαι ταῖς ἐμαῖς τύχαις πρὸς ἐπίδειξιν ἀρετῆς μᾶλλον ἢ πρὸς ἀποπλήρωσιν ὀργῆς. σώσεις μὲν γὰρ ἱκέτην σόν, ἀπολεῖς δ' Ἑλλήνων πολέμιον γενόμενον." 5 ταῦτ' εἰπὼν ὁ Θεμιστοκλῆς ἐπεθείασε τῷ λόγῳ, προσδιελθὼν τὴν ὄψιν ἣν εἶδεν ἐν Νικογένους καὶ τὸ μάντευμα τοῦ Δωδωναίου Διός, ὡς κελευσθεὶς πρὸς τὸν ὁμώνυμον τοῦ θεοῦ βαδίζειν, συμφρονήσειε πρὸς ἐκεῖνον ἀναπέμπεσθαι· μεγάλους γὰρ ἀμφοτέρους εἶναί τε καὶ λέγεσθαι βασιλέας. 6 ἀκούσας δ' ὁ Πέρσης, ἐκείνῳ μὲν οὐδὲν ἀπεκρίνατο, καίπερ θαυμάσας τὸ φρόνημα καὶ τὴν τόλμαν αὐτοῦ· μακαρίσας δὲ πρὸς τοὺς φίλους ἑαυτὸν ὡς ἐπ' εὐτυχίᾳ μεγίστῃ, καὶ κατευξάμενος αἰεὶ τοῖς πολεμίοις τοιαύτας φρένας διδόναι τὸν Ἀρειμάνιον, ὅπως ἐλαύνωσι τοὺς ἀρίστους ἐξ ἑαυτῶν, θῦσαί τε τοῖς θεοῖς λέγεται καὶ πρὸς πόσιν εὐθὺς τραπέσθαι καὶ νύκτωρ ὑπὸ χαρᾶς διὰ μέσων τῶν ὕπνων ἐκβοῆσαι τρίς· "ἔχω Θεμιστοκλέα τὸν Ἀθηναῖον."

29. Ἅμα δ' ἡμέρᾳ συγκαλέσας τοὺς φίλους εἰσῆγεν αὐτόν, οὐδὲν ἐλπίζοντα χρηστὸν ἐξ ὧν ἑώρα τοὺς ἐπὶ θύραις, εὐθὺς ὡς ἐπύθοντο τοὔνομα παριόντος αὐτοῦ, χαλεπῶς διακειμένους καὶ κακῶς λέγοντας. 2 ἔτι δὲ Ῥωξάνης ὁ χιλίαρχος, ὡς κατ' αὐτὸν ἦν ὁ Θεμιστοκλῆς προσιών, καθημένου βασιλέως καὶ τῶν ἄλλων σιωπώντων, ἀτρέμα στενάξας εἶπεν· "ὄφις Ἕλλην ὁ ποικίλος, ὁ βασιλέως σε δαίμων δεῦρο ἤγαγεν." 3 οὐ μὴν ἀλλ'

who he was, and, in reply to the interpreter's question, he said [2] "My lord, I who have come to you am Themistocles the Athenian, now an exile pursued by the Greeks. It was owing to me that the Persians suffered much harm; but owing to me also they derived even more benefits, since I prevented the Greeks from pursuing them, once Greece was made safe and the rescue of my homeland allowed me the opportunity to do your side some favour as well. [3] As for me, I have to accept anything which may be appropriate to my present state of misfortune. So I have come here ready either to receive your favour, if you are graciously willing to be reconciled, or to beg for mercy if you still harbour resentment. [4] But you should take the actions of my enemies as evidence for the services I have rendered the Persians, and take advantage now of my misfortunes to make a display of your magnanimity rather than to satisfy your thirst for revenge. In the former case you will be saving the life of a man who is your suppliant, in the latter you will be putting to death someone who has become an enemy of the Greeks."

[5] Having said this, Themistocles invoked the divine in support of his argument, describing the vision he had seen in the house of Nicogenes and the oracle given by Zeus at Dodona, by which he had been commanded to proceed to the "namesake of the god". He said he had concluded from this that he was being sent to the King, since both were indeed Great Kings and were so addressed. [6] On hearing this the Persian King did not reply to him directly, although he was struck with admiration at his bold and spirited approach. But in conversation with his friends he congratulated himself on what he held to be a supreme piece of good fortune, and he prayed the god Arimanius to ensure that his enemies always were given minds of this sort, so they would keep driving their best men away from them. Then, so it is said, he sacrificed to the gods and at once embarked on a drinking session, and during the night, in the midst of his sleep, he shouted out three times in sheer joy: "I have Themistocles the Athenian".

29. At daybreak he called his friends together and had Themistocles introduced. Themistocles was not expecting any favourable outcome, after seeing that, as soon as the guards at the palace gates learned the name of who it was that was going in, they adopted a threatening and abusive attitude towards him. [2] Moreover Roxanes the Chiliarch growled in a low voice, as the approaching Themistocles came alongside him (the King was seated and the others were standing in silence), "You cunning Greek snake, it is the King's lucky spirit that has brought you here." [3] In spite of this, when he

εἰς ὄψιν ἐλθόντος αὐτοῦ καὶ πάλιν προσκυνήσαντος, ἀσπασάμενος καὶ προσειπὼν φιλοφρόνως ὁ βασιλεύς, ἤδη μὲν διακόσια τάλαντα ὀφείλειν ἔφησεν αὐτῷ· κομίσαντα γὰρ αὐτὸν ἀπολήψεσθαι δικαίως τὸ ἐπικηρυχθὲν τῷ ἀγαγόντι· πολλῷ δὲ πλείω τούτων ὑπισχνεῖτο καὶ παρεθάρρυνε καὶ λέγειν ἐδίδου περὶ τῶν Ἑλληνικῶν ἃ βούλοιτο παρρησιαζόμενον. 4 ὁ δὲ Θεμιστοκλῆς ἀπεκρίνατο, τὸν λόγον ἐοικέναι τοῦ ἀνθρώπου τοῖς ποικίλοις στρώμασιν· ὡς γὰρ ἐκεῖνα καὶ τοῦτον ἐκτεινόμενον μὲν ἐπιδεικνύναι τὰ εἴδη, συστελλόμενον δὲ κρύπτειν καὶ διαφθείρειν· ὅθεν αὐτῷ χρόνου δεῖν. 5 ἐπεὶ δ' ἡσθέντος τοῦ βασιλέως τῇ εἰκασίᾳ καὶ λαμβάνειν κελεύσαντος, ἐνιαυτὸν αἰτησάμενος καὶ τὴν Περσίδα γλῶτταν ἀποχρώντως ἐκμαθὼν ἐνετύγχανε βασιλεῖ δι' αὐτοῦ, τοῖς μὲν ἐκτὸς δόξαν παρέσχε περὶ τῶν Ἑλληνικῶν πραγμάτων διειλέχθαι, πολλῶν δὲ καινοτομουμένων περὶ τὴν αὐλὴν καὶ τοὺς φίλους ὑπὸ τοῦ βασιλέως ἐν ἐκείνῳ τῷ χρόνῳ, φθόνον ἔσχε παρὰ τοῖς δυνατοῖς, ὡς καὶ κατ' ἐκείνων παρρησίᾳ χρῆσθαι πρὸς αὐτὸν ἀποτετολμηκώς. 6 οὐδὲ γὰρ ἦσαν αἱ τιμαὶ ταῖς τῶν ἄλλων ἐοικυῖαι ξένων, ἀλλὰ καὶ κυνηγεσίων βασιλεῖ μετέσχε καὶ τῶν οἴκοι διατριβῶν, ὥστε καὶ μητρὶ τῇ βασιλέως ἐς ὄψιν ἐλθεῖν καὶ γενέσθαι συνήθης, διακοῦσαι δὲ καὶ τῶν μαγικῶν λόγων τοῦ βασιλέως κελεύσαντος. 7 ἐπεὶ δὲ Δημάρατος ὁ Σπαρτιάτης αἰτήσασθαι δωρεὰν κελευσθεὶς ᾐτήσατο τὴν κίταριν ὥσπερ οἱ βασιλεῖς ἐπαράμενος εἰσελάσαι διὰ Σάρδεων, Μιθροπαύστης μὲν ἀνεψιὸς ὢν βασιλέως εἶπε τοῦ Δημαράτου τῆς τιάρας ἁψάμενος· "αὕτη μὲν ἡ κίταρις οὐκ ἔχει ἐγκέφαλον ὃν ἐπικαλύψει· σὺ δ' οὐκ ἔσῃ Ζεὺς ἐὰν λάβῃς κεραυνόν·" 8 ἀπωσαμένου δὲ τὸν Δημάρατον ὀργῇ διὰ τὸ αἴτημα τοῦ βασιλέως καὶ δοκοῦντος ἀπαραιτήτως ἔχειν πρὸς αὐτόν, ὁ Θεμιστοκλῆς δεηθεὶς ἔπεισε καὶ διήλλαξε.

9 λέγεται δὲ καὶ τοὺς ὕστερον βασιλεῖς, ἐφ' ὧν μᾶλλον αἱ Περσικαὶ πράξεις ταῖς Ἑλληνικαῖς ἀνεκράθησαν, ὁσάκις δεηθεῖεν ἀνδρὸς Ἕλληνος, ἐπαγγέλλεσθαι καὶ γράφειν ἕκαστον, ὡς μείζων ἔσοιτο παρ' αὐτῷ Θεμιστοκλέους. 10 αὐτὸν δὲ τὸν Θεμιστοκλέα φασὶν ἤδη μέγαν ὄντα καὶ θεραπευόμενον ὑπὸ πολλῶν, λαμπρᾶς ποτε τραπέζης αὐτῷ παρατεθείσης, πρὸς τοὺς παῖδας εἰπεῖν· "ὦ παῖδες, ἀπωλόμεθα ἄν, εἰ μὴ ἀπωλόμεθα." 11 πόλεις δ' αὐτῷ τρεῖς μὲν οἱ

had come face to face with the King and had prostrated himself again, the King welcomed him and spoke to him kindly, declaring that he already owed him two hundred talents, for, since he had delivered himself up, it was only right that he should receive the reward offered to whoever brought him in. And he promised a great deal more than this, reassured him, and invited him to say with complete frankness whatever he wished about the affairs of Greece. [4] Themistocles replied that human speech was like embroidered tapestries. Like them, it too displayed its pictures only when it was well spread out, but when it was tucked up it obscured and deformed them. [5] For this reason, he said, he needed time. The King was pleased with this comparison and told him he could take time. Themistocles asked for a year, and in that time he learnt Persian sufficiently well to have audiences with the King all by himself. He led those outside the room to believe that his conversations concerned only Greek affairs. But during that period many innovations were being introduced by the King at court, and they affected his favourites, and so Themistocles incurred the jealousy of the nobles for supposedly having dared to use his freedom of speech with the King to their disadvantage. [6] Certainly the marks of honour he received were in no way merely like those given to other foreigners. He actually took part in the King's hunts, and in his household pastimes (to such an extent that he even came face to face with the Queen Mother and became her close friend), and, at the King's command, he was even instructed in the doctrines of the Magi.

[7] When Demaratus the Spartan was told to choose a gift for himself he asked that he might enter Sardis and ride through it in state, wearing on his head the tiara as the Persian kings do. At this Mithropaustes, a cousin of the King, touched Demaratus' tiara and said, "This tiara has no brains to cover; you will not become Zeus just by holding a thunderbolt." [8] The King, angry at his request, expelled Demaratus from his company, and seemed to be implacably set against him. But Themistocles pleaded on Demaratus' behalf, and it was he who persuaded the King to be reconciled with him. [9] It is said as well that later kings of Persia, in whose reigns Persian affairs became more intermingled with those of Greece, used to promise in writing, every one of them, whenever they wanted a Greek adviser, that he would have more influence with them than Themistocles.

[10] Themistocles himself, so they say, after he had become an important personage courted by many people, observed to his children one day, when a superb banquet was set before him, "My children, we would be ruined now, if we had not been ruined before." [11] Three cities (according to most

πλεῖστοι δοθῆναι λέγουσιν εἰς ἄρτον καὶ οἶνον καὶ ὄψον, Μαγνησίαν καὶ Λάμψακον καὶ Μυοῦντα· δύο δ' ἄλλας προστίθησιν ὁ Κυζικηνὸς Νεάνθης καὶ Φανίας, Περκώτην καὶ Παλαίσκηψιν εἰς στρωμνὴν καὶ ἀμπεχόνην.

30. Καταβαίνοντι δ' αὐτῷ πρὸς τὰς Ἑλληνικὰς πράξεις ἐπὶ θάλατταν Πέρσης ἀνὴρ Ἐπιξύης ὄνομα, σατραπεύων τῆς ἄνω Φρυγίας, ἐπεβούλευσε, παρεσκευακὼς ἔκπαλαι Πισίδας τινὰς ἀποκτενοῦντας, ὅταν ἐν τῇ καλουμένῃ κώμῃ Λεοντοκεφάλῳ γενόμενος καταυλισθῇ. 2 τῷ δὲ λέγεται καθεύδοντι μεσημβρίας τὴν Μητέρα τῶν θεῶν. ὄναρ φανεῖσαν εἰπεῖν· "ὦ Θεμιστόκλεις, ὑστέρει κεφαλῆς λεόντων, ἵνα μὴ λέοντι περιπέσῃς. ἐγὼ δ' ἀντὶ τούτου σε αἰτῶ θεράπαιναν Μνησιπτολέμαν." 3 διαταραχθεὶς οὖν ὁ Θεμιστοκλῆς προσευξάμενος τῇ θεῷ τὴν μὲν λεωφόρον ἀφῆκεν, ἑτέρᾳ δὲ περιελθὼν καὶ παραλλάξας τὸν τόπον ἐκεῖνον ἤδη νυκτὸς οὔσης κατηυλίσατο. 4 τῶν δὲ τὴν σκηνὴν κομιζόντων ὑποζυγίων ἑνὸς εἰς τὸν ποταμὸν ἐμπεσόντος, οἱ τοῦ Θεμιστοκλέους οἰκέται τὰς αὐλαίας διαβρόχους γενομένας ἐκπετάσαντες ἀνέψυχον· 5 οἱ δὲ Πισίδαι τὰ ξίφη λαβόντες ἐν τούτῳ προσεφέροντο, καὶ τὰ ψυχόμενα πρὸς τὴν σελήνην οὐκ ἀκριβῶς ἰδόντες ᾠήθησαν εἶναι τὴν σκηνὴν τοῦ Θεμιστοκλέους κἀκεῖνον ἔνδον εὑρήσειν ἀναπαυόμενον. 6 ὡς δ' ἐγγὺς γενόμενοι τὴν αὐλαίαν ἀνέστελλον, ἐπιπίπτουσιν αὐτοῖς οἱ παραφυλάττοντες καὶ συλλαμβάνουσι. διαφυγὼν δὲ τὸν κίνδυνον οὕτω καὶ θαυμάσας τὴν ἐπιφάνειαν τῆς θεοῦ, ναόν τε κατεσκεύασεν ἐν Μαγνησίᾳ Δινδυμήνης καὶ τὴν θυγατέρα Μνησιπτολέμαν ἱέρειαν ἀπέδειξεν.

31. Ὡς δ' ἦλθεν εἰς Σάρδεις καὶ σχολὴν ἄγων ἐθεᾶτο τῶν ἱερῶν τὴν κατασκευὴν καὶ τῶν ἀναθημάτων τὸ πλῆθος, εἶδε καὶ ἐν Μητρὸς ἱερῷ τὴν καλουμένην ὑδροφόρον κόρην χαλκῆν, μέγεθος δίπηχυν, ἣν αὐτὸς ὅτε τῶν Ἀθήνησιν ὑδάτων ἐπιστάτης ἦν, ἑλὼν τοὺς ὑφαιρουμένους τὸ ὕδωρ καὶ παροχετεύοντας, ἀνέθηκεν ἐκ τῆς ζημίας ποιησάμενος· εἴτε δὴ παθών τι πρὸς τὴν αἰχμαλωσίαν τοῦ ἀναθήματος, εἴτε βουλόμενος ἐνδείξασθαι τοῖς Ἀθηναίοις, ὅσην ἔχει τιμὴν καὶ δύναμιν ἐν τοῖς βασιλέως πράγμασι, λόγον τῷ Λυδίας

writers) were given to him for his bread, wine, and fish, namely Magnesia, Lampsacus, and Myus; in addition Neanthes of Cyzicus and Phanias mention two more, namely Percote and Palaiscepsis, for his bedding and clothing.

30. When he was returning to the Aegean coast on his mission to deal with Greek affairs, a Persian, Epixyes by name, who was the governor of Upper Phrygia, organised an attempt on his life. A long time before he had procured the services of some Pisidians, who were to kill Themistocles whenever he reached the village called Lion's Head and stopped for the night there. [2] But the story goes that, while he was taking a midday siesta, the Mother of the Gods appeared to him in a dream and said, "Themistocles, you must avoid a lion's head, so as not to fall into the clutches of a lion. In return for this warning I ask you to give me Mnesiptolema to be my maidservant." [3] Themistocles was much disturbed by this, and in consequence, having offered a prayer of thanks to the goddess, left the main road and took another, more roundabout, route. Then, having bypassed that place, he set up camp when night had already fallen.

[4] There one of the pack animals, which were carrying his tent, fell into the river, and Themistocles' attendants were drying the curtains, which had got soaking wet, by spreading them out on a line. [5] At that moment the Pisidians approached, swords in hand, but, since the light of the moon did not allow them to see clearly, they supposed that the drying things were the tent of Themistocles, and that they would find their quarry sleeping inside. [6] But when they got close, and started to lift up the curtains, the guards pounced on them and arrested them. In this way Themistocles escaped the danger, and, because he was so impressed at the appearance of the goddess, he built a temple in Magnesia in honour of Cybele Dindymene, and assigned his daughter Mnesiptolema to be her priestess.

31. When he had arrived at Sardis and was viewing in his spare time the architecture of the temples and the large number of dedicatory offerings inside them, he saw in the temple of the Mother the so-called Water-carrier. This was a bronze female figure, two cubits tall, which he himself had dedicated when he was superintendent of the water supply at Athens. He had had it made and paid for out of the fines levied on those he had convicted of drawing off and diverting the public water. Either because he was rather upset that this votive offering was now in captivity, or because he wanted to demonstrate to the Athenians just how much honour and power he

σατράπῃ προσήνεγκεν, αἰτούμενος ἀποστεῖλαι τὴν κόρην εἰς τὰς Ἀθήνας. 2 χαλεπαίνοντος δὲ τοῦ βαρβάρου καὶ βασιλεῖ γράψειν φήσαντος ἐπιστολήν, φοβηθεὶς ὁ Θεμιστοκλῆς εἰς τὴν γυναικωνῖτιν κατέφυγε, καὶ τὰς παλλακίδας αὐτοῦ θεραπεύσας χρήμασιν, ἐκεῖνόν τε κατεπράυνε τῆς ὀργῆς, καὶ πρὸς τἆλλα παρεῖχεν αὑτὸν εὐλαβέστερον, ἤδη καὶ τὸν φθόνον τῶν βαρβάρων δεδοικώς. 3 οὐ γὰρ πλανώμενος περὶ τὴν Ἀσίαν ὥς φησι Θεόπομπος, ἀλλ' ἐν Μαγνησίᾳ μὲν οἰκῶν, καρπούμενος δὲ δωρεὰς μεγάλας καὶ τιμώμενος ὅμοια Περσῶν τοῖς ἀρίστοις, ἐπὶ πολὺν χρόνον ἀδεῶς διῆγεν, οὐ πάνυ τι τοῖς Ἑλληνικοῖς πράγμασι βασιλέως προσέχοντος ὑπ' ἀσχολιῶν περὶ τὰς ἄνω πράξεις.

4 Ὡς δ' Αἴγυπτός τ' ἀφισταμένη βοηθούντων Ἀθηναίων καὶ τριήρεις Ἑλληνικαὶ μέχρι Κύπρου καὶ Κιλικίας ἀναπλέουσαι καὶ Κίμων θαλασσοκρατῶν ἐπέστρεψεν αὐτὸν ἀντεπιχειρεῖν τοῖς Ἕλλησι καὶ κωλύειν αὐξανομένους ἐπ' αὐτόν, ἤδη δὲ καὶ δυνάμεις ἐκινοῦντο καὶ στρατηγοὶ διεπέμποντο, καὶ κατέβαινον εἰς Μαγνησίαν ἀγγελίαι πρὸς τὸν Θεμιστοκλέα, τῶν Ἑλληνικῶν ἐξάπτεσθαι κελεύοντος βασιλέως καὶ βεβαιοῦν τὰς ὑποσχέσεις, 5 οὔτε δι' ὀργήν τινα παροξυνθεὶς κατὰ τῶν πολιτῶν, οὔτ' ἐπαρθεὶς τιμῇ τοσαύτῃ καὶ δυνάμει πρὸς τὸν πόλεμον, ἀλλ' ἴσως μὲν οὐδ' ἐφικτὸν ἡγούμενος τὸ ἔργον, ἄλλους τε μεγάλους τῆς Ἑλλάδος ἐχούσης στρατηγοὺς τότε καὶ Κίμωνος ὑπερφυῶς εὐημεροῦντος ἐν τοῖς πολεμικοῖς, τὸ δὲ πλεῖστον αἰδοῖ τῆς τε δόξης τῶν πράξεων τῶν ἑαυτοῦ καὶ τῶν τροπαίων ἐκείνων, ἄριστα βουλευσάμενος ἐπιθεῖναι τῷ βίῳ τὴν τελευτὴν πρέπουσαν, ἔθυσε τοῖς θεοῖς, καὶ τοὺς φίλους συναγαγὼν καὶ δεξιωσάμενος, 6 ὡς μὲν ὁ πολὺς λόγος αἷμα ταύρειον πιών, ὡς δ' ἔνιοι φάρμακον ἐφήμερον προσενεγκάμενος, ἐν Μαγνησίᾳ κατέστρεψε, πέντε πρὸς τοῖς ἑξήκοντα βεβιωκὼς ἔτη, καὶ τὰ πλεῖστα τούτων ἐν πολιτείαις καὶ ἡγεμονίαις. 7 τὴν δ' αἰτίαν τοῦ θανάτου καὶ τὸν τρόπον πυθόμενον βασιλέα λέγουσιν ἔτι μᾶλλον θαυμάσαι τὸν ἄνδρα, καὶ τοῖς φίλοις αὐτοῦ καὶ οἰκείοις διατελεῖν χρώμενον φιλανθρώπως.

32. Ἀπέλιπε δὲ Θεμιστοκλῆς παῖδας ἐκ μὲν Ἀρχίππης τῆς Λυσάνδρου τοῦ Ἀλωπεκῆθεν Ἀρχέπτολιν καὶ Πολύευκτον καὶ Κλεόφαντον, οὗ καὶ Πλάτων ὁ φιλόσοφος ὡς ἱππέως

enjoyed in the King's service, he submitted a proposal to the governor of Lydia requesting him to return the statue to Athens. [2] But the barbarian official was enraged by this, and declared that he would write a letter to the King. So Themistocles, in his alarm, had recourse to the harem, and, by winning the favour of the satrap's concubines with gifts of money, succeeded in soothing his anger. In his subsequent activities he exhibited greater caution, seeing that even now he had to fear the jealousy of the barbarians.

[3] Hence he did not travel all over Asia, as Theopompus says, but remained at his residence in Magnesia, enjoying substantial gifts and receiving honours equal to those offered to the highest Persian nobility. For a long period he lived there without any apprehension, since the king paid no attention at all to Greek affairs, being preoccupied with the condition of the interior of his empire. [4] But, eventually, Athenian assistance in the revolt of Egypt, and the fact that Greek triremes were now sailing as far east as Cyprus and Cilicia, and that Cimon was in control of the high seas, forced him to change his policy, and to fight back against the Greeks and try to halt their menacing expansion. Then at last forces started to be mobilised and generals dispatched in all directions, and messages came down to Magnesia addressed to Themistocles, saying that the King commanded him to make good his promises, by applying himself seriously to the Greek problem. [5] But Themistocles was not moved by any feelings of anger against his fellow citizens, nor was he excited by the thought of all the status and power he would have in conducting the war. It is possible that he considered his task was simply not accomplishable, since Greece had some great generals at that time, particularly Cimon, who was enjoying wonderful success in his military operations. But it was most of all out of reverence for the glory of his own achievements and for the triumphs he had won in those days that he made the excellent decision to put a fitting end to his life. So he made a sacrifice to the gods, and then, having gathered his friends about him and clasped their hands in farewell, [6] he drank bull's blood, according to most sources, though some writers say he gave himself a quick-acting poison. He died in Magnesia at the age of sixty-five, having spent most of his life in political and military leadership. [7] They say that the King, on learning the reasons for Themistocles' death, and the manner of it, felt more admiration than ever for the man and continued to treat his friends and relatives with kindness.

32. Themistocles left three sons by Archippe, the daughter of Lysander of the deme Alopece. These were Archeptolis, Polyeuctus, and Cleophantus, whom Plato the philosopher mentions as being an excellent horseman, but in

ἀρίστου, τἆλλα δ' οὐδενὸς ἀξίου γενομένου, μνημονεύει. 2 τῶν δὲ πρεσβυτάτων Νεοκλῆς μὲν ἔτι παῖς ὢν ὑφ' ἵππου δηχθεὶς ἀπέθανε, Διοκλέα δὲ Λύσανδρος ὁ πάππος υἱὸν ἐποιήσατο. θυγατέρας δὲ πλείους ἔσχεν, ὧν Μνησιπτολέμαν μὲν ἐκ τῆς ἐπιγαμηθείσης γενομένην Ἀρχέπτολις ὁ ἀδελφὸς οὐκ ὢν ὁμομήτριος ἔγημεν, Ἰταλίαν δὲ Πανθοίδης ὁ Χῖος, Σύβαριν δὲ Νικόδημος ὁ Ἀθηναῖος. 3 Νικομάχην δὲ Φρασικλῆς ὁ ἀδελφιδοῦς Θεμιστοκλέους, ἤδη τετελευτηκότος ἐκείνου, πλεύσας εἰς Μαγνησίαν ἔλαβε παρὰ τῶν ἀδελφῶν, νεωτάτην δὲ πάντων τῶν τέκνων Ἀσίαν ἔθρεψε.

4 Καὶ τάφον μὲν αὐτοῦ λαμπρὸν ἐν τῇ ἀγορᾷ Μάγνητες ἔχουσι· περὶ δὲ τῶν λειψάνων οὔτ' Ἀνδοκίδῃ προσέχειν ἄξιον, ἐν τῷ Πρὸς τοὺς ἑταίρους λέγοντι φωράσαντας τὰ λείψανα διαρρῖψαι τοὺς Ἀθηναίους - ψεύδεται γὰρ ἐπὶ τὸν δῆμον παροξύνων τοὺς ὀλιγαρχικούς -, ἅ τε Φύλαρχος, ὥσπερ ἐν τραγῳδίᾳ τῇ ἱστορίᾳ μονονοὺ μηχανὴν ἄρας καὶ προαγαγὼν Νεοκλέα τινὰ καὶ Δημόπολιν, υἱεῖς Θεμιστοκλέους, ἀγῶνα βούλεται κινεῖν καὶ πάθος, οὐδ' ἂν ὁ τυχὼν ἀγνοήσειεν ὅτι πέπλασται. 5 Διόδωρος δ' ὁ περιηγητὴς ἐν τοῖς Περὶ μνημάτων εἴρηκεν ὡς ὑπονοῶν μᾶλλον ἢ γιγνώσκων, ὅτι περὶ τὸν μέγαν λιμένα τοῦ Πειραιῶς ἀπὸ τοῦ κατὰ τὸν Ἄλκιμον ἀκρωτηρίου πρόκειταί τις οἷον ἀγκών, καὶ κάμψαντι τοῦτον ἐντός, ᾗ τὸ ὑπεύδιον τῆς θαλάττης, κρηπίς ἐστιν εὐμεγέθης καὶ τὸ ἐπ' αὐτῇ βωμοειδὲς τάφος τοῦ Θεμιστοκλέους. 6 οἴεται δὲ καὶ Πλάτωνα τὸν κωμικὸν αὐτῷ μαρτυρεῖν ἐν τούτοις·

ὁ σὸς δὲ τύμβος ἐν καλῷ κεχωσμένος
τοῖς ἐμπόροις πρόσρησις ἔσται πανταχοῦ,
τούς τ' ἐκπλέοντας εἰσπλέοντάς τ' ὄψεται,
χὠπόταν ἅμιλλ' ᾖ τῶν νεῶν θεάσεται.

τοῖς δ' ἀπὸ γένους τοῦ Θεμιστοκλέους καὶ τιμαί τινες ἐν Μαγνησίᾳ φυλαττόμεναι μέχρι τῶν ἡμετέρων χρόνων ἦσαν, ἃς ἐκαρποῦτο Θεμιστοκλῆς Ἀθηναῖος, ἡμέτερος συνήθης καὶ φίλος παρ' Ἀμμωνίῳ τῷ φιλοσόφῳ γενόμενος.

other respects a good-for-nothing. [2] Of his two eldest sons Neocles died while still a boy, from the bite of a horse, and Diocles was adopted by his grandfather Lysander. He had several daughters, of whom Mnesiptolema, born to his second wife, was married to Archeptolis, her half-brother by a different mother, Italia married Panthoides the Chian, and Sybaris married Nicodemus the Athenian. [3] After Themistocles' death his nephew Phrasicles sailed to Magnesia and was given Nicomache in marriage by her brothers, and he also adopted the youngest of all the children, Asia.

[4] The Magnesians have a splendid tomb of Themistocles in their market place. As for his actual remains, one should not pay any attention to Andocides when he says in his *Address to his Comrades* that the Athenians stole them and scattered them about. He is telling lies in order to incite the oligarchs against the democracy. Phylarchus, too, virtually erects a theatrical machine within his history, as though it were a tragedy, and, by producing before our eyes a Neocles and a Demopolis, supposedly Themistocles' sons, stages a scene purely to stir up emotions. Even the man in the street could not fail to realise that this story is a fabrication. [5] But Diodorus the Topographer, in his work *On Tombs*, has stated, though as an inference rather than something he knows for sure, that near the great harbour of the Piraeus a sort of elbow juts out from the promontory facing Alcimus, and, as you round this and come inside where the sea is calmer, you see a large stone base, and the altar-shaped monument upon it is the tomb of Themistocles. [6] Moreover, he thinks that Plato the comic poet testifies in support of his view in these lines:-

"Your tomb is built up on a lovely site.
It will be a place to which the merchant seamen
will shout greetings wherever they are going.
It will have a view of both the outward
and the inward bound sailors,
And it will be a spectator of every trireme race."

For the direct descendants of Themistocles there were also certain honours which have been maintained at Magnesia right down to my time, and these were enjoyed by a Themistocles of Athens, who became my companion and friend in the school of Ammonius the philosopher.

Commentary.

The numerical references in the left hand margin conform to the standard division of the text into chapters and sections (Sintenis), which is to be found in the Budé and Teubner editions. The Loeb edition of Perrin, rather confusingly, follows a different division of the chapters into sections (that of Bekker). The words in bold type (*lemmata*) are from the translation.

Chapters 1–2
This first section of the *Life* is concerned with Themistocles' origins, family, education, and experiences as a youth, factors which for Plutarch the biographer always had a vital bearing on his subject's subsequent character and career.

1.1 **But**: All the manuscripts have δὲ as the second word of the text, though "but" seems odd and unnecessary at the beginning of the first sentence. It is bracketed as an interpolation by some editors (e.g. Flacelière [1972], 34). Others suppose that an introductory paragraph, setting out Plutarch's reasons for comparing Themistocles and Camillus, which originally formed the beginning of this *Life*, has been lost (for this sort of opening or *prooimion* see e.g. *Nicias 1*, and, in a more extended form, *Cimon* 1–3, *Pericles* 1–2). Thus this was not originally the first sentence. It is true that some *Lives* start without any such introduction (e.g. *Aristides, Alcibiades).* It was obviously not an invariable requirement. However, the hypothesis of a lost opening paragraph to the *Themistocles* is made more plausible by the fact that with the pair *Themistocles/Camillus* Plutarch has not attached a comparison (σύγκρισις) of the two lives at the end. This is unusual. Only three other pairs of *Lives* (out of twenty two) do not have a concluding *synkrisis*.

The main points of similarity between Themistocles and Camillus are that both supposedly came from comparatively undistinguished families, both were skilful commanders, who rescued their cities after they had been captured and occupied by barbarian enemies, and both were exiled (though Camillus was exiled before, Themistocles after, his greatest triumph). There is a detailed discussion of this particular issue by David Larmour (Larmour, 1992), and a good account of *synkrisis* in general in the *Lives* by C.B.R. Pelling in *Miscellanea Plutarchea, Quad. Fil. Ferr.* 8 (1986), 83–96.

1.1 **his father Neocles**: Plutarch follows Herodotus, 7.143 (the earliest reference to Neocles in extant literature), on the name of Themistocles' father. It is confirmed by the ostraca evidence (see 5.7 note on ostracism). Themistocles is styled "son of Neocles" (his "patronymic") on numerous inscribed ostraca (cast against him in the 480s and 470s), which have been found in the Athenian *agora*, on the Acropolis, and in the Ceramicus (see e.g. Lang

[1990], nos. 664–1049, Willemsen and Brenne, *AM* cvi [1991], 147–56). Some examples of these are photographed in Lenardon (1978), plates 6–13, facing p. 128.

Plutarch's comments that Themistocles family was "humble", and that Neocles was "not particularly distinguished", may be thought to be supported by the fact that nothing at all is known about Neocles, apart from his name. However, Plutarch is directly contradicted on this point by Cornelius Nepos, *Themistocles 1.2*: *Pater eius Neocles generosus fuit*, "his father Neocles was of noble birth", and he himself goes on to admit, a few lines below, that Themistocles "had a connection with" the (aristocratic) *genos* of the Lycomidae (see 1.4 note; and cf. the implications of Lysias 30.27–8). Nothing can be inferred from the name itself of Themistocles' father. It could just as easily mean "youthful fame" as "new fame". It does not necessarily imply a recent rise in the family fortunes (see F.D. Harvey, *Historia* 29 [1980], 110–11).

The overall (and rather misleading) impression Plutarch creates in chapters 1–3, of Themistocles rising from humble origins to great political power purely through his own natural ability and determination, may be motivated by a desire to make a parallel between Themistocles and Camillus (cf. *Camillus* 2.1), as Larmour suggests (1992, 4180–82). In creating his picture he also makes use of a strongly anti-Themistocles tradition, propagated by his political enemies, which seems to have become well established in Athens by the mid to late fifth century. This can be clearly seen in Herodotus' portrayal of Themistocles throughout Book 8 of his *Histories* (see 1.1 notes on **illegitimate** and **Habrotonon**).

1.1 **from the deme Phrearrhioi:** This was one of the 139 demes or districts into which the territory of Athens and Attica had been divided for political and administrative purposes by Cleisthenes in his reforms of 508/7 (*Ath. Pol.* 21.4–5; see e.g. Whitehead [1986], 17–21). Accepted membership of a deme (through enrolment into the deme register) became the key criterion for qualification as an Athenian citizen, and a citizen's deme-name, or "demotic", which was inherited, and, subsequently, not dependent on place of residence, became part of his "official" name (along with his patronymic). The location of Phrearrhioi has been fairly certainly established (see E. Vanderpool, 'A Lex Sacra of the Attic deme Phrearrhioi', *Hesperia* 39 [1970], 47–53; J.S. Traill, *The Political Organisation of Attica, Hesperia* Supplement XIV [1975], Map 2; Whitehead [1986], xxiii). It lies in southern Attica, on the inland road to Sunium, and was the biggest deme of its tribe, Leontis (Whitehead [1986], 370–71).

Plutarch's assertion that Neocles' deme (and through him, therefore, that of Themistocles) was Phrearrhioi has been confirmed by the Themistocles ostraca (see previous note on **Neocles**) whenever his demotic is inscribed. At the time of Cleisthenes' reforms Themistocles can hardly have been more than a teenager (see 31.4 note), living with his father on the family estate in Phrearrhioi. Hence Neocles acquired, and Themistocles inherited, this demotic. Later on, Themistocles seems to have resided in a different deme, Melite (see 22.2 note), which, as a city deme, was more conveniently situated for a political activist.

1.1 **the tribe Leontis:** As part of his reforms in 508/7 Cleisthenes divided the citizen population into ten new tribes, roughly equal in population, named after traditional national heroes, and the demes were assigned in varying numbers to each of these (*Ath. Pol.* 21.1–4, 6).

1.1 **through his mother he was illegitimate:** At the time when Themistocles was born, νοθεία, "illegitimacy", could mean only that Neocles and Themistocles' mother were not legally married, and that he was a bastard child. This is possible, but unlikely, given the length and prominence of Themistocles' political career, and the fact that there is no hint of this sort of illegitimacy anywhere in Herodotus' narrative, even though he happily retails many other defamatory traditions about Themistocles (see 2.6, 7.6, 12.4, 16.2 notes).

Plutarch, however, considers Themistocles' illegitimacy to be the consequence of his mother's non-Athenian nationality. But this is an anachronistic view, since it was only after Pericles' nationality law in 451 (*Ath. Pol.* 26.4, *Pericles* 37.2–3) that children of a marriage between an Athenian father and a non-Athenian mother were disqualified from citizenship and considered to be *nothoi*, illegitimate. In fact, in the sixth and early fifth century it seems to have been quite common for members of the Athenian aristocracy to marry well connected non-Athenian, even non-Greek, wives (Cleisthenes' mother was a Sicyonian, Cimon's a Thracian; see Hdt. 6.39, 131, *Cimon* 4.1). So, if Themistocles' mother *was* a Thracian or a Halicarnassian, he would not for that reason have been a *nothos*, provided his parents were legally married.

1.1 **"Habrotonon ... the great Themistocles":** This apparent epitaph, which takes the form of an elegiac couplet (a hexameter followed by a pentameter), is quoted by Athenaeus, 13.576c, and attributed to the orator Amphicrates' *On Famous Men* (a work probably of the first century B.C, now lost; see Frost [1980], 62). It also appears in the *Palatine Anthology* (*AP* 7.306). If Phanias actually *denied* (as Plutarch suggests) that Themistocles' mother's name was Habrotonon, it must go back at least to the later fourth century (see 1.2 note).

However, the name Habrotonon actually carried strongly prejudicial overtones (as is made clear by Athenaeus in the above passage, though not by Plutarch here). It was a name characteristic of a slave girl or a *hetaira*, and it suggested easy sexual availability (cf. *Moralia* 753D; there is a character of that name and profession in Menander's *The Arbitration*). The clear implication is that Themistocles' mother was not just foreign, but a slave and a prostitute as well. The supposed epitaph is therefore almost certainly not genuine. It may originally have been concocted as part of a malicious anti-Themistocles tradition, vigorously propagated by his political enemies from the 460's on, some of which is reproduced by Herodotus in Book 8 of his *Histories* (see 2.6, 7.6, 12.4, 16.2 notes).

Again, there is a very different tradition in the account of Nepos (*Them.* 1.2): *uxorem Acarnanam civem duxit, ex qua natus est Themistocles*, "he (Neocles) married a citizen of Acarnania, from whom was born Themistocles". The appearance here of the word *civem* (citizen) is a little puzzling, given that Greek women did not exercise positive citizenship rights in Athens or Acarnania (on the western coast of mainland Greece), or anywhere else as far as we know. But it may derive from a tradition established specifically to refute the smear that Themistocles' mother was a slave (see next note).

1.2 **Phanias ... Euterpe ... Neanthes ... Halicarnassus:** Phanias of Eresus in Lesbos was a contemporary and fellow countryman of Theophrastus (Strabo 13.2.4), and a pupil of Aristotle. He was writing in the 330's (Suda s.v. Φανίας), and he is cited five times by Plutarch in this *Life* (1.2, 7.7, 13.5, 27.8 and 29.11) – more than any other writer. He seems to have written extensively about Themistocles (see introductory note on chs. 26–29), and he was clearly one of Plutarch's main sources in the *Themistocles*. However, Plutarch does not always seem to be fully convinced about Phanias' reliability, and his story about Themistocles' alleged human sacrifice before Salamis is demonstrably untrue (see 13.2–5 and notes).

Neanthes of Cyzicus wrote a *Hellenica* in the third century B.C., and mentioned Themistocles' mother in the third and fourth books (Athenaeus 13.576d). Neanthes presumably followed Phanias' version of the name and origins of Themistocles' mother, with the addition simply of the name of her supposed home town in Caria.

Wherever it originated, this version seems to have been designed to re-establish the respectability of Themistocles' mother. Euterpe is not so obviously a slave woman's name, and Halicarnassus, the birth place of Herodotus, had a large Greek population. Almost certainly the true name and provenance of Themistocles' mother were never publicly recorded. Plutarch himself tells us (*Alcibiades* 1.3) that the names of the mothers of such prominent Athenians as Nicias, Demosthenes, Lamachus, Phormio, Thrasybulus and Theramenes were all unknown.

1.3 **Cynosarges:** This was a γυμνάσιον, public exercise-ground, situated south-east of the *agora*, just outside the city walls (Frost [1980], 63). Its association with bastards is referred to at *Moralia* 750F, and attested by Demosthenes 23.213, and Athenaeus 234e (citing Polemon).

1.3 **he ... removed the distinction:** This is probably another invented story from the discrediting tradition (see 1.1 note on **Habrotonon**). S.C. Humphreys has suggested ('The *Nothoi* at Kynosarges', *JHS* 94 [1974], 88–95), that, in consequence of Pericles' restrictive citizenship law in 451, a number of upper class Athenian boys with non-Athenian mothers, who had not yet been enrolled in their demes as citizens, found themselves disfranchised as technically "illegitimate", and so deliberately and defiantly adopted Heracles as their patron, and the gymnasium of Cynosarges as their social centre. It is possible that, at the time, this association was presented by them and their families as a restoration of the "original and exclusive" character of Cynosarges, which Themistocles had deliberately altered for his own selfish motives, since he wished to obscure the fact of his own, out of wedlock, illegitimacy.

1.4 **connection with the Lycomidae ... initiation-shrine of Phlya:** A very important piece of information. The deme Phlya is situated about nine kilometres north of the Athenian *agora*. It was here that the *genos* (strictly speaking a clan, rather than a single family) of the Lycomidae had their estate and private shrine (see 15.2). Neocles was presumably a member of a cadet branch of the family which had moved before 508 to the more distant Phrearrhioi (see Davies [1971], no. 6669, p. 212). The Lycomids appear (like the Eumolpids) to have exercised important priestly functions. Mystery rites were performed at their shrine, and hymns by Musaeus sung to Demeter (Pausanias 1.22.7, 4.1.5–7). Phlya was also a venue for altars of Apollo, Artemis, Dionysus, and Ge (Pausanias 1.31.4).

The Lycomids seem to have had a long-standing feud with the Alcmaeonids, who, after the pollution they had incurred as a result of Megacles' massacre of Cylon and his supporters in the later seventh century, had been successfully prosecuted by a Myron *of Phlya* (*Ath. Pol.* 1.1, *Solon* 12.3). Thus this high profile advertisement by Themistocles of his Lycomid credentials was very appropriate to his own hostile relationship with the Alcmaeonids in the 480's and 470's (see 22.4, 23.1 notes).

1.4 **as Simonides has recorded:** The famous poet, Simonides of Ceos (c.550 – c.460), was a close friend of Themistocles (cf. 5.6–7, 15.4, Cicero *De Finibus* 2.104). It is likely that he composed a commemorative epigram, and that this was inscribed on the chapel wall after its restoration by Themistocles.

2.1 **by nature intelligent:** Themistocles' σύνεσις, intelligence, is also emphasised by Thucydides (1.138.3). Note the deliberate word repetition in 2.1–3 (συνετός ... σύνεσιν), and see 3.4 note.

2.3 **manifested a great passion, far beyond his years:** The point Plutarch is making in the first part of this chapter is that, from his earliest days, Themistocles demonstrated a natural predilection for the *political* aspects of education, e.g. composing forensic exercises, as against the liberal or cultural aspects, e.g. music. Hence we should accept Madvig's correction, ὑπερερῶν, of the manuscript reading ὑπερορῶν here (so also Flacelière [1972], 36, and in the Budé edition [1961], 103). The sense is that Themistocles, who was reluctant to learn the character-forming elements of education, had *by contrast* a great passion ("far beyond his years") for those elements which develop intelligence (σύνεσις) and practical efficiency (πρᾶξις). Compare 2.1, "by nature intelligent", "life of action and politics".

Frost (1980), 66, follows Perrin (1948), 4, in retaining ὑπερορῶν (="disregarding"), and this reading is supported also by H. Martin in *AJP* 85 (1961), 192–95. But it is hard to see how "disregarding" can give the sense required by the context. The word ὑπερερῶ is unattested elsewhere, but it is a natural formation, and ὑπερέραμαι is found in Aelian, *VH* 12.1.

2.3–4 **liberal ... so-called liberal:** The word repetition of ἐλευθέριον... ἐλευθερίοις is no doubt deliberate, the connotations of the word underlining the contrast with Themistocles' own supposedly discreditable origins (see 1.1 notes on **Neocles** and **Habrotonon**).

2.4 **he was forced to defend himself rather brusquely:** This anecdote goes back to the near contemporary writer, Ion of Chios (named as its author at *Cimon* 9.1), who was a friend and admirer of Themistocles' post-war political enemy, Cimon (*Cimon* 5.3, *Pericles* 5.3; see 5.4, 20.4 notes). It may therefore be authentic. The populist Themistocles was perhaps not unhappy to play up to the suggestion that he lacked the accomplishments characteristic of a "true gentleman" (cf. Ar. *Wasps* 959).

2.5 **Stesimbrotus says ... pupil of Anaxagoras ... Melissus:** Stesimbrotus of Thasos, a Homeric rhapsode and scholar (Plato *Ion* 530C–D, Xen. *Symposium* 3.6), who perhaps taught at Athens in the later fifth century, wrote a work entitled *On Themistocles, Thucydides* [the son of Melesias], *and Pericles* (Athenaeus 589d–e), which is cited or referred to by Plutarch on numerous occasions (e.g. *Themistocles* 4.5, 24.6–7, *Cimon* 4.5, 14.4, 16.1, 16.3, *Pericles* 8.9, 13.16, 26.1, 36.6). To judge from these references the work seems to have been a partisan and unreliable pamphlet, hostile to Themistocles and Pericles, and complimentary to Cimon and Thucydides.

Anaxagoras of Clazomenae (c.500–c.428) was a famous rationalist philosopher who lived for many years in Athens, where he became the teacher and close friend of Pericles (*Pericles* 4–6). Melissus of Samos (see next note) is described as a philosopher by Plutarch at *Pericles* 26.3.

2.5 **not adhering to correct chronology:** Plutarch can show awareness of chronological inaccuracies in his sources (cf. 27.1–2 and notes), and can correct them effectively when he wishes, in this case by using a simple comparative method. Pericles, a generation later than Themistocles, was well known to have been a friend of Anaxagoras, and also to have commanded the

Athenian forces at the time of the siege of Samos in 440–39, when Melissus was one of the Samian generals (Thuc. 1.116–17, *Pericles* 26.1–4).

For the chronology of Themistocles' life (a much disputed issue) see 31.4 note.

2.6 **Mnesiphilus the Phrearrhian:** This man appears in the narrative of Herodotus (8.57–8), where he is presented as being the first to see the vital necessity for the Greeks of fighting a naval battle at Salamis, and as communicating this view to Themistocles. Themistocles thereupon adopted his plan, and put it before Eurybiades, the overall commander, as though it were his own, without acknowledging its provenance. This characteristically anti-Themistocles story, in which he claims the credit which belongs to someone else, is part of a tradition which colours Herodotus' whole account of Themistocles in Book 8 of the *Histories* (see 7.6, 12.4 16.2 notes). It is almost certainly a fiction disseminated by Herodotus' Athenian informants, in particular the Alcmaeonids. Plutarch is highly critical of it in *Malice* 869D–E, and ignores it in his own account of the debate (11.2–6). Here Mnesiphilus appears as an influential tutor and adviser of Themistocles *in his youth.* This provides Themistocles with a direct link to the political wisdom of the great Solon, whose disciple Mnesiphilus had supposedly been (cf. *Moralia* 154C). However, that relationship seems unlikely on chronological grounds (see next note). The tradition was perhaps invented in the late fourth and third century B.C. philosophical schools, when it became a requirement for every great statesman to have had a (preferably well-known) mentor in his youth.

Nevertheless, Mnesiphilus himself is no invention. He was a historical figure, prominent enough politically to have ostraca cast against him (14 have been found in the Ceramicus deposit). Frost argues (*Historia* 20 [1971], 20–25) that he was a candidate when Megacles was ostracised in 487/6, though it is possible that these ostraka date from the 470's rather than the 480's. The ostraca confirm Plutarch's statement that his deme was Phrearrhioi, the same as that of Themistocles (1.1 note, 5.5). It thus seems reasonable to assume that Mnesiphilus was a political associate of Themistocles, even if he was not his boyhood guru.

2.6 **Solon:** The famous Athenian statesman, lawgiver, and poet of the early sixth century, whose reforms are traditionally dated to 594/3. A veritable pillar of σοφία, wisdom, he was subsequently regarded as one of the Seven Sages (Hdt. 1.29, Diog. Laert. 1.1.40).

2.6 **his successors ... forensic skills ... "sophists":** By the later fifth century litigants had to plead their cases in person before large juries in the Athenian *dikasteria*, courts of law (cf. 5.7 note on **Aristides**). Litigation was very common. It thus became necessary for all citizens to acquire at least some rudimentary oratorical techniques ('forensic skills'). The so-called σοφισταί, sophists, successfully exploited this demand. Plutarch's apparently rather critical attitude towards this development in the nature of σοφία is probably influenced by Plato's fierce hostility to sophists (see e.g. *Gorgias* 463A–465C).

2.8 **disinheritance by his father:** This story is found in Nepos (*Them.* 1.2): *a patre exheredatus est*, "he was disinherited by his father" – the disinheritance acts as an incentive for Themistocles to reform his ways and become a great statesman – and it had become a rhetorical commonplace by the time of the Elder Seneca (*Controversiae* 1.8.6). Despite Plutarch's firm rejection of the story here, it remained current in later times (cf. Aelian *VH* 2.12). As a matter of fact, disinheritance was very rare in Athens. It could only occur as the result of the formal renunciation (ἀποκήρυξις) by a father of his son. But this involved severe legal problems (see e.g. MacDowell [1978], 91).

2.8 **the old triremes:** This story is, strictly speaking, anachronistic, since the first Athenian triremes, as distinct from more primitive oared ships, were not built until 483 (Thuc. 1.14.3, *Ath. Pol.* 22.7). However, it has an important symbolic function in the narrative, pointing forward to what is to become a key policy of Themistocles, and a major theme in the *Life*, the commitment to a powerful Athenian navy (cf. 4.1–4, 7.1, 8.1, 10–17).

Chapters 3–5

This section is concerned with Themistocles' early career, before Xerxes' invasion of Greece. The linking motif is his political rivalry with Aristides. The central, and crucial, event is his Naval Bill (3.5–4.3).

3.1 **urge to achieve fame:** See 3.4, 5.3–5, 18.1–9 and notes.

3.1 **Aristides, son of Lysimachus:** This is the first mention in this *Life* of Themistocles' great rival and political opponent, Aristides. Here Aristides is presented as already a member of the political establishment, now about to be challenged by the young Themistocles. However, we have good evidence that Themistocles had been elected eponymous archon in 493/2 (Dionysius of Halicarnassus *AR* 6.341), four years *before* Aristides (489/8; see Develin [1989], 57).

The supposed stark contrast (briefly alluded to in this chapter) between the upright Aristides, whose political support allegedly came from the upper classes, and the unscrupulous Themistocles, popular with the common people, is a major theme in Plutarch's *Life of Aristides* (e.g. chs. 2–4, 6). It is, however, an over-simplification. There can be no doubt that the two were political rivals (cf. Hdt. 8.78–9). But the view that there was a rigid division between classes, and that this determined the nature of political life in early fifth century Athens, a view which goes back at least to the time of Aristotle (cf. *Ath. Pol.* 28.2), is almost certainly false, and there is every reason to doubt the black and white *moral* contrast between the two men which is found in the *Aristides*. We know, for example, that Aristides willingly cooperated with Themistocles in the deception of the Spartans over the rebuilding of Athens' city walls (see 19.2 note).

3.2 **Stesileos ... Ceos ... Ariston:** This story appears in more detail at *Aristides* 2.2–4. It is probably a fabrication, which owes its origin to the Hellenistic view that everything a great man did could be traced back to the influences of his childhood (cf. 2.6 note). Romantic colour could then be supplied to taste. Ariston was a Peripatetic philosopher, perhaps head of the Lyceum, who wrote in the later third century B.C. He came from Ceos. Hence, no doubt, his interest in the story.

3.3 **incite to ... radical decisions ... political reforms:** This view of Themistocles as a prototype "demagogue" is found in more detail at 4.4 and 19.1–6. It probably goes back to oligarchic propaganda of the late fifth century, which presented Themistocles as the ideologically motivated founder of radical democracy (see 4.4, 19.3 notes).

3.4 **desire for fame ... ambition ... still a young man ... Marathon:** This anecdote is designed to illustrate Themistocles' innate and lifelong φιλοτιμία, ambitious desire for fame and honour (cf. 5.3–5, 18.1–9 and notes), which is, together with σύνεσις (see 2.1 note), his major characteristic for Plutarch in this *Life* (see e.g. the analysis of H. Martin, *TAPA* xcii [1961], 326–34). Plutarch seems to have been fond of the anecdote, which is found also at *Theseus* 6.9, *Moralia* 84C and 800B. However, the implication that Themistocles was too young to fight at Marathon is directly contradicted at *Aristides* 5.4, where Themistocles is presented as the commander of his tribal regiment in that battle (and as rivalling Aristides in bravery). As a matter of fact, if Themistocles had been elected archon in 493/2 (see 3.1 note), he must have fought at Marathon in 490, probably as some sort of officer.

3.4 **Miltiades:** The Philaid Miltiades, the father of Cimon (see 5.4, 20.4 notes), had been the heroic victor of the battle of Marathon in 490, the greatest hoplite infantry success in Athenian history (Hdt. 6.103–115). He died in 489, after an unsuccessful expedition against Paros (Hdt. 6.135–6).

3.5 **the rest ... Themistocles ... the threat to come:** Here Themistocles demonstrates his σύνεσις (see 2.3, 3.4 notes). Plutarch expands on a comment of Thucydides (1.14.3), to the effect that the Persian invasion "was expected" (by Themistocles). In his narrative it becomes a point of contrast between Themistocles (alone) and everyone else. He goes on to present the "Aeginetan threat" argument as merely a stratagem on Themistocles' part. Herodotus (7.144), following the anti-Themistocles tradition (see 2.6 note), which denied his foresight, says simply that the ships were built for the war with Aegina (implying it was the only consideration), but were not in fact used for that purpose. Of the three versions, that of Thucydides probably comes closest to the truth. For most Athenians the Aeginetan threat was the main consideration, but fear of Persia was also a factor for at least some of them.

4.1 **customary practice of the Athenians:** This tradition is also found in Nepos (*Them.* 2.2), who refers specifically to an annual share-out, *cum pecunia publica, quae ex metallis redibat, largitione magistratuum quotannis interiret*, "when the public funds, which came from the mines, were being squandered by the authorities in distributions every year". However, our earliest source, Herodotus, says nothing about this (7.144). He refers only to an *intention* on the Athenians' part to distribute the large sum of money which had accrued to the "state treasury" (τὸ κοινόν) from the Laureum silver mines. Herodotus seems to be followed by the author of the *Ath. Pol.*, who implies it was purely a one-off situation in 483/2 (22.7). He refers to a surplus of 100 talents, apparently coming from one specific strike, which certain persons proposed should be distributed to the people.

On the other hand Herodotus himself elsewhere (3.57) tells us that the people of Siphnos used to share out amongst themselves *every year* the surplus from their gold and silver mines. This accorded with a traditional Greek view, that the *polis* was a sort of limited company, and the citizens were its shareholders. We know little or nothing about the functions and capacity of the Athenian treasury in the pre-Persian War period, but it does not seem that the notions of a state budget or an accumulated reserve fund had yet developed, as they had in Pericles' day (see e.g. M.M. Austin and P. Vidal-Naquet, *Economic and Social History of Ancient Greece* [English trans., 1977], 118–20). It is possible, therefore, that on this point Nepos and Plutarch are drawing on a valid independent tradition, and that the Herodotean version is affected by bias (see 2.6 note). If Themistocles had had to argue against a *traditional* practice, then his success was all the more creditable.

4.1 **the only man brave enough to come before the assembly:** Again, Themistocles is presented as unique (see 3.5 and note). This is the first appearance in the *Life* of any recorded historical activity on Themistocles' part. Themistocles' Naval Bill can be dated to 483/2 (*Ath. Pol.* 22.7). Plutarch omits to mention a number of other attested events during Themistocles' early life, in which he was either directly or indirectly involved (see Frost [1980], 73–80). This is not because he was unaware of them, but because at this point narratological considerations are primary. The Naval Bill was a defining moment for Athens, so Plutarch selects and highlights it.

4.1 **silver mines at Laureum:** This was the name given to the whole of the metal-rich region of Attica south of a line between Anaphlystus and Thoricus, ending in Cape Sunium. The mines had apparently been worked from distant antiquity (Xen. *Ways and Means* 4.2), but presumably there had been a recent increase in yield. They were publicly owned, but worked by private contractors, and they supplied the silver used for the state coinage. Their importance in the early fifth century is attested by Aeschylus *Persians* (472 B.C), line 238, where they are described as "a treasure of the earth". Themistocles' deme, Phrearrhioi (see 1.1 note), was on the fringes of this district, and it is possible that, through his family contacts, he had more accurate information than most about how much silver was available at a particular time.

4.1 **the war against the Aeginetans ... number of their ships:** This conflict with Aegina, an island in the Saronic Gulf about ten miles from the coast of Attica, seems to have been going on intermittently for some considerable time (cf. Hdt. 5.81–89, 6.87–93), and it would appear that, overall, the islanders had indeed been having the better of it. Only a few years earlier the Athenians had had to borrow 20 ships from the Corinthians (bringing their total fleet up to 70) to fight against the Aeginetans and, even then, they had been singularly unsuccessful (Hdt. 6.89, 93). The war was brought to an end shortly before Xerxes' invasion, when the resisting Greek states agreed to halt any ongoing conflicts they had with one another (Hdt. 7.145; see 6.5 note). Interestingly, the Aeginetans, who had medised in 491 (Hdt. 6.48), proved themselves the bravest fighters of all at Salamis (see 17.1 and note).

4.2 **Darius or the Persians:** Darius was certainly dead by 483/2. He had been succeeded as king of Persia by his son, Xerxes. The most likely date is late 487 or early 486 (see Frost [1980], 84–85, for the calculations). The Athenians thus must have been aware of it at least three years before their debate on the Naval Bill. Plutarch has simply not bothered to think chronologically here. Contrast 2.5 and, especially, 27.1, where he is forced to do so because of a major source conflict.

4.3 **one hundred triremes were built:** Plutarch follows a tradition for the number of new ships which goes back at least to the time of Aristotle (*Ath. Pol.* 22.7). Herodotus (7.144) states that two hundred ships were built, but it is generally thought that this is a mistake, the figure coming from the supposed *total* number of Athenian ships at the time of Salamis (Hdt. 8.1, 44, 46, 61). They already had fifty ships in the early 480's (Hdt. 6.89; see 4.1 note). Nepos appears to think they had no ships at all before the Naval Bill, as a result of which they built one hundred, and then added another hundred in 480 (*Them.* 2.2, 8, 3.2).

4.4 **directing its course to the sea ... nearest neighbours ... "steadfast hoplites":** As Frost (1980), 85, points out, Themistocles cannot possibly have argued in 483/2, a mere seven years after the great hoplite victory at Marathon, that the Athenians were no match *even for their Greek neighbours* in infantry. Not very long before that, their army had decisively defeated their neighbours, the Boeotians and the Chalcidians, both on the same day (Hdt. 5.77). The view is more appropriate to the period of the Peloponnesian War (cf. the very similar words of the "Old Oligarch", [Xenophon]

Constitution of the Athenians 2.1 [see 19.3 note]), and it is not a completely fair representation of Athenian strategic thinking even then. Its attribution to Themistocles probably stems from oligarchic propaganda put out in the later fifth century and subsequently, which represented Themistocles as deliberately building up the Athenian navy for ideological purposes (see 3.3, 19.3–6, and notes). Not surprisingly, perhaps, we learn that one of Plutarch's sources for this section was the anti-democrat Plato. The phrase quoted is from *Laws* 706C.

4.4 **"Themistocles robbed ... a rower's cushion and an oar":** The source of this quotation is unknown. Its tendentious character is self-evident. However, the incidental implication that those who qualified as hoplites on the property census could, and did, serve as rowers in the Athenian navy when necessary is interesting (see 19.5 note).

4.5 **opposition in the assembly from Miltiades ... as Stesimbrotus records:** For Miltiades see 3.4 note. It is not entirely clear whether "in achieving this" refers back to 4.3, the Naval Bill itself, or to 4.4, Themistocles' alleged transformation of the Athenians into sailors (something which the great hoplite hero Miltiades might well be thought to have opposed). In fact Miltiades had died in 489, some six years before Themistocles' Naval Bill, after a failed expedition against Paros (Hdt. 6.135–6), and thus cannot have opposed Themistocles in an assembly debate on it or its possible consequences. It has been suggested (E.S. Gruen, "Stesimbrotus on Miltiades and Themistocles", *CSCA* 3 [1970], 91–8) that Stesimbrotus dated the opposition of Miltiades to 493/2, when he returned from the Chersonese (Hdt. 6.41, 104) and Themistocles was archon (3.1 note). But at that date Themistocles could not be said to have achieved success in his naval policy, if he had one. The fact is that Stesimbrotus was notoriously unreliable on matters of both fact and chronology, as Plutarch himself points out (2.5, 24.6, and notes).

4.5–6 **integrity and purity of the citizen body ... philosophers to consider ... salvation ... facts proved ... by ... Xerxes ... in my opinion:** This is an interesting passage. Plutarch openly ("in my opinion") challenges the influential views of Plato (and other anti-democrats). He points out firstly, in answer to the criticism of *Laws* 706C–D (cf. also *Gorgias* 519A), that, whether or not the philosophical argument that the Athenian dependence on naval power had a corrupting effect on the citizen body of the state has any force (and he does not commit himself on this), what really matters is that, in practice, the entire Greek world was saved from becoming Xerxes' slaves by their navy. Secondly, in rebuttal of the argument at *Laws* 707B–D, he asserts that, in fact, Salamis was a far more decisive victory for the Greeks than Marathon or Plataea. In arguing that Mardonius' infantry force, which was left behind after Salamis, performed a mere holding function to cover Xerxes' retreat, he actually goes beyond what the facts seem to have warranted (Hdt. 8.101, 107), and what even the Athenians were subsequently prepared to claim (cf. Thuc. 1.73.5–74.1). Indeed, it contradicts what he himself says about Plataea at 16.6. Nevertheless, his commonsense view of the paramount importance of the victory at Salamis is to be commended.

Chapter 5 is a largely anecdotal chapter, in which the anecdotes (six in all) are intended to illustrate three important aspects of Themistocles' character and behaviour; his love of money and possessions (sections 1–2), his *philotimia* (3–5), and his political populism (6–7). It is of the nature of anecdotes that they cannot be historically authenticated, though they can sometimes be shown to be invented. However, the chapter does conclude with a reference to an important attested event of Themistocles' pre-war career, the eclipse of his main political rival, Aristides (see chs. 3–5 introductory note).

5.1 **Others ... accuse him of ... meanness ... used to sell even the victuals:** One of these critics may have been Timocreon of Rhodes (see 21.3–7 and notes).

5.2 **Diphilides the horse breeder:** Διφιλίδης is the reading of S. This is preferable to Φιλίδης of the other manuscripts, where the first syllable of the name has probably been lost after the preceding connective δὲ. Diphilides cannot be identified from other sources, but a family interest in horse-breeding and riding (a pastime affordable only by the very rich) is attested at 32.1 (Themistocles' son, Neocles, died from a horse's bite), and by Plato, *Meno* 93C–D (another son, Cleophantus, was an excellent horseman).

5.3 **desire to be famous:** For the Greeks *philotimia* (see 3.4, 18.1–9, and notes) was not necessarily a characteristic to be deplored (cf. Xen. *Mem.* 3.3.13). Plutarch's point (which could perhaps be made more clearly) in this and the next two anecdotes is that Themistocles' *youthfulness* and obscure background at the time made his behaviour seem pushy and pretentious.

5.3 **Epicles the lyre player of Hermione:** Like Diphilides, this Epicles is not mentioned anywhere else. Hermione, in the Argolid, was the neighbour of Troezen, the state to which the Athenians evacuated their women and children at the time of Salamis (see 10.5 note).

5.4 **on a visit to Olympia ... trying to rival Cimon:** Cimon, son of Miltiades (3.4, 4.5), became a leading political opponent of Themistocles after the Persian wars (see 20.4 and note). The Olympic festival was held every four years. It is not clear to which festival this anecdote refers. A visit by Themistocles to that of 476 is reported at 17.4 (see note). However, that was at a period when he was universally regarded as the victor of Salamis, and could in no way be described as "not yet a person of note". Indeed he had been a "person of note" since at least 493/2 (his archonship; see 3.1 note), several years before the young Cimon had become head of the Philaid family (see 3.4 note on Miltiades).

5.4 **who belonged to a great house:** The Philaids were certainly one of the grandest of all Athenian aristocratic families (see 3.4 note; *Cimon* 4.1–2, 5.3–4, Hdt. 6.34). For the supposedly humble origins of Themistocles see 1.1 and note.

5.5 **when he won a victory as a choregus:** An interesting piece of information, from the only anecdote in the chapter with any verifiable details. Plutarch presumably saw this choregic inscription for himself, in the precinct of Dionysus (cf. *Aristides* 1.3, *Nicias* 3.3). Adeimantus was archon in 477/6 (Develin [1989], 67), Phrynichus was the most famous tragedian of the day (cf. Hdt. 6.21). The play was probably his *Phoenician Women*, which dealt with the battle of Salamis (like Aeschylus' *Persians*, written four years later). However, the story does not illustrate Plutarch's point very well. By 476 Themistocles was at the height of his fame throughout Greece. The setting up by such a man of a simple commemorative plaque, after financing the training of the chorus of a successful tragedy at the Dionysia, would hardly have been regarded as a striking example of *philotimia*.

χορηγῶν is here used in a technical sense, "being a choregus", unlike χορηγίας("fortune") at 5.1, which foreshadows it. The *choregia* was a civic duty imposed on the richest citizens. Choregi for tragedies and comedies were chosen by the archon (*Ath. Pol.* 56.3), though it was possible to volunteer (Lysias 31.1–5).

5.5 **Themistocles of Phrearrhioi:** See 1.1 note.

5.6–7 In the final section of the chapter Plutarch explains how Themistocles was able politically to defeat his great rival Aristides (see 3.1 and note). Aristides was removed from Athens by the process of ostracism. Ostracism was a populist weapon (see note on 5.7), and Themistocles was able to exploit it, since he had become very popular with οἱ πολλοί, "the common people". The point is underlined by ring composition, τοῖς πολλοῖς coming at both the beginning and end of the section. Plutarch gives two reasons for this development on Themistocles' part. Firstly, he had a photographic memory (cf. Cicero *De Senect.* 21), which enabled him to demonstrate the common touch by greeting everyone by name on sight. Secondly, he gained widespread popularity by being a fair judge.

5.6 **showing himself to be a reliable judge ... contractual disputes:** Although the word Plutarch uses here, κριτής, does not necessarily indicate an *official* position, it seems probable (*pace* Frost [1980], 89) that Plutarch (or his source) assumed that Themistocles' popular judgements were those of an Athenian magistrate. συμβόλαια were legally enforceable contracts, usually of a financial kind, between individuals, and adjudication in the case of disputes arising therefrom was a matter for the nine archons (see 5.7 note). In the anecdote which follows, which is inserted to illustrate the point that Themistocles was a reliable judge, he is described as "serving as a *strategos* (general)". This is probably a slip (see next note), but it does indicate that Plutarch, or the anecdote compiler, thought of Themistocles as having an official role in these adjudications.

The presentation here of Themistocles as an honest, and therefore popular, judge is interesting. It is at variance with the more usual picture of Themistocles, in contrast to Aristides the Just, using office to dispense favours to his friends (cf. e.g. *Aristides* 2.5 [= *Moralia* 807A], 4.3; see 3.1 and 5.7 notes on Aristides).

5.6 **serving as a general ... Simonides of Ceos:** For Simonides see 1.4, 15.4 notes. This anecdote also appears at *Moralia* 185D, 534E, and 807B, where the context implies, more plausibly, that Themistocles was acting as an archon (note here ἀστεῖος ἄρχων). "General" seems to be a slip. For the *strategoi* see 6.1–2 note.

5.7 **On another occasion he made fun of Simonides ... abuse the Corinthians:** This second anecdote is quite irrelevant to Plutarch's purpose, which is to demonstrate Themistocles' methods of gaining popularity. It has been inserted here simply because it depicts another exchange between Themistocles and Simonides. "Abuse" is an exaggeration. There was a line of Simonides to the effect that "Troy does not hate the Corinthians", because they had supposedly fought on both sides in the Trojan War (*Dion* 1.1, schol. Pindar *O.* 13.78; cf. Aristotle *Rhet.* 1363a15). In fact Simonides also praised Corinth fulsomely (*Malice* 872D–E).

5.7 **having portraits made:** The Greek word used here, εἰκών, probably refers to a portrait bust (see 22.3 note on εἰκόνιον).

5.7 **secured a majority ... and:** The word which Plutarch uses here, and at 11.1, καταστασιάζειν, literally means "defeat by means of a political faction", and seems to imply that Themistocles acquired a loyal political following and a block vote he could rely on. This is unlikely. The ostracism procedure did allow for some preliminary organisation, since there was an interval of about two months between the decision to hold an ostracism and the vote itself (see 22.4 note). Ostraca (see next note) could be prepared in advance, as can be seen from the "Themistocles Hoard" (191, all inscribed with his name), which was found in a well on the north slope of the Acropolis (see e.g. O. Broneer, *Hesperia* 7 [1938], 212–52). However, the vast majority of citizens probably just voted (one man, one vote) according to their perceptions and prejudices on the day of the poll, *ostrakophoria*. In this case it was the way Themistocles wanted, but majority support could never be guaranteed.

5.7 **Aristides ... banished by ostracism:** For Aristides see 3.1–3, 11.1, and notes. For ostracism, so called because the candidates' names were inscribed on pieces of pottery, *ostraka*, see 22.5 note. It involved a ten year period of exile. The ostracism of Aristides is attested by Herodotus (8.79), and dated by *Ath. Pol.* 22.7 to 483/2, the same year as Themistocles' Naval Bill (4.1–3 and notes). Plutarch repeatedly asserts (*Them.* 11.1, 12.6, *Arist.* 7.1) that Themistocles was responsible for Aristides' ostracism, and, although neither Herodotus nor the author of the *Ath. Pol.* make the connection explicit, it does seem implicit in their narratives. The natural inference was also drawn by Nepos, or his source (*Aristides* 1.2): *a Themistocle collabefactus testula illa exsilio decem annorum multatus est*, "having been undermined by Themistocles, he was punished with ten years exile by the well-known potsherd vote".

Ostracism was essentially an unpopularity poll, and, if Themistocles was "responsible" for Aristides' ostracism, it must have been by fanning popular resentment against him by a word of mouth propaganda campaign. It has often been suggested that Aristides' unpopularity in 483/2 was the consequence of his unsuccessful opposition in the assembly to Themistocles' Naval Bill earlier in the year. Ostracisms were held in the eighth prytany (out of ten) of the official Athenian year, i.e., roughly, late March (see 22.4 note). Aristides had fought in the great hoplite victory at Marathon, and might therefore be thought to have been suspicious of an out-and-out naval strategy. It has also been suggested (e.g. by Frost [1980], 84, 90) that Aristides was the leader of a pro-Aegina group at Athens.

But it is odd that Plutarch nowhere *states* that Aristides had opposed the Naval Bill, and the evidence that Aristides spent his period of exile in Aegina is tenuous, to say the least (Demosthenes 26.6 merely reports this as something which "they say"). It may well be that Aristides' unpopularity in 483/2 had more to do with internal politics.

At *Aristides* 7.1. Plutarch says that Themistocles attacked Aristides for acting in an unconstitutional fashion in his administration of justice, alleging that he had "done away with the popular courts by judging and deciding all cases by himself", and that he had thereby "surreptitiously secured a monarchy for himself". We do not know Plutarch's source for this information, and there is an anachronism, as Frost points out [1980], 91), in his employment of the word δικαστήρια, since these "popular courts" had not yet been established in the 480's. However, this does not by itself wholly invalidate the tradition Plutarch is reproducing. Though the administration of justice in most cases was still in the hands of the nine archons, acting individually in their capacity as judges (cf. *Aristides* 4.2–3), Solon had long ago established a right of appeal against an archon's verdict to some sort of wider judicial body (*Solon* 18.2–3, *Ath. Pol.* 9.1). This was probably called the *Heliaea* (and was the whole assembly sitting in a judicial capacity), though the anachronistic use by our sources of the term *dikasteria* is common. It may be that Aristides, who had been eponymous archon in 489/8 (Develin [1989], 57), had been obstructing, or at least could plausibly be accused of having obstructed, the litigant's right to appeal against his verdict in cases which he had been adjudicating. This is perhaps the historical context into which we can place the tradition that *Themistocles* was a scrupulously fair and popular judge (see 5.6 and note).

A further reason for Aristides' unpopularity in 483/2 may have been a perceived connection with the "accursed" Alcmaeonid family (cf. *Aristides* 2.1), who were widely believed to have sent a treasonable signal to the Persian camp just before Marathon (Hdt. 6.121, 124). Abusive tags added onto two Aristides ostraca, quoted in Meiggs and Lewis (ML, 42), accuse him of medism and ill-treatment of suppliants.

Chapters 6–9

This section of the *Life* is concerned with those events of the war in which Themistocles was involved, before the evacuation of Athens and Attica and the battle of Salamis. **Chapter 6** narrates four praiseworthy, patriotic actions taken by Themistocles in the period leading up to the start of military operations in summer 480.

6.1–2 Epicydes, son of Euphemides: As it stands, this story, which is found twice elsewhere in Plutarch (*Nic.Crass.comp.* 3.3, *Moralia* 185A), but in no other writer, seems unhistorical. It is introduced by the vague λέγουσιν ("they say"), which perhaps indicates that it lacked a reputable written source, and it assumes that the Athenians in 480 had a single supreme military commander (contrast 18.6), whereas in fact they had no less than ten *strategoi*, generals, who were annually elected as a board (*Ath. Pol.* 22.2), and had equal powers with one another (see e.g. K.J. Dover, *JHS* 80 [1960], 72–3). Plutarch makes a similar mistake at *Aristides* 8.1. The anachronism here may be due to a desire to make a parallel between Themistocles and Camillus, with both being chosen as military supremos (so Larmour [1992], 4191; see 1.1 note). Plutarch's chronological vagueness at the beginning of the chapter is also suspicious. It is not clear whether the election is that held in spring 481 (for the year 481/0) after Xerxes had set out from Susa, or that of spring 480 (for 480/79) after he had sent demands from Sardis to the Greek states for earth and water (tokens of submission), and then started his march from there to the Hellespont (winter 481/0, spring 480). If there is anything at all historical in the story it may be that, *after the election*, Themistocles arranged that he, and not one of the other members of the board of *strategoi*, should lead the Athenian contingent which was sent to Tempe in early summer 480 (Hdt. 7.173; see 7.2 note). Epicydes, however, is not attested anywhere else, and further suspicion is aroused by the fact that in the story he functions as the prototype of later fifth century demagogues such as Cleon. Hence it has been suggested that Plutarch's source here was Theopompus (so Frost [1980], 95; see 19.1 note).

6.3–4 bi-lingual speaker ... interpreter: There are historical problems about this story too. Herodotus tells us (7.32, 133) that Xerxes did not send heralds in winter 481/0 to Athens or Sparta, because Darius' heralds had been put to death in these two cities in 491 (a highly discreditable action, which, significantly, he does not record in its proper place in his narrative, at 6.48). We cannot assume that Plutarch has simply misdated this story, since he clearly implies that the interpreter was a Greek, not a Persian herald. Furthermore, Pausanias tells us that the Athenian responsible for the deaths in 491 was Miltiades, not Themistocles (3.12.7). It is possible that an alternative version, designed to exculpate the Athenians, was concocted about who was killed in 491 (cf. Frost [1980], 96), and that Plutarch has misdated this variant. More likely, Plutarch is following a tradition about Themistocles which we do not otherwise know of.

6.4 treatment of Arthmius of Zeleia: This decree was inscribed on a bronze plaque or *stele* on the Acropolis in the fourth century (Dem. 9.41–2). It is "quoted" several times by fourth century orators (Dem. 19.271, Aeschines 3.258, Dinarchus 2.24 and 25). Meiggs (1972), 508–9, has produced an approximate text. However, the decree was moved not by Themistocles, but by Cimon (schol. on Aelius *Aristides* 3.327, quoting Craterus as his source). Craterus compiled a valuable collection (συναγωγή) of Athenian decrees in the early third century B.C., copying directly from the inscribed stones. His collection is sometimes cited by name by Plutarch (e.g. *Arist.* 26.1–2, *Cimon* 13.5; see 23.1. note), though he does not seem to be using it here. The decree has been wrongly attributed to Themistocles by Plutarch, or his source, probably because the orator Aeschines, after referring to the decree, goes on to ask his audience rhetorically whether Themistocles and the dead of Marathon would not be in mourning if they could see what was happening now (3.259).

A reference in the text of the decree to "Athens' allies" indicates that it was passed later than the establishment of the Delian League in winter 478/7. The most likely date is suggested by Meiggs (1972), 511 (following Cary, *CQ* xxix [1935], 177–80), who assigns it to the early 460's, and connects Arthmius' mission with the intrigues of the Spartan regent, Pausanias, who was based at Colonae in the Troad (Thuc. 1.131.6), not far from Zeleia, in Hellespontine Phrygia, and the Persian governor's headquarters at Dascylium. This was a period when, after the ostracism of Themistocles, Cimon's political influence in Athens was at its height.

6.4 inscribed ... on the list of those outlawed: The Greek word ἀτίμους (from ἄτιμος) cannot here mean "disfranchised", "without citizenship rights", since Arthmius was not an Athenian citizen. It has its earlier sense of "outlawed", i.e. someone who had lost his personal rights and who thus could be killed with impunity. For this "untamed" sense of the word see Rhodes (1981), 158, 222, 282–83, on *Ath. Pol.* 8.5, 16.10, 22.8.

6.5 **greatest of all his achievements:** Plutarch saves the best till last, and describes Themistocles' ending of the current inter-Greek wars as his greatest (pre-war) achievement, because, unlike the other actions mentioned in this chapter, this one did not involve financial skulduggery or violence, real or threatened.

A formal decision to end all Greek against Greek wars is attested by Herodotus, 7.145. It was taken by delegates at a conference at the Isthmus, probably in autumn 481. But he says nothing of any Themistoclean role in this decision. Plutarch naturally wishes to emphasize the role of his protagonist. He may also be trying to create another parallel between Themistocles and the "conciliatory" Camillus (cf. Larmour [1992], 4192–93). However, even if there is some unhistorical exaggeration on his part here, it is reasonable to assume that Themistocles did take the lead in persuading the Athenians to give up their conflict with the Aeginetans (see 4.1 and note), who themselves were no doubt leaned on by the Spartans.

6.5 **Cheileos the Arcadian:** Presumably this is the same man as Cheileos the Tegean, who, according to Herodotus (9.9), followed by Plutarch at *Malice* 871F, was effective in persuading the Spartans ephors to send out an army in summer 479, in response to the demands of an Athenian embassy. Herodotus says he had the most influence of any foreigner at Sparta. However, there is nothing in Herodotus or the other surviving sources about any role played by him in 481. This detail is tacked on rather awkwardly by Plutarch at the end of the chapter, and λέγουσι,"they say", is suspiciously vague (see 6.1 note). Nevertheless, there is no reason to think he has invented it. For a similar tacked-on detail, but with a named source (Stesimbrotus), see 4.5.

7.1 **to embark on their triremes ... leave their city:** The famous Delphic oracle, not mentioned here by Plutarch (see 10.3 note), had already been delivered and interpreted (cf. Hdt. 7.140–3). But at that stage the Athenian decision must have been to resist the coming invasion, using the fleet in particular, and to evacuate the city *if and when it became necessary*. It is highly unlikely that Themistocles would have proposed an evacuation of the city even before the Tempe expedition (see 7.2 note), and Herodotus' narrative at 7.173–4 says nothing about any such proposals. He does, however, tell us that the expeditionary force sent to Tempe went by sea as far as Halus in southern Thessaly, and this *may* be the source of Plutarch's error here. More likely the chronological distortion is deliberate, to highlight a key narrative motif (see 2.8, 3.5, 4.1, 4.4 notes).

7.1 **face the barbarians at sea as far away from Greece as possible:** An odd comment. Does Plutarch imply that Themistocles wanted to send the fleet *en* *masse* to attack Xerxes' forces as they crossed the Hellespont? There is no hint of such an unlikely plan in the other sources.

7.2 **Tempe ... in defence of Thessaly ... not yet thought to be taking the Persian side:** The narrow vale of Tempe, where the river Peneus flows between Mounts Olympus and Ossa, was regarded as a strategically vital pass guarding the entrance to northern Thessaly, and it was a natural decision by the Greeks to make this the initial defensive position, probably in May 480. Herodotus (7.173) confirms that Themistocles was the commander of the Athenian contingent. Plutarch alludes rather cryptically here to the most powerful family in Thessaly, the Aleuadae, who, according to Herodotus (7.6, 130), had "medised" from the start, even before Xerxes sent his demands for earth and water as tokens of surrender (7.32, 132). The abandonment of the position, after only a few days, is explained by Herodotus (7.173) as due to the discovery that there was another traversable pass to the north and west of Olympus, by which the Persians could by-pass Tempe. After this the rest of the Thessalians also medised. However, such a gross error of strategic intelligence on the Greeks' part, when no fewer than 10,000 hoplites were being committed, seems remarkable, and we may perhaps suspect that medising in Thessaly had spread well beyond the Aleuadae even before the expedition was sent.

7.2 **with a fleet to guard the straits at Artemisium:** 127 ships, according to Herodotus, with a further 53 arriving later, as well as 20 Athenian ships manned by crews from Chalcis (8.1, 14). The strategy was to block the straits (between the southern end of Magnesia on the mainland and the northern tip of Euboea) to prevent the Persian fleet from by-passing Thermopylae, where the Greek land forces were holding the narrow pass between the mountains and the sea (see 9.1 note). However, the "Themistocles Decree", from Troezen (text and commentary in ML, 48–52; translation in Crawford and Whitehead [1983], 224–25), records a decision taken to send only 100 ships to Artemisium (and 100 to Salamis). There has been much discussion about the authenticity of this document (cf. e.g. Frost [1980], 102–04, Podlecki [1975], 147–67; see 10.4 note) which appears to be in conflict with Herodotus on the timing of the evacuation decision. Evacuation is provided for in the Decree, whereas Herodotus says this did not take place until *after* the defeat of Thermopylae and the withdrawal from Artemisium). The Decree as we have it has been thought to be a later, fourth century compilation, and, at best, to paraphrase a number of originally separate decisions made on different occasions by the Athenian assembly, which were subsequently all rolled into one and attributed to the proposal of Themistocles. However, it is a reasonable hypothesis that the text does, among other things, record (though not always *verbatim*) the original decree proposed by Themistocles and passed by the assembly in the late spring of 480. It may well be that a detailed plan for the evacuation was drawn up before the Artemisium campaign, but not put into effect until after it, when evacuation could no longer be avoided, and that the Athenians, perhaps under pressure from the Spartans, subsequently modified their battle plan, and added to the Artemisium contingent most of the ships originally earmarked for Salamis.

7.3 **exceeded that of all the rest:** At Salamis there were 180 Athenian ships, plus 20 which they supplied to the Chalcidians, out of a grand total of 380 (Hdt. 8.44, 48, 82), or 310 (Aeschylus *Persians* 339–40). See 14.1 note.

7.3 **Themistocles voluntarily surrendered his own command to Eurybiades:** Spartan command of both land and naval forces is attested by both Herodotus (7.159, 8.2) and Thucydides (1.18.2). But this issue had been settled, with Athenian acceptance, almost a year earlier, before the embassy sent to Gelon of Syracuse (7.161, 8.3). Plutarch is again sacrificing chronology to dramatic effect here, to keep Themistocles in the narrative spotlight, though it is likely that Themistocles had earlier been the man responsible for persuading the assembly to accept Spartan command at sea (see 6.5 note).

7.5 **Eurybiades was terrified:** Herodotus says that *all* the Greeks were frightened at first (8.4), and that they only found out about the encircling squadron *after* the Euboeans' act of bribery (8.7–8). Plutarch again dramatises the situation, focussing on the supreme commander from the start, and making his panic seem more justifiable.

7.5 **two hundred ... beyond Sciathos:** Their intention was to sail right round Euboea, returning up the Euripus strait to attack the Greeks at Artemisium in the rear.

7.6 **to Eurybiades, as Herodotus has recorded:** Plutarch's use here of the plural definite article plus περί (literally, "those around") before the name may be periphrastic (cf. 26.1 note), equivalent simply to writing the name alone (see LSJ, s.v.περί, C.2). Herodotus, in the passage which Plutarch explicitly refers to, makes no mention of any associates of Eurybiades (8.45); hence my translation here. However, Plutarch may be delicately hinting at the story recorded by Herodotus immediately afterwards (which Plutarch has suppressed), that Themistocles gave three talents of the Euboeans' money to the Corinthian commander, Adeimantus (cf. 11.5 note).

The story as it appears in Herodotus is flagrantly anti-Themistocles, part of the hostile tradition which strongly colours his narrative throughout Book 8 of the Histories (see 2.6, 12.4, 16.2 notes). Themistocles takes thirty talents from the Euboeans, gives five to Eurybiades and three to the Corinthian Adeimantus as bribes, and keeps the rest for himself! Plutarch doctors Herodotus' account, so there is no mention of Adeimantus (cf.11.2 note), and the bribe is given in its entirety to Eurybiades. Thus for Plutarch Themistocles' action demonstrates, not fraudulent deception, but prudent intervention. The name of the Euboean emissary, Pelagon, is a detail not found in Herodotus. It adds verisimilitude to the narrative.

As a matter of historical fact, it is very unlikely that, however numerous the enemy appeared to be at Artemisium, Eurybiades would have contemplated withdrawal, since that would have left his fellow Spartan commander, Leonidas, in a hopelessly exposed position at Thermopylae (see 9.1 note). Conversely, after Thermopylae had fallen, the fleet had no choice but to withdraw from Artemisium (as Plutarch points out at *Malice* 867D).

7.6 **Architeles ... captain:** The word used by Plutarch, τριήραρχος, here translated as "captain", literally means "trireme commander" (cf.12.8, 15.3). It is also used by Herodotus (8.93) with reference to the Athenian ship captains at Salamis. Trierarchs became key figures in the Athenian navy in the second half of the fifth century, when they were required to be financially responsible for the running costs of their allocated trireme (see e.g. Ar. *Knights* 913–8). However, this is unlikely to have been the case in 480 (see next note). We do not hear of this Architeles elsewhere, and the anecdote is almost certainly unhistorical.

7.6 **sacred ship:** In the late fifth century the Athenians had two special "sacred" ships, the Paralus and the Salaminia, manned by elite crews who were paid above the regular rate (Harpocration s.v. Πάραλος). These were used for official state missions, including the conveyance of delegates to religious festivals, though they could also be pressed into service as regular warships (Thuc. 3.31.1, 77.3). However, it is not clear when they were first instituted. We do not hear of them before the start of the Peloponnesian War in 431, and it is arguable whether they were in existence as early as 480 (cf. Hdt. 6.87; Jordan [1975], 157ff.). Furthermore, the supposed insistence of the crew on being paid on the spot is anachronistic at the time of Artemisium. Such payment on campaign, and the associated problems when it was not promptly forthcoming, became characteristic of the Athenian navy only after the emergence and development of the Delian League, when squadrons were on active service and away from Athens for long periods of time (cf. e.g. Thuc. 8.45.2).

Plutarch himself seems to harbour some doubts about this story, to judge from the slightly distancing "at any rate" in the final sentence. But he uses it because, like the previous story, it portrays Themistocles as employing dubious means, not to enrich himself, but to secure a desirable objective for the Greeks as a whole.

7.7 **Phanias of Lesbos:** An important source for Plutarch in this *Life* (see 1.2, 13.5, 27.8, 29.11 and notes).

8.1 **battles ... did not produce a decisive result:** According to Herodotus' account (8.9–18) there were two smaller engagements at Artemisium on successive evenings, in which the Greeks were victorious, followed by a full-scale battle on the third day, in which both sides sustained losses, though the Persians suffered more severely, and in which the Athenians particularly distinguished themselves. The subsequent Greek withdrawal was prompted by the news of the defeat at Thermopylae (8.21).

Plutarch gives vent to some patriotic moralising here, but, interestingly, his idea of the character of a naval battle at this period, with the emphasis on collision and boarding rather than manoeuvring and tactical skills, probably represents the reality pretty accurately (see 14.2 note).

8.2 **Pindar:** Born at Cynoscephalae in Boeotia in 518, and thus a fellow-countryman of Plutarch, Pindar came from an aristocratic background, and wrote eulogistic odes for rich patrons, both individuals and cities. He was said to have annoyed his fellow Boeotians, who had medised in 480, by praising Aeginetan courage at Salamis (*Isthmian* 5), and by his famous dithyramb in honour of Athens (fr. 76). These lines on Artemisium, probably from the same poem, are quoted frequently by Plutarch (e.g. *Moralia* 232E, 250E, 552B, 867C).

8.3–4 **Artemisium ... temple of Artemis:** The beach and temple are referred to by Herodotus (7.176), but there is no reason to doubt that Plutarch had also personally visited the site and read the inscription. He had stayed in the nearby resort town of Aedepsus on the N.W. coast of Euboea (*Moralia* 667C). The site of the temple has been identified, near modern Pefki (see Frost [1980], 110, H.G. Lolling, *Ath. Mitt.* 8 [1883], 7–23).

8.3 **Hestiaea ... Olizon ... Philoctetes.** For Hestiaea, in Northern Euboea, see next note. Olizon, once a possession of the hero Philoctetes (*Iliad* 2.717–8), is the rocky curling "tail" of the promontory of Mount Pelion, on the northern side of the strait of Artemisium.

8.5 **elegiac poem ... inscribed:** This epitaph, not mentioned by Herodotus, is also quoted by Plutarch at *Malice* 867F. It has sometimes been attributed to Simonides. However, the formulaic expression παῖδες Ἀθηναίων, "(brave) sons of the Athenians", sounds like a conscious imitation of Pindar's παῖδες Ἀθαναίων quoted at 8.2, and there is a distinct boastfulness about an epitaph in which only those who set up the memorial are praised in it, which seems inappropriate in 480 (cf. the reaction to Pausanias' boastful inscription at Delphi, recorded by Thuc. 1.132.2–3). The phrase "when the army of the Medes was destroyed" indicates at least that the epitaph cannot have been composed immediately after Artemisium, and it may well be that it was not in fact inscribed until the mid-440's, after the Athenians had put down a revolt in Euboea and occupied the territory of Hestiaea (Thuc. 1.114.3).

9.1 **bringing up the rear in recognition of their bravery:** Herodotus merely says that the Greeks withdrew, Corinthians first, Athenians last (8.21). It is possible that the rear position in the retreat was regarded as a post of honour, but it is more likely that it simply made tactical sense for by far the largest single squadron to cover the most dangerous point of the line.

9.1 **Thermopylae ... Leonidas lay dead:** The Spartan king Leonidas, commanding the Greek infantry forces, had the task of defending the pass at Thermopylae, where the road from northern Greece edges between the mountains of Trachis and the Euripus strait. The position was eventually turned by treachery, and Leonidas and his 300 Spartans died to a man and became a legend (Hdt. 7.201–228)

9.2 **conspicuous messages engraved on stones:** This story goes back to Herodotus (8.22), who quotes the text of the message and surmises its double motive. Herodotus, however, seems to mean that Themistocles left these messages only in the coastal area around Artemisium, in the places where drinking water was to be found. Plutarch goes further. In the event the messages had no effect on the performance of the Ionians (Hdt. 8.85), but they may have helped to reinforce the anti-Ionian prejudices of the Phoenicians (cf. Hdt. 8.90).

If we accept the authenticity of this detail, there are interesting implications for the question of the degree of popular literacy in early fifth century Greece (see e.g. F.D. Harvey, *REG* 79 [1966], 585–635, Rosalind Thomas, *Literacy and Orality in Ancient Greece* [Cambridge, 1992], 128–57). For the propaganda to be effective it must have been expected that many of the rank and file Ionian sailors, not just a handful of officers, would be able to read the messages. The conclusion seems to be that a reasonable degree of literacy was widespread, at least in the Ionian Greek cities (see 10.5 note).

9.2 **who were their ancestors:** It was widely believed that the Ionian cities had been founded originally by settlers from Athens (Herodotus 5.97, 9.97, Thuc. 1.12.4).

9.3 **burning the towns of the Phocians:** Phocis was badly devastated by the Persian army, possibly because of Thessalian ill-will (Hdt. 8.31–3). But there was no way it could be successfully defended (see 9.4 note).

9.3 **a stand in Boeotia:** The chief city of Boeotia, Thebes, had medised, according to Herodotus (7.132), as soon as it received Xerxes' demand for earth and water in winter 481/0, and the Theban contingent at Thermopylae was only there under duress, and they surrendered as soon as they could (7.205–22). After the war Thebes was to some extent rehabilitated (see 20.3 note), on the dubious grounds that its medising had been the work of only a small but powerful clique (cf. Hdt. 9.87–88, Thuc. 3.62.3–4). For Plutarch, as a Boeotian, Thebes' medising role during Xerxes' invasion was an embarrassing problem, which he slides over here. He does attempt a defence, attacking Herodotus' credit, at *Malice* 864D–867F.

9.4 **building a wall across the Isthmus:** i.e. between the Corinthian and the Saronic gulfs. This was in fact the only defensible position left *on land*, though it does seem that, after Thermopylae, the Peloponnesians had adopted something of a bunker mentality (cf. Hdt. 8.40, 56–63, 78–80).

9.4 **betrayal ... left in an isolated position:** Herodotus says that the Athenians had "expected" that a stand would be made in Boeotia. But after Thermopylae had fallen, there was no way, given the defection of Thebes, that an effective stand could have been made anywhere on the Greek mainland north of the Isthmus, including Attica, and most Athenians must have realised this. To heighten the drama Plutarch's narrative here and in chapter 10 suggests that a considerable period of time elapsed between the loss of Thermopylae and the actual evacuation of Athens, which, in his account, had still not been agreed to, even in principle. In fact the Persians reached Attica within a week (Hdt. 8.50–1).

9.5 **the temples of their gods and the tombs of their forefathers:** Plutarch here brings out very effectively just what the abandonment of the city and the *land* of Attica meant to the ordinary Athenians, the vast majority of whom were peasant farmers. Their distress was all the more severe because of the widely held belief that they alone of the Greeks were "autochthonous" – they had never lived anywhere else (Hdt. 7.161, Thuc. 1.2.5, 2.36.1, Euripides *Medea* 824–26). The reading of S, ἡρῷα (=hero-tombs), is less apposite here, with πατέρων (contrast *Camillus* 31.3).

Chapters 10–17

This section is devoted to Themistocles' role in the battle of Salamis, a victory universally regarded in antiquity as the greatest triumph of his career. These chapters thus constitute both the climax of the first half of the narrative, and the centrepiece of the *Life* as a whole.

10.1 **like a playwright deploying machinery in a tragedy:** Plutarch seems fond of this comparison, which he uses to pour scorn on supposedly supernatural interventions. These may come in the form of unlikely stories within historical narratives (cf. 32.4 [Phylarchus], *Malice* 870C [Herodotus]), or as real life attempts to impress and manipulate superstitious public opinion (as here, and at *Lysander* 25.1). The reference is to the theatrical μηχανή, a sort of crane positioned behind the backdrop (σκηνή). It was used to swing divine characters into view, and lower them onto the stage, so they could be thought of as arriving "out of the blue" (cf. e.g. Euripides *Helen* 1642ff.).

Plutarch is closely following the account of the snake's disappearance given by Herodotus (8.41), which also refers to the oracle (see next note), but Herodotus does not bring Themistocles into the story, and indeed there was no need to resort to subterfuge by this stage, with Xerxes' army fast closing in on Attica. The Athenians were already persuaded, and the disappearance of the snake must simply have been regarded as final confirmation of the need to do what they were already doing.

10.1 the snake ... disappeared from its sacred enclosure: This was probably the Erechtheum, the temple of Erechtheus on the Acropolis. The snake was identified with the hero Erechtheus, or Erichthonius (cf. Pausanias 1.24.7, Ar. *Lysistrata* 759).

10.2 choice offerings ... each day: These were honey cakes (Hdt. 8.41).

10.3 the oracle ... a wooden wall: This is Plutarch's first mention of the famous oracle and Themistocles' interpretation of it. We might have expected a reference to it in the narrative at the beginning of chapter 7 (see 7.1 note), since Herodotus (7.141–3) makes it clear that the Athenians had been given the oracle much earlier, probably in late 481, before Xerxes' invasion had begun. However, Plutarch's preferred, and more dramatic, picture is one of Themistocles trying for a considerable time to persuade his countrymen to agree to an evacuation of the city, using every possible argument, and succeeding only at the very last minute. Hence the chronological rearrangement.

The expression "wooden walls" (which alone would not be destroyed) occurred in the second, more favourable, oracle (Hdt. 7.141), and after the war it rapidly became proverbial (cf. Ar. *Knights* 1040).

10.3 the god: i.e. Apollo.

10.4 he proposed a decree: For the so-called Themistocles Decree see 7.2 note. Plutarch had almost certainly seen a copy of this decree, a text of which goes back at least to the fourth century (cf. Dem. 19.303), but he seems here to be quoting from memory. He reproduces from line 5 the expression "Athena who guards Athens" (though he writes "Athenians" – a manuscript reading which should not be altered), with its archaic, ritual epithet for Athena, μεδεούσῃ (cf. Ar. *Knights* 723). But then he diverges considerably from the text of the decree with "each man providing as best he could for the safety of his children, wife, and slaves", instead of "the Athenians should place their children and wives in Troezen ... and the old men and moveable property on Salamis" (lines 6–11). This is probably because he has been influenced by Herodotus' narrative at 8.41, where a proclamation is made to the effect that "everyone should get his children and members of his household to safety as best he could". In Herodotus, however, this seems to come at the moment when the Athenians *activated* a decision in principle which had been taken earlier (7.144).

Incidentally, the assertion at *Ath. Pol.* 23.1 (see 10.6 note) that, on the eve of Salamis, "the generals made a proclamation that each man should see to his own safety", with its imputation of official panic, is not found elsewhere, and does not square with the picture of an organised and orderly evacuation presented by Herodotus and the Themistocles Decree (see 10.6 note).

10.5 evacuated ... children and wives to Troezen: Perhaps not surprisingly, given its provenance (see 7.2 note), Troezen is the only place of refuge specified in the Themistocles Decree. Herodotus (8.41) says that "most" went to Troezen (so Plutarch here), but adds that some went to Salamis or Aegina. Presumably those who had delayed to the last minute could only be ferried to the nearest safe havens.

Troezen, on the north coast of the Argolid, was traditionally the birth place of Theseus (*Theseus* 3–4), and his maternal grandfather, Pittheus, had been its founder. This explains the special arrangements the Troezenians were prepared to make for Athens in this emergency. Troezen was staunchly loyal during the war, sending five ships to Salamis (Hdt. 8.43) and 1000 hoplites to Plataea (Hdt. 9.28).

10.5 **two obols a day:** Plutarch's text does not specify "daily", but two obols would not have lasted long as a one-off payment. The allowance was probably given to each citizen's family.

10.5 **to pick the ripe fruit:** It was now mid-September (see 11.1 note), harvest time.

10.5 **voted ... to pay teachers' fees:** If Plutarch is reporting the Troezenian decree accurately, this is important evidence for the existence of early fifth century public education (cf. Hdt. 6.27 [Chios]; H.I. Marrou, *History of Education in Antiquity* [English trans., New York, 1956], p.72). The story recorded at 9.2 (see note) implies that literacy was widespread by 480, at least among the Ionians.

10.5 **Nicagoras proposed the decree:** Nicagoras is an otherwise unknown Troezenian. A copy of the decree was later kept at Athens, since the orator Hyperides had it read out in court in the 320's (3.32–3).

10.6 **Areopagus ... Aristotle ... Cleidemus:** The Areopagus, so called because it met on the hill of Ares, was the oldest council of state at Athens. It was composed of ex-archons, who qualified for life membership at the end of their year of office (cf. Wallace [1985, 1989], especially 70–93). Cleidemus was a fourth century Atthidographer, or local historian of Athens and Attica, whose work is now lost.

Neither of these two apparently rival versions of an emergency funding operation, immediately before Salamis, has much historical credibility. It is not mentioned in Herodotus' account, and it seems extremely unlikely that, having decided in principle on an evacuation and naval mobilisation much earlier, the Athenians had not stockpiled supplies on Salamis, or made provisions for the crews' rations for a reasonable period when the fleet embarked for Salamis. The idea of cash payments for naval service at this period seems anachronistic (see 7.6 note), and there is no other evidence for any rivalry at this time between Themistocles and the Areopagus, a council of which he was himself, as an ex-archon, a member (see 23.6 note [end]).

The Aristotelian version (*Ath. Pol.* 23.1–2), which alleges despair on the part of the *strategoi*, is motivated by the author's dubious and probably unhistorical belief that the council of the Areopagus, whose influence had been in decline since the reforms of Cleisthenes, salutarily regained a position of power as a result of its steadfastness at the time of the Salamis campaign, a "leadership" which it retained until it was stripped of most of its powers by the reforms of Ephialtes in 462/1 (*Ath. Pol.* 25–26.1).

The Cleidemus version is equally unhistorical – a mass embarcation from Athens in 480 must have departed mainly from the beach at Phaleron (see 12.2 note), not from the Piraeus, which had not yet been converted into *the* great harbour of Athens, which it subsequently became (see 19.3–4 and notes).

It is likely that these two versions go back to a mid-fifth century propaganda battle at Athens between two groups, who should perhaps be called "conservatives" (pro-Areopagus and Cimon) and "radicals" (pro-Themistocles and Ephialtes), rather than oligarchs and democrats. The claim of the conservatives seems to have been that, though Themistocles' responsibility for winning the battle of Salamis could not be denied, the Areopagus deserved the most credit for enabling the Athenians to fight it in the first place by distributing vital funds. This was then countered by the radicals with the version Plutarch found in Cleidemus – that it was Themistocles who was responsible for this funding operation as well. Cleidemus himself probably wrote earlier than Aristotle, or whoever was the author of the *Ath. Pol.* (so Thomsen [1964], 85–89). But the rival versions almost certainly did not originate with either author.

10.9 A pitiful sight ... the many citizens who were being left behind because of old age: Herodotus (8.51) says that only "a few Athenians", stewards of the temples on the Acropolis and poor people, stayed behind. Similarly Nepos (*Them.* 2.8): *arcem sacerdotibus paucisque maioribus ... tradunt*, "they left the citadel to the priests and a few older citizens". Presumably those who were too old or infirm (or too destitute) to travel stayed, and there must have been some who, for religious reasons, did so by choice. They put up fierce, though short-lived resistance (Hdt. 8.52–3). But it is hard to believe they were very numerous, as Plutarch here claims. Hence some editors (e.g. Flacelière [1972], 58, and in the Budé edition [1961], 114) have emended πολλοί, the unanimous manuscript reading here, to πολὺν. This gives the sense "those who were left behind ... very pitiful sight". This may be correct. However, I am inclined to agree with Frost (1980), 122, who argues in favour of retaining the manuscript reading, on the grounds that Plutarch is here employing narratological licence, to add drama and colour to the departure scene.

10.10 Xanthippus, the father of Pericles: He had been ostracised in 484, and returned, along with Aristides and others, in accordance with the Recall

Decree (see 11.1 and note, *Ath. Pol.* 22.6, 22.8). He played a leading role in the campaigns of 479 (Hdt. 8.131, 9.114, 120).

The story about his faithful dog is found also at *Cato maior* 5.4. It apparently goes back to the fourth century B.C. (Aristotle and Philochorus cited as sources by Aelian, *NA* 12.35). Here it adds detail and pathos to the narrative. However, its historical value is uncertain, as it could be attached to any prominent Athenian of the time.

11.1 he saw that the citizens missed Aristides ... therefore proposed a decree: That the Athenians before Salamis passed a decree recalling those who had been ostracised is attested by *Ath. Pol.* 22.8 and Andocides 1.77, 107. However, of the literary sources, only Plutarch here says that the decree was proposed by Themistocles. There is no mention of Themistocles in the above passages, or in Nepos, *Aristides* 1.5–2.1, and Plutarch himself does not attribute responsibility to Themistocles when he refers to the recall of Aristides at *Aristides* 8.1.

But Plutarch may be right about Themistocles' responsibility. He obviously would not want to mention Themistocles at *Aristides* 8.1, since throughout that *Life* he is keen to draw a contrast between the virtuous, upright Aristides and the unscrupulous, self-seeking Themistocles (see 3.1, 5.7 notes). The Themistocles Decree (see 7.2 note) seems to refer to at least a preliminary stage in a recall of the ostracised (lines 44–47) and, given Themistocles' obvious political influence in Athens at this period, it is not unreasonable to assume that he personally proposed the Recall Decree in the assembly.

Plutarch is vague about the precise date of the Recall Decree here, though his implication is that it came at the last minute. He is a little more specific at *Aristides* 8.1 ("when Xerxes was marching through Thessaly and Boeotia against Attica"), i.e. after the loss of Thermopylae, and only a few days before the final evacuation and mobilisation. A last minute recall also seems to be implied by Herodotus at 8.78–9, where Aristides is represented as travelling from Aegina to Salamis immediately before the battle, as though he was only just at that moment returning from ostracism, and by Nepos, *Aristides* 1.5–2.1. On the other hand *Ath. Pol.* 22.8 dates the Recall Decree to the archonship of Hypsichides, i.e. 481/0 (see Rhodes [1981], 281). The recall thus occurred at least three months before the battle of Salamis, which, according to Plutarch *Camillus* 19.6, was fought on 20th Boedromion 480 (= 28th September; see Frost [1980], 123–26, for a plausible reconstruction of the chronology of the Salamis campaign). A date for the recall in early summer, shortly after the Tempe expedition, is also implied by the inclusion of a clause dealing with the ostracised in the Themistocles Decree.

According to *Ath. Pol.* 22.8 "all" those ostracised, of whom there were at least five (22.4–7), were allowed to return. We know that Xanthippus and

Aristides did so, and that they played prominent roles in the military campaigns of 480 and 479. The Alcmeonid Megacles probably returned too (according to Lysias, 14.39, he was ostracised twice), though he is not mentioned in any military capacity by Herodotus, presumably because the Athenians did not trust him enough for that, after the Alcmeonid family's suspected treachery at the time of Marathon (Hdt. 6.121–124). However, the first *ostracisé,* Hipparchus, son of Charmus, seems not to have returned. We are told that he was condemned to death *in absentia* on a treason charge (Lycurgus, *Against Leocrates* 117). If true, this suggests he had by this time followed in the tracks of his maternal grandfather, the ex-tyrant Hippias, and joined the King's entourage.

What was the motivation behind the Recall Decree? It is likely that the Athenians (*pace* Plutarch) were not so much yearning for Aristides' company as seriously worried that he and the other ostracised exiles, all senior political figures with connections and supporters in Athens, might "medise" at the crunch. Hence it was of paramount importance to get them back in the fold.

In 480 there was nothing unthinkable, or inherently shocking, about opting for Persia. As well as non-Athenians like the Spartan king Demaratus and the high ranking Eretrians, Euphorbus and Philagrus, Athenians such as Hippias and his relatives and Dicaeus had already done so (Hdt. 6.101, 8.65). Others, like Aeschines and Agesias, were going to do so (*Aristides* 13.1–4). Aristides and the others, if unrecalled, might well have decided to back what seemed likely to be the winning side, and join the other distinguished exiles in Xerxes' camp, thus creating dangerous doubts and suspicions about their connections back home. Hence in the Themistocles Decree action about the ostracised is to be taken "so that all Athenians might be united in opposing the barbarian".

11.1 **those who had been removed from Athens for a specific period:** Plutarch's expression here, τοῖς ... μεθεστῶσιν (cf. 5.7, μετέστησεν) was probably suggested by the text of the Themistocles Decree, which has τοὺς μεθεστηκότας (line 45). Ostracism involved exile for a period of ten years (*Aristides* 7.5).

Frost (1980), 126–28, argues that the Recall Decree in 480 was in fact an amnesty decree applying to all exiles, not just the ostracised. This view, however, is certainly not supported by the language of *Ath. Pol.* 22.8 or the Themistocles Decree, both of which attach the Recall Decree specifically to the ostracised, as does Plutarch here. In addition, it seems clear at *Aristides* 8.1 that "the law" which the Athenians "repealed" when they voted for the return of "the exiles" is specifically the law of ostracism, which Plutarch has been discussing in the whole of the previous chapter. The strong implication is that "the exiles" are specifically those who had been exiled by the ostracism procedure. The orator Andocides (1.77) quotes the Decree of Patroclides of

405, which extended an amnesty to several categories of exiles at that time. This refers back to the Recall Decree of 480, but not in a precise way, and it does not imply that the Recall Decree applied to all classes of exiles. It is true that in his comments later in the same speech Andocides claims that it did (1.107). But this is extremely unreliable evidence. Andocides' history is seriously deficient in 1.107, as he confuses Xerxes' invasion with the Marathon campaign. Furthermore, he naturally wishes to make this claim about the Recall Decree, since that would then supply a convenient precedent for his own case, which in fact had nothing to do with exile by ostracism.

11.2 Eurybiades held the overall command: See 7.3 and 7.5 notes. Plutarch makes the Spartan Eurybiades the focus of opposition to Themistocles, and the chief proponent of a retreat to the Isthmus. However, there is no suggestion in Herodotus' account (8.56–63) that Eurybiades was particularly faint-hearted, and it is the Corinthian commmander, Adeimantus, with whom Themistocles has his pointed exchanges (cf. 24.1 note). This version may be a mere slip on Plutarch's part (though his memory is better at *Moralia* 185B), but it is more likely to be deliberate. Plutarch wants to keep the spotlight on the two protagonists, Themistocles and the overall commander Eurybiades, rather than diffuse the dramatic effect by introducing other characters like Adeimantus and Mnesiphilus, who in Herodotus' account had actually suggested the plan to Themistocles in the first place (see 2.5 note).

11.2 memorable remarks: See ch. 18 introductory note, and 18.1, "well-known stories".

11.3 lifted up his stick as if to strike him: The stick was both the symbol of authority carried by Spartan commanders, and an instrument of chastisement (cf. Thuc. 8.84.2, Xen. *Hell.* 2.13.11). This anecdote is not in Herodotus' account, and appears first in Plutarch (cf. *Moralia* 185B).

11.5 but someone objected: In Herodotus this is Adeimantus, but Plutarch wants to keep the Corinthian out of it, partly for dramatic reasons (see 11.2 note), and partly to correct Herodotus' alleged anti-Corinthian bias (see 7.6 note, and cf. *Malice* 870B–871C).

11.5 a man who did not have a city was not qualified to instruct those who did to ... abandon their native lands: What Adeimantus actually said, in Herodotus' account, was that such a man had no right to make a proposal in the war council at all (8.61). Plutarch's version is less effective. Presumably the implication is that, by fighting at Salamis instead of nearer to their own cities, the Peloponnesians are "abandoning" them.

11.5 such lifeless things: The idea that men (and, here, ships), are more important than walls and buildings was as old as Alcaeus (fr. 29).

11.5 city and a territory ... not inferior: According to Herodotus (8.62), Themistocles threatened that the Athenians would go and settle at Siris, on the south coast of Italy. Themistocles himself did have an interest in the Greek

West (see 24.7 note), but it is unlikely that a mass emigration to such a distant site had seriously been envisaged by the Athenians in 480. The story probably dates from after the settlement of Athenian colonists at the nearby site of Thurii in 444/3 (Diodorus 12.9–11).

11.5 **Eurybiades was struck by the frightening thought:** Plutarch merely implies here what is made explicit by Herodotus (8.63), that it was as a result of Themistocles' direct threat, that the Athenian navy would sail away, that Eurybiades changed his mind and decided to stay and fight at Salamis. Instead he ends the chapter with another example of Themistocles' repartee, and at 12.1 reports a story that the decision was finally made in response to a favourable omen. In fact, it is likely that at least two close allies of Sparta, the Aeginetans and Megarians, with more than 50 ships between them (Hdt. 8.45), were as keen as the Athenians to fight at Salamis rather than at the Isthmus, which would have meant evacuating their own cities.

11.6 **the Eretrian commander ... like the cuttlefish:** This story, like that at 11.3, is unattested before Plutarch. The implication is one of cowardice, and the allusion is presumably to the capture of Eretria by the besieging Persians in 490 (Hdt. 6.101). But the criticism is not particularly apt, since the Eretrian resistance in 490 had been fierce, and the town had only been captured by treachery. In 480 the survivors still contributed seven ships to fight at Artemisium and Salamis.

The word μάχαιρα must mean "sword" here (as at *Camillus* 22.6, 40.4). Euboean swords were famous (cf. Archilochus fr. 3, quoted by Plutarch, *Theseus* 5.3), and, according to Aristotle, *HA* 524 b23ff., the anatomy of the cuttlefish included a long piece of hard cartilage which resembled a sword.

R. Flacelière (*REA* 50 [1948], 211–17) connects the remark with the emblem stamped on Eretrian coins before 446. His interpretation is perhaps over-ingenious, as the emblem (a fine example in C.M. Kraay, *Greek Coins* [New York, 1966], plate 121, no. 369 [reverse side]) would appear to be an octopus, rather than a cuttlefish or squid.

12.1 **Themistocles ... speaking from the upper deck of his ship, an owl was observed to fly ... from the right:** Herodotus (8.58) says that Themistocles visited Eurybiades on his ship, and persuaded him to call the commanders together at "the council place" (συνέδριον). He gives no indication of where this was, but it was not likely to have been on, or beneath the prow of, Themistocles' ship.

The story of the owl omen is not found in Herodotus' account of the battle of Salamis, though we would have expected it to be there if it had been current in his day. The original version of the story seems to have put the sighting of a lucky owl just before the battle of Marathon in 490 (Ar. *Wasps* 1086, Ammonius *On Altars* [*FGH* 361 F5]), where, as Athena's bird and their national emblem, it is more appropriate as a spur specifically for *Athenians.* The detail was subsequently attached to Salamis and Themistocles.

For the Greeks the right was the lucky side (cf.13.3). However, in the story as it stands it is rather vaguely defined. Presumably the owl appeared on Themistocles' right, rather than on the right of the audience who were facing him.

12.2 **bay of Phalerum:** This bay, to the east of Piraeus, in effect no more than a gently sloping sandy beach, functioned as the early harbour of Athens. It was now the main base for Xerxes' fleet (Hdt. 8.67).

12.2 **the arguments of Themistocles drained out of the minds of the Greeks:** Like Herodotus (8.70, 74–6), Plutarch presents the deceptive message sent by Themistocles to Xerxes as something which was kept secret from the rest of the Greek commanders, thus forcing them against their wishes to fight in the narrow straits at Salamis (see 12.4 note). Since Herodotus had previously (8.64) recorded a formal decision taken earlier by the Greek council of war to stay and fight at Salamis, it was necessary for him to introduce a fresh bout of panic into his narrative at this point. This version is followed by Plutarch here.

12.3 **position in the narrow straits:** The Greek fleet was drawn up by Salamis town. It is clear (cf. Hdt. 8.60) that, as well as being outnumbered, their ships were heavier and less manoeuvrable than those of their enemy. Hence it would be doubly to their advantage to fight in narrow, confined waters.

12.3 **Themistocles ... planned and organised the Sicinnus affair:** Plutarch follows the account of Herodotus (8.75–6) closely. The earliest version (472 B.C.) of this famous story is to be found in Aeschylus *Persians*, lines 353–73 (see 14.1 note). It seems unreasonable to doubt its authenticity, in substance if not in details, since Aeschylus, a participant in the battle, was writing within eight years of the actual event, for an audience most of whom must have themselves participated in what was by far the most formative experience of their lives. Furthermore, it is hard to understand why Xerxes should have gone to the trouble of stationing armed men on the islet of Psyttaleia (in the mouth of the Salamis straits) during the evening, as he clearly did (Hdt. 8.76, 95, Aeschylus *Persians* 447–64), if he had not believed, wrongly, that the Greeks would be attempting to make a precipitate withdrawal from the straits, and that there might be a battle there, perhaps during the night.

12.4 **Sicinnus ... a Persian ... prisoner of war ... tutor of his children:** The name Sicinnus is given by Herodotus (8.75), who also calls him the tutor, παιδαγωγός, of Themistocles' children. However, Herodotus refers to him not as a Persian prisoner of war, but as a household slave, οἰκέτης, of unspecified nationality. Nepos (*Them.* 4.3) follows Herodotus on this point (*de servis suis quem habuit fidelissimum ad regem misit*, "he sent the most faithful slave he had to the king"), though he does not give the messenger a name. In Aeschylus, *Persians* 355, the Persian messenger, addressing Queen Atossa, says merely that the man was a "Greek from the Athenian camp". Diodorus (11.17.1) is even vaguer, supplying neither the name, nationality nor occupation of the messenger, "he persuaded a certain man to desert to Xerxes".

Plutarch is alone in describing him as a "Persian prisoner of war". Almost certainly this is a mistake, the result partly of a failure of memory (as usual, he "knows" Herodotus from his reading, but does not have the text in front of him), and partly of confusion with the tradition he followed for the identity of the bearer of the second, post-Salamis, message (see 16.5 note). Although some Persians had been captured before the battle of Artemisium (Hdt. 7.194–5), there can hardly have been time for them to have been allocated to individual Greek owners, let alone to have become tutors to their children.

If the messenger's name was Sicinnus, he may have been a Phrygian, since, according to Arrian, the original Sicinnis was supposedly a nymph of the Phrygian goddess Cybele (for whom see 30.2 note), and a satyric dance was named after her (*FGH* 156 F106). Phrygian slaves were common enough in the Greek world. If Sicinnus was Hellenised and trusted enough to be the tutor of Themistocles' children, it would be natural for a Persian messenger in Aeschylus' drama, reporting to the Persian queen, to refer to him as a "Greek". To enhance his credibility, it is possible that the messenger, as an Asiatic, could speak at least some words of Persian.

12.4 **He sent him to Xerxes secretly:** This is the picture presented by Herodotus (8.70, 74–6), followed by Diodorus (11.17.1, 4) and Nepos (*Them.* 4.3–5), i.e. that the deceptive message was kept a secret from the rest of the Greeks, and was intended to have the effect of forcing them to fight at Salamis by leaving them no other option (see 12.2 note)

However, there is not the slightest suggestion in our earliest account, Aeschylus *Persians* 353–73 (see 12.3, 14.1 notes), that the message was not known about by the other Greek commanders, and, indeed, a number of factors tell strongly against the Herodotean version.

All the sources agree that, on the following morning, the Greek navy presented a united front, fighting with enthusiasm and in good order. This is not what we would have expected if most of the contingents had been tricked and forced to fight where they did not want to. Furthermore, after the battle, Themistocles was publicly honoured by the Spartans for his "cleverness" (Hdt. 8.124). This must have referred to the ruse by which he induced Xerxes to commit his fleet to a battle in an unfavourable position. But the Spartans would surely not have wished to call attention to, let alone publicly honour, something which had also been a deception of themselves. It is thus a fair inference that no such deception had occurred.

Naturally, in his message Themistocles had to *pretend* to Xerxes that the other Greeks knew nothing about his apparent act of betrayal. That was part of the subterfuge, and as such an agreed part of the text. Subsequently, when Themistocles had been driven into exile and had sought sanctuary with the Persian King (see chs. 26–29), it was easy, now that he had been discredited, for his political enemies at home to claim that his Salamis message to Xerxes had *in fact* been a secret one, and that Themistocles had deceived his fellow Greeks as much as he had deceived Xerxes. These enemies, particularly Cimon and the Alcmaeonid family (see 20.4, 22.4, 23.1 notes) seem to have been the ultimate source of much of the hostile account of Herodotus in Book 8 (see 2.6, 7.6, 16.2 notes).

12.5 Xerxes ... was delighted. He immediately issued an order: The most difficult problem about the deceptive Salamis message tradition is not to explain why the messenger was believed. No doubt, as Diodorus says (11.17.1), it was just what Xerxes wanted to hear. Rather it is to explain why he was believed *and then allowed simply to go away* (Hdt. 8.76). In Xerxes' entourage there were many hard-headed and well informed Greek exiles (see 29.7 note), who would certainly have wished to question closely, using torture if necessary, this confidant of such an important apparent renegade. It is hard to believe (*pace* Frost [1980], 145) that his story would have been accepted if he had just shouted it from his boat, and then made off immediately.

It is interesting that neither Aeschylus (*Persians* 361–2) nor Diodorus (11.17.1–2) says that the bearer of the message was allowed to get away after delivering it (nor indeed does Plutarch here). Herodotus does say so, but that is because, in his account, it is the self-same Sicinnus who is used again by Themistocles to deliver a second secret message, after the battle (8.110; see 16.5 note), and who subsequently operates as one of Themistocles' agents in extorting money from islanders who had medised (8.112).

It would certainly have added considerably to the deceptive message's credibility if the messenger had *himself* believed Themistocles' story, and stayed with the Persian side after delivering it, in the deluded expectation that he would be soon joined by his master. Such a degree of duplicity will be familiar to readers of the espionage novels of John Le Carré. The existence of a tradition that this was indeed what happened is perhaps implied by the words of Diodorus (whose account almost certainly derives from the fourth century writer Ephorus) – "he persuaded a certain man to desert (αὐτμολῆσαι) to Xerxes" (11.17.1). However, the assertion of Herodotus (8.75), that "afterwards" Themistocles got Sicinnus enrolled as a new citizen of Thespiae in Boeotia, if true, would appear to rule out this hypothesis. That he returned to the Greek side was, it seems, a checkable story, but did Herodotus bother to check it by a visit to Thespiae?

12.5 **two hundred ships ... block the straits completely:** This encircling manoeuvre, to block the western entrance to the Salamis straits as well as the eastern, seems to be attested by Aeschylus, *Persians* 368 (Herodotus, 8.76, is not very clear on this point). According to Diodorus (11.17.2) Xerxes gave this task to the Egyptian squadron, which traditionally numbered two hundred ships (Hdt. 7.89, Diodorus 11.3.7).

12.5 **encircling the islands:** It is hard to make any sense of this plural. What island other than Salamis could be encircled? The phrase περιβαλέσθαι ... τὰς νήσους may be a conscious reminiscence of *Aristides* 8.2, περιβαλοῦσαι τόν τε πόρον ἐν κύκλῳ καὶ τὰς νήσους κατεῖχον where the plural "islands" is again used rather loosely (to denote the islet of Psyttaleia, in the eastern mouth of the straits [see 12.6 note]).

12.6 **Aristides ... the first to be aware of it:** More details are provided at *Aristides* 8.2, where it is clear that Plutarch is following the account of Herodotus (8.79, 81). Aristides had come from Aegina, and his ship had with difficulty slipped through the Persian blockade. Herodotus' account implies (wrongly, see 11.1 note) that this was the actual moment when Aristides returned from exile. In fact the position of authority Aristides seems to have enjoyed in the action on Psyttaleia (Hdt. 8.95, *Aristides* 9.1–2) strongly suggests that he was an elected *strategos* for the year 480/79. These elections were normally held in the spring.

It has been suggested that Aristides had spent his period of exile (he had been ostracised in 483/2) in Aegina (see 5.7 note). But the evidence for this is weak (Dem. 26.6, Aristodemus 1.4), and may be no more than a faulty inference from the Herodotus passage. Athens and Aegina had been engaged in intermittent hostilities over many years (see 4.2 note), and for a leading Athenian politician to choose to spend his exile there would surely have been seen back home as an unacceptably provocative act.

Almost certainly Aristides had been on some sort of official mission to Aegina, immediately before the battle of Salamis. However, this cannot have had anything to do with the ferrying over to Salamis of the national heroes of Aegina, statues of Aeacus and his sons (see 15.2 note), since that must surely have been an exclusively Aeginetan affair. It is more likely that Aristides' mission had been concerned with arrangements for the reception of Athenian refugees, possibly involving the use of public money. The last minute evacuees seem to have gone to Salamis and Aegina rather than to Troezen (see 10.5 note, Hdt. 8.41).

There is no reason to doubt the central element of the story, i.e. Aristides' dramatic last-minute arrival, by which the fact of the Persian blockade was confirmed, though it is possible that his ship had actually put him ashore on the south coast of Salamis (i.e. outside the Persian blockade), and that he had made his way to the Greek base at Salamis town overland.

12.6 **a man to whom he was no friend:** Plutarch echoes the words of Herodotus (8.79). For Aristides and Themistocles see 3.1, 5.7, 11.1 and notes.

12.7 **noble character ... as one who had greater credit ... than himself:** See 3.1 note. This supposed admission (cf. also *Aristides* 8.5) is found in Herodotus' account (8.80). In reality, what made Aristides' contribution significant was the fact that he had just witnessed the blockade personally. In Herodotus' account (which Plutarch follows here, though not at *Aristides* 8.6, 9.1), the Greek commanders remain unconvinced, and are only finally persuaded when a deserting Tenian ship brings them a full account of the enemy's position (see next note).

12.8 **trireme of Tenedos ... Panaetius:** The text should not be emended. Τενεδία is a simple mistake by Plutarch, and a good example of how he "knows" a passage in Herodotus (cf. 12.4 note), but does not check his own account directly against a written text. He correctly remembers the name of the captain as given by Herodotus. But Herodotus says the ship was "of Tenos", and this is confirmed by the evidence of the Serpent Column, a war memorial set up at Delphi (ML no. 27, p. 58 = Crawford and Whitehead [1983], no. 115B, p. 229), where the name "Tenians" appears (it is apparently a later addition to the list), but "Tenedians" does not.

13.1 **Xerxes took his seat ... golden seat:** This seat (δίφρος) was probably not a massive throne, but a portable stool (so Frost [1980], 149, quoting Dinon [*FGH* 690 F26 = Athenaeus 514a–b]). Neither Aeschylus (*Persians* 466–7) nor Herodotus (8.90) refers to a throne, and it is much more likely that Xerxes intended, and was equipped, to move about in his carriage, together with his secretaries, to whichever spot on the Attic coastline gave the best and closest view of the action.

13.1 **Phanodemus ... the Heracleum:** Phanodemus was an Athenian, who played a prominent part in public life at Athens in the second half of the fourth century and wrote an Atthis, a local history of Athens and Attica. The temple of Heracles has not been identified, but it was probably situated on the rocky headland of Mount Aegaleos, which overlooks the narrowest part of the straits. This would have afforded Xerxes an excellent view of the actual location of the battle (see next but one note), though he could not have been absolutely sure of that in advance (see above note). This also seems to be where Herodotus locates Xerxes' seat, though his description is much vaguer (8.90): "below the (top of the) mountain opposite Salamis (town)".

13.1 **Acestorides ... the so-called "Horns":** Acestorides came, apparently, from Megalopolis, and wrote a treatise *On Cities*. He is cited for the early history of Eleusis by the scholiast at Sophocles *Oedipus at Colonus* 1053 (cf. *FGH* 334 F22). However, this is a much less likely location. The Horns are situated at the western end of Eleusis bay, and from there Xerxes' secretaries would have needed telescopic vision to observe and record the details of the battle which Herodotus says they did (8.88–90).

13.1 the events of the battle as they happened: It seems clear from all our accounts that the battle was actually fought within the straits, north of the promontory of Cynosura, which juts out eastwards from a point on the island just south of Salamis town, the Greek base. This means that, presumably early in the morning, the Persian fleet moved *further forward* from the position it had occupied during the night, when it had been commanded to guard the entrance to the strait in the area around the islet of Psyttaleia, since it was expected that the Greeks would try to break out of the straits during the night.

This turned out to be a disastrous tactical mistake, and it is hard to see why Xerxes should have ordered such a risky manoeuvre. Frost (1980), 148, suggests overconfidence on Xerxes' part. But one might have expected him, when nothing at all had happened during the night, to have started to wonder about the veracity of Themistocles' message. His crews were tired, and hungry for their breakfast. Both Herodotus (8.83) and Aeschylus (*Persians* 386–405) suggest the action began first thing in the morning, without time for any tactical conferences between Xerxes and his admirals. A detail in Herodotus' account may help to explain what happened. At 8.84 he says that after getting under way the Greek ships were attacked and backed astern before driving forward again. This detail does not appear in Aeschylus' account, and in Herodotus the backing movement is presented as the result of (initial) fear. But it may in fact have been a deliberate ploy. A number of Greek ships, presumably not the whole fleet, may have been sent out at dawn to round the promontory of Cynosura, attract the attention of the enemy, and then back water up the straits, thus luring the Persian fleet into the confined waters north of Cynosura (where the battle was actually fought). Hence the men Xerxes had stationed on Psyttaleia (just *outside* the straits) became irrelevant to the conflict when it began in earnest.

13.2 conducting a sacrifice ... three prisoners of war: This human sacrifice story, which Plutarch tells us comes from Phanias of Eresus (see 1.2 note), appears also at *Aristides* 9.1–2 and *Pelopidas* 21.3. However, it has no historical credibility. That is not because the very idea of human sacrifice by Greeks at this period is inconceivable (see e.g. the ancient scholars "lists" of such sacrifices, discussed by D.D. Hughes, *Human Sacrifice in Ancient Greece* [London, 1991], 115–30), but because the story involves a chronological impossibility. Plutarch does not here explain when these Persian prisoners had been acquired, but at *Aristides* 9.2 he tells us that they had been among those captured by Aristides in the fighting on Psyttaleia. But both Aeschylus (*Persians* 447–64) and Herodotus (8.95) make it clear that this military action did not occur until *after* the naval battle had begun, and Plutarch himself seems to follow this chronology at *Aristides* 9.1.

13.2 **Sandauce, the King's sister, and Artayctes:** These names presumably come from Phanias. The daughter of Darius, the sister of Xerxes who lost her sons in the battle of Salamis, is called Mandane by Diodorus (11.57.1–2). Artayctes was the name of the Persian governor of Sestos (Hdt. 9.116–8), but Herodotus does not say that this man was Xerxes' brother-in-law.

13.3 **Euphrantides the seer:** Euphrantides is not heard of elsewhere, but the presence of μάντεις, both before and during Greek military action in the Persian wars, is well attested (cf. Hdt. 7.221, 228, 9.33).

13.3 **a sneeze ... on the right hand side:** A sneeze at a critical moment, being something involuntary, was considered to be a heaven-sent, favourable omen (cf. *Odyssey* 17.545, Xen. *Anab.* 3.2.9). For the right as the lucky side see 12.1 note.

13.3 **Dionysus the Flesh Eater:** Literally, the "Raw-Eater". This is an attested cult-epithet of Dionysus (cf. Alcaeus fr. 129, *AP* 9.524.25), whose rites involved the eating of raw animal flesh by his frenzied Maenad followers (cf. Euripides *Bacchae* 139). Though false, Phanias' story, and his use of this epithet, does suggest there was a contemporary belief that, at one time, these rites had involved human sacrifice and the eating of human flesh (cf. Porphyry *De Abstin.* 2.55).

13.4 **Themistocles was stunned:** Plutarch attributes to Themistocles the same instinctive reaction towards the idea of human sacrifice as he himself has. But, adaptable as ever (see 27.4 note), Themistocles is prepared to go along with it in order to bolster the morale of the rank and file at a critical moment, just as he had exploited their superstitious beliefs about the Acropolis snake to secure a necessary political end, the evacuation of the city (10.1–2).

13.5 **at any rate ... Phanias ... learned man, and well acquainted with works of history:** For Phanias see 1.2 note. Despite paying a compliment to Phanias' knowledge of history, Plutarch seems to suggest that he has some doubts about the veracity of this story. He uses the same slightly distancing expression (μὲν ὂυν)with regard to Phanias' authority at 7.7.

14.1 **the playwright Aeschylus ... in his tragedy *The Persians*:** This play was produced in early 472, less than eight years after the battle of Salamis, and performed before a large audience of Athenians, most of whom must have participated in that battle. According to the fifth century writer Ion of Chios (*FGH* 392 F7 = schol. *Persians* 432) Aeschylus himself had fought in the battle. Hence the section of the play which is concerned with the actual battle (lines 350–471), which takes the form of a report brought to Queen Atossa, Xerxes' mother, by a Persian messenger, is a most valuable piece of evidence for any historical reconstruction of what actually happened, representing, as it does, what must have been the generally accepted contemporary version of events.

14.1 writes as follows: Plutarch's quotation of Aeschylus *Persians* 341–43 is slightly inaccurate, but Plutarch invariably quotes from memory, and the text should not be changed to conform fully to that of Aeschylus (cf. 12.8 note). The reading here of S, normally the most reliable manuscript, νη-ῶν ἦγε, is unmetrical. I follow the tradition represented by U and A.

14.1 a thousand ships ... two hundred and seven especially fast ones: It is not completely clear in the Aeschylus passage whether the 207 ships are regarded as additional to, or a part of, the 1000. Probably the latter. However, it soon became the accepted view that the 207 were additional, hence the total of 1207 given by Herodotus (7.89, 184). This figure is certainly a gross exaggeration, which perhaps derives from the assumption that a "normal" Persian naval expedition involved a fleet of 600 ships (cf. Hdt. 4.87, 6.9, 95). Furthermore, Herodotus' claim (8.66), and Aeschylus' implication, that the fleet was just as large at Salamis as it had been before its losses due to storms (7.190, 8.13), and earlier battles (7.194, 8.11, 16), is patently absurd. All we can say for sure is that the Persian fleet at Salamis still much outnumbered that of the Greeks, which totalled 380, according to Herodotus 8.48, 82 (only 310, according to Aeschylus *Persians* 339–40; or 300, Nepos *Them.* 3.2). These are much more credible figures, for the simple reason that each Greek state knew at first hand the size of its own contingent, and so the overall total could be worked out with a fair degree of accuracy.

14.2 Athenian contingent ... one hundred and eighty: Plutarch derives this figure from Herodotus (8.44), for whom 200 is a constant figure for the total numbers of the Athenian fleet from the time of the Themistocles' Naval Bill (7.144) to Salamis, where the Chalcidians manned 20 of these 200 ships (8.46), as they had at Artemisium. 200 is also the figure given in the Themistocles Decree, lines 14, 19, 32, 37 (see 7.2, 16.4 notes), and by Nepos (*Them.* 3.2).

14.2 eighteen marines ... archers ... hoplites: The presence of marines on board the Athenian ships in 480 is attested by the Themistocles Decree, lines 23–26, where the figures given are 10 hoplites (called simply ἐπιβάται) and 4 archers per ship. Plutarch's figures are probably taken from the text of the Decree (see 10.4 note), and the discrepancy is simply the result of a slight slip of memory on his part (i.e. 14 plus 4, instead of 10 plus 4).

It seems to have been customary for Greek warships in the early fifth century to carry a fair number of marines – the Chian contingent at the battle of Lade in 494 had 40 per ship (Hdt. 6.15). At Salamis the Athenians may have reduced the usual number of marines in order to man a greater number of ships. The naval battles of the Persian War were won by the tactics of deliberate collision, boarding and fighting on deck (cf. 14.4), rather than by the deployment of more sophisticated rowing skills involving speed and manoeuvrability, which only became characteristic of the Athenian navy later in the fifth century.

14.3 **Themistocles appears to have judged the best time ... breeze ... swell rolls through the straits. :** Plutarch is our only authority for this stratagem on Themistocles' part. At first sight the story might seem plausible, but in fact it must be a fiction. The accounts of both Aeschylus and Herodotus strongly suggest that the battle started very soon after dawn, and not at some unspecified hour later in the day. It is not obvious that the effects of wind and swell would be more adverse for tall ships than for small ones. But the crucial objection is that, at this date, the Greek ships were in fact bigger and heavier, as well as slower, than those of the Phoenicians (cf. Hdt. 8.10, 60). It may be that Plutarch made the story up himself, on the grounds that "the just cause must have the smaller ships" (so W.W. Tarn, "The Fleet of Xerxes", *JHS* 28 [1908], 208 note 28). But this would be unusual in the *Themistocles*, and the use here of δοκεῖ (cf. 1.3) suggests he had some authority for it.

14.3 **Ariamenes:** This seems to be a non-existent personage. The name is probably a mistake for Ariabignes, son of Darius and half-brother of Xerxes, who commanded the Asiatic Greeks, and was killed at Salamis (Hdt. 7.97, 8.89). Plutarch, or his source, compounds the confusion at *Moralia* 488C–F, where this same supposed "Ariamenes" is described as having disputed the Persian throne with Xerxes on Darius' death. Herodotus tells us that the name of Xerxes' rival at the time of the succession was Darius' eldest son, Artabazanes (7.2–3).

14.4 **Ameinias of the deme Deceleia ... Socles of Pallene:** The manuscripts here have Σωκλῆς ὁ Πελιεύς or ὁ Πεδιεύς, but neither of these epithets provides him with a demotic which corresponds to a recognised Athenian deme. Perrin (1948, 42) adopts the suggestion of F. Blass, Παιανιεύς (= "of Paeania"). This is possible, but Flacelière's suggestion, Παλληνεύς (= "of Pallene"), is better (1972, 67; 1961, 119). Herodotus (8.84, 93) refers to an Ameinias *of Pallene* as one of two Athenian captains who performed the most distinguished service at Salamis. He says nothing of Socles, but does mention a Sophanes *of Deceleia* as the Athenian hero of the battle of Plataea (9.73).

What seems to have happened here is that Plutarch, though "following" Herodotus, has mistakenly transposed the demotics of these two Athenians, got the name of one of the protagonists slightly wrong (writing "Socles" instead of "Sophanes"), and associated his heroism with the wrong battle. This is a particularly striking example of the biographer's indifference to accurate *minutiae* within a story. What matters is the focus of attention, here Ariamenes and his fate.

Herodotus says of Ameinias that he was the first to engage with an enemy ship, and subsequently chased the ship of Artemisia (8.84,93). Diodorus has an improved version, which makes him sink the Persian flagship and kill their admiral (11.27.2). He also makes Ameinias the brother of Aeschylus, an implausible identification, given that Aeschylus belonged to a different deme, Eleusis. Plutarch was either unaware of this tradition, or, more likely, deliberately rejected it.

14.4 **Artemisia:** This "warrior-queen" is a figure made famous by Herodotus in his account of the Salamis campaign (cf. 7.99, 8.68, 87–8, 101–103). She was actually Greek on both her parents' sides, being at the time of Xerxes' invasion both daughter and widow of previous tyrants of Halicarnassus. Her dynasty continued in power at Halicarnassus down at least to the time of Herodotus (cf. Suda s.v. Ἡρόδοτος).

There seems no reason to doubt that she did command a naval detachment at Salamis (a mere five ships), but whether she, rather than her son Pisendelis, was the ruling tyrant at Halicarnassus is more debatable. It is understandable that Herodotus, as a Halicarnassian, should wish to highlight her role at Salamis, but he grossly exaggerates her ease of access to, and influence with, Xerxes.

15.1 **Eleusis ... Thriasian plain ... Iacchus, god of the Mysteries:** The reference is to the annual procession of initiated citizens from Athens to Eleusis in western Attica, on the first day of the festival of the Eleusinian Mysteries, held in late September. Iacchus was probably originally a minor deity associated with the cult, whose name led him to be connected with Dionysus (Bacchus). His statue was carried in the procession and a hymn, the "Iacchus song", was sung in his honour (*Alcibiades* 34.3–4, Ar. *Frogs* 314–413). In 480, because of the evacuation of Athens and Attica, both the procession, which passed through the Thriasian plain on the road to Eleusis, and the festival itself had been cancelled.

15.1 **great light ... sound ... cloud:** Herodotus tells the story of this portent in some detail (8.65). It was supposedly seen by two Greek exiles in Xerxes' entourage, Demaratus, the ex-Spartan king, and an Athenian, Dicaeus, son of Theocydes, who understood its significance. Plutarch's source (possibly, in this case, popular tradition rather than a written account), has "improved" on the version in Herodotus in a number of details. Herodotus puts the portent on some unspecified day shortly before the battle, whereas Plutarch says it occurred on the same day, during the course of the fighting. The traditional date of Salamis was the 20th of the Attic month Boedromion (*Camillus* 19.6), and Plutarch assigns this date also to Iacchus' procession (*Camillus* 19.10). However, according to a third century A.D. inscription (*Syll.*[3] 885.19), the Eleusinian procession was held on the 19th of Boedromion (see Frost [1980], 123–26). Plutarch makes the dust cloud travel all the way to Salamis, and then actually settle on the Greek ships; in Herodotus it is merely seen to move "towards" Salamis.

Interestingly, the portent is not mentioned anywhere in Aeschylus *Persians* (see 14.1 note), despite a strong emphasis in the messenger's speech on the importance of the role of the gods in defeating Xerxes (345–54). This may well be because the story, though current by the later fifth century, had not yet been invented in 472. The suggestion of Frost (1980), 157–8, that Aeschylus did not wish to risk getting into trouble again with the Athenians, by referring to the apparent intervention of Iacchus at Salamis, is not very plausible. It is true that Aristotle suggests (*Nic. Eth.* 1111a10) that Aeschylus had been criticised for inadvertently "revealing" Mystery cult secrets, presumably in one of his dramas. But Aristotle provides no details of titles or dates, and, in any case, the story of the Iacchus portent and the cloud manifestation, to judge from the version we have, did not involve the revelation of any forbidden secrets.

15.2 phantoms ... of armed men coming from Aegina ... sons of Aeacus: Peleus and Telamon were the actual sons of Aeacus (*Theseus* 10.2–3). But probably Achilles, son of Peleus, and Ajax, son of Telamon, are alluded to as well. Herodotus says that the statues of these national heroes of Aegina were sent for after the decision was made to fight at Salamis, and that the ship bringing them arrived just as the battle was about to begin (8.64, 83). Because of the proximity of this detail in Herodotus' narrative to his story of the Iacchus portent, Plutarch has introduced it here, though in his account the heroes come, not as statues, but in the form of another miraculous epiphany. Plutarch may be "adapting" Herodotus for dramatic reasons, but it is possible that there was an alternative tradition to the one in Herodotus, i.e. that the effigies did *not* arrive before the battle, but that the heroes were able to manifest their support in a different way, as apparitions. Herodotus himself admits that the blockade of the straits was completed the previous evening, when Aristides and the Tenian deserters came to confirm there was no way through (8.78–82). If so, it is hard to see how an Aeginetan ship could still have got through to Salamis town early the following morning.

15.3 Lycomedes ... dedicated it to Apollo the Laurel-wearer at Phlya: Plutarch has mistakenly attributed Lycomedes' moment of glory to Salamis. In fact it was at Artemisium that Lycomedes, son of Aeschraeus, had been the first to capture an enemy ship (Hdt. 8.11). Flacelière has suggested (1972, 68) that Plutarch's mistake arose because he had seen this figurehead dedication in the temple of Phlya, with an inscription which read simply ἀπὸ Μήδων, 'taken from the Medes", and had consequently assumed it came from Salamis. This is possible. Plutarch did sometimes visit sites to confirm or embellish a story (cf. 8.3, 22.3 notes). But it is more likely that this is just another careless mistake about names, like the one at 14.4 (see note).

Both Lycomedes' name, and the location of the temple in which he dedicated the figurehead, make it virtually certain that he was a member of the Lycomid genos, who had their private chapel in the deme Phlya (see 1.4 note). His was probably the main branch, rather than the cadet branch of the family (to which Themistocles belonged), which had its estates at Phrearrhioi (see 1.4 note; Davies [1971], 346–7). Phlya seems to have been a district rich in cults (Pausanias 1.31.4), and this temple of Apollo, like the Lycomid family shrine, was decorated with frescoes.

The tradition that the heroes of the two great naval battles of 480 were both Lycomids was doubtless a central element in the political propaganda war waged by the supporters of the Lycomid Themistocles against the Philaid Cimon and his friends at Athens in the 460's and 450's (see 22.4, 23.1 notes).

15.4 **narrow straits:** Though neither of our two main accounts of the actual battle at Salamis (Aeschylus *Persians* 388–471, Herodotus 8.84–94) gives an adequate explanation of the course of the fighting, it is clear that having to fight *in confined waters*, which forced them to funnel their attack, and limited their manoeuvrability, caused serious problems for Xerxes' large navy (cf. *Persians* 413–4, Herodotus 8.89, Thuc. 1.74.1).

15.4 **as Simonides has said:** Plutarch has already cited Simonides at 1.4 (see note), and retailed two anecdotes about him and Themistocles at 5.6–7. It is clear that he was a friend and admirer of Themistocles. The reference here is probably to his *Seafight at Salamis* (the title is given by the Ambrosian *Life of Pindar* and the Suda s.v. Σιμωνίδης.). This was a poem in either the lyric or elegiac metre. However, the Greek words Plutarch uses here, down to the end of the chapter, are not in any kind of metre (though ἐνάλιον is a poetic word). Plutarch must therefore be paraphrasing, rather than quoting *verbatim*, unlike e.g. his direct quotations of Simonides in *Malice*, 869C–871B.

15.4 **good judgment and cleverness:** If Simonides used the word δεινότης (= "cleverness"), or a word of similar sense, that is strong confirmatory evidence that there was a deceptive message sent before the battle, and that it was not kept a secret from the other Greeks (see 12.4 note). After the battle the Spartans honoured Themistocles for his wisdom and his δεξιότης (Hdt. 8.124; see 17.3 note), a word which has very much the same sense as δεινότης.

16.1 **Xerxes ... started to build moles:** Extensive modern building in this area of the Attic coastline has ruled out the possibility of discovering any traces of an ancient mole, if there ever was one. The story goes back to Herodotus (8.97), though in his account the mole-building was just a ruse on Xerxes' part to deceive the Greeks about his intentions, and to boost morale on his own side, since he always intended to withdraw his forces back across the Hellespont. However, for Plutarch, Xerxes is still in a fighting mood, and the mole building is a serious project designed to facilitate an infantry attack on Salamis. Plutarch's version is necessitated by his view, expressed later in this chapter (16.2–6), that it was only because of Themistocles' successful stratagem of a *second* message that Xerxes was persuaded to withdraw himself and some of his forces from Greece.

Neither version is very plausible. There could have been no serious possibility of a successful attack on Salamis *via* a mole after the disastrous naval defeat. Even at its narrowest point the strait between the mainland and Salamis is nearly a mile wide, and, without naval superiority, a mole-building project would have been military suicide. Conversely, it is hard to see why such a time- and energy-consuming project should have been undertaken merely as a ruse, to mask the retreat, since it would not have taken the Greeks more than a few hours to realise the true situation once the retreat had started.

Presumably it was these considerations which led to the emergence of a third version (Ctesias 26, Strabo 9.1.13), that Xerxes attempted to built a mole *before* the battle. This however is even more unlikely. Before Salamis Xerxes had no reason to doubt the ability of his massive navy to crush the Greek fleet. The last thing he would have wanted would have been to hold up the expedition through a difficult and unnecessary engineering project.

The story of a mole may be an exaggeration, based on the remains of some temporary pier or landing stage constructed by Xerxes' engineers just before the battle, but it is probably safest to reject it completely.

16.2 Themistocles, by way of drawing out Aristides' view ... destroy the bridge of boats: The earliest version of this story of a second (post-Salamis) message is to be found in Herodotus (8.108–110). Herodotus also records a change of mind on Themistocles' part about the wisdom of the Greek fleet sailing at once to the Hellespont. But there are some significant differences of detail in his version. Aristides does not appear in it at all, and Themistocles puts his initial proposal to a conference of the Greek naval commanders at Andros. He is opposed and overruled by the Spartan Eurybiades, supported by the other Peloponnesians. Themistocles' apparent change of heart is expressed in a speech which he subsequently makes to "the Athenians", but he is not being honest with them. He has an ulterior motive for advising them against engaging in an immediate pursuit, as he wants to be able to make a claim on Xerxes' favour, if, at some time in the future, he should get into trouble at home. He then sends his second message, but it is a secret one, not known about by anyone other than his own henchmen, and in it he claims that he already has prevented the Greek pursuit. This strongly anti-Themistocles story is characteristic of Herodotus' slanted picture throughout Book 8 of his Histories (see 2.6, 7.6, 12.4 notes).

For Plutarch here, on the contrary, the second message, sent apparently from Salamis, is a clever and patriotic stratagem on Themistocles' part, fully supported by his great rival Aristides, which achieves its desired objective, to get Xerxes and at least a large part of his forces out of Greece as quickly as possible. As we might expect (see 3.1 note), Plutarch's version of the story at

Aristides 9.6 is less favourable to Themistocles, and rather closer to that of Herodotus. After Aristides opposes Themistocles' initial proposal that the fleet should sail at once to the Hellespont, Themistocles seems to change his mind, as he does here. However, in the *Aristides* Plutarch does not portray the second message as a jointly agreed patriotic stratagem, but as a secret initiative by Themistocles, who claims in it that he *has turned back* the Greeks, and so saved the King.

16.5 **one of the royal eunuchs ... among the prisoners of war ... Arnaces ... to tell the King:** The Greeks believed that eunuchs were regarded as especially trustworthy among the *barbaroi* (Hdt. 8.105). We do not know what Plutarch's authority was for these details (given also at *Aristides* 9.4) about the name and occupation of the bearer of the second message, though his source seems to have been followed by the later second century A.D. writer, Polyaenus, who refers to "another eunuch, Arsaces" (1.30.4) – the variant spelling is not significant.

This is the third occasion in this *Life* on which Plutarch has referred to Persian prisoners of war on the Greek side (cf. 12.4, 13.2 and notes), and in each case there are strong reasons to doubt his statement. We might well wonder what a royal eunuch was doing on board a fighting ship involved in a vital naval battle.

According to Herodotus (8.110), followed by Justin 2.13.5 ("the same slave"), this second message was taken by a group of men including Themistocles' slave Sicinnus, who had been the bearer of the famous pre-Salamis message (8.75). However, it is hard to believe that a second message could have been taken by the very man who had been responsible for delivering the first deceptive message, as a result of which Xerxes' fleet had been decisively defeated at Salamis. No one could have expected Xerxes to believe him. If Sicinnus delivered the first message, he cannot have been involved in the taking of the second, and *vice versa*.

This consideration is presumably the reason why Plutarch (or his source), who follows Herodotus on Sicinnus as the name of the first message-bearer (see 12.4 note), here gives the bearer of the second message a different identity (though he too is described as a prisoner of war).

Diodorus (11.19.5) calls the second message-bearer "the tutor of Themistocles' children" (i.e., presumably, Sicinnus), but he is vague about the identity of the bearer of the first message:– "he persuaded a certain man to desert to Xerxes" (11.17.1). Nepos (*Them.* 5.1) also refers to this second message, but says nothing about the identity of its bearer, who may or may not have been for him the same man as the first message-bearer, whom he describes as "the most trustworthy of Themistocles' slaves" (*Them.* 4.3).

Despite the unanimity of our sources (cf. also Thucydides 1.137.4) it is very difficult to believe in the historicity of this second message, whatever its supposed purpose, and whatever the identity of the putative messenger. In the immediate, bitter, aftermath of his shock defeat at Salamis it is most unlikely that Xerxes or his advisers would have been prepared to accept any further supposedly confidential message emanating from anyone on the Greek side, let alone Themistocles, or that any Greek commander could have believed that he would.

I have discussed the origins and development of the tradition of Themistocles' supposed second message to Xerxes more fully in *Acta Classica* 38 (1995), 57–69.

17.1 **Herodotus tells us that ... the Aeginetans proved themselves the bravest:** Plutarch probably has in mind both 8.93 and 8.122. The former passage does not seem to refer to the awarding of a specific prize, but rather to the "general view" which was taken after the battle. At some subsequent stage (it is not clear exactly when and how) a prize was awarded, to the Aeginetans, which they were required by Apollo at Delphi to hand over to him. There seems to have been a patriotic tradition in Athens in the later fifth century that it was the Athenians who won, or at least should have won, the state prize for valour at Salamis (cf. *Malice* 871C, Thuc. 1.74.1, Isocrates *Panegyricus* 71–98), but that they were deprived of it because of the machinations of the Spartans (Diodorus 11.27.2).

There is no reason to doubt the authority of Herodotus (rightly followed here by Plutarch) on this point. The Athenians contributed the greatest number of ships, and Themistocles' tactical genius, but the prize was for those who had fought most bravely, and Herodotus' account testifies to the valour of the Aeginetans (8.84, 86, 90–92), which was doubtless regarded as all the more praiseworthy after they had medised in 491 (6.48).

17.1 **that everyone awarded the first prize for individuals to Themistocles, albeit unintentionally:** Plutarch is referring to the story at Hdt. 8.123–24, though Herodotus says only that the *majority* of the commanders put Themistocles second, not all of them. This meeting of the Greek commanders was held at the Isthmus, their last action before the fleet broke up for the winter, and their vote was taken at the altar of Poseidon, doubtless to invest it with the extra authority which came from the implied divine sanction on the electors (cf. *Pericles* 32.3). The prize for individual performance seems to have been limited to the *commanders* of the various national contingents. Diodorus (11.27.2) says that the individual prize was awarded to an Athenian, Ameinias (see 14.4 note), but that is probably just a faulty inference from Herodotus 8.93, a passage which seems to refer not to a formal prize–giving, but to a general view expressed immediately after the battle (see previous note).

17.3 **the Lacedaemonians invited him down to Sparta:** These honours are described at Herodotus 8.124 (and attested also by Thucydides, 1.74.1, and

Diodorus, 11.27.3), where we are told that the Spartans awarded Themistocles an olive crown in honour of his wisdom, σοφία (the word used by Plutarch here), and his cleverness, δεξιότης (see 15.4 note). Plutarch is almost certainly right in saying that Themistocles was "invited" to Sparta. Herodotus, in accordance with his generally unfavourable picture of Themistocles in Book 8, is less complimentary – Themistocles was welcomed at Sparta, but "he went there immediately after failing to win the prize at the Isthmus, because he wanted to be honoured".

17.3 **an escort of three hundred young men:** This élite corps of youths, the Spartan kings' bodyguard in battle, were called "knights", but fought as infantry (Hdt. 8.124, Thuc. 5.72.4). Their name seems to have been a survival from very much earlier times, since the Spartans had no cavalry force in recorded history until 424 (Thuc. 4.55.2). The corps presumably rode horses on ceremonial occasions, like this escort for Themistocles. This must have been an immensely significant honour from the Spartans' point of view. It is no wonder they felt so aggrieved at Themistocles' behaviour a year or so later (see 19.3, 20.4 notes).

17.4 **when the next Olympic Games were being celebrated:** This story is referred to by Pausanias, 8.50.3. However, the Olympic festival of 480 had actually taken place before Salamis (Hdt. 8.26). Plutarch, in his eagerness to provide a striking and concrete illustration of Themistocles' popularity after the victory, the greatest moment of his life, has jumped forward in time by nearly four years, to the festival of 476. At this point it is clearly narrative and dramatic, rather than chronological, considerations which are uppermost .

Chapter 18

This chapter provides an interlude in the narrative, and gives the reader a chance to pause and draw breath after the climax reached at the end of chapter 17. Structurally it is very similar to chapter 5, in that it comprises a series of anecdotes (many of which are found elsewhere in Plutarch's writings), nine in all, which purport to illustrate what Plutarch regarded as Themistocles' most prominent character trait – his *philotimia* (cf. 3.4, 5.3 and notes), a keen desire to be noticed, admired and honoured. Apart from the first one, they all involve a remark or comment on Themistocles' part (cf. 18.9 ἀποφθέγμασι, "sayings"). Plutarch compiled a collection of *apophthegmata* (*Famous Sayings of Kings and Commanders*) at *Moralia* 172A–236E, 240C–242D. This includes the *Sayings of Themistocles* (17 in all), at 184F–185F. The collection was probably originally compiled to provide his busier patrons, like the emperor Trajan, with some easily digested light reading, and he seems to have drawn on his *Sayings of Themistocles* for most of the material of this chapter.

As a matter of fact, not all the anecdotes in this chapter do illustrate Themistocles' *philotimia* (as distinct from his gift for repartee) particularly well, and one cannot help feeling that the chapter has not been given very careful thought.

18.1 **elected admiral:** This story, which is found only here, is an invention. ναύαρχος (admiral) was not an official post in fifth century Athens, and in the Greek world it was not (and is not) necessary to delay business deliberately in order to create artificially an atmosphere of frantic activity.

18.2 **some Persian corpses:** For the story cf. *Moralia* 808F. The reference is to the coastline of Attica after the battle of Salamis. For gold ornaments found on Persians killed in battle cf. Herodotus 9.80 (at Plataea).

18.3 **Antiphates:** Cf. *Moralia* 185C. For the supposed homosexual proclivities of Themistocles in his youth see 3.2.

18.4 **the Athenians ... treated him like a plane tree:** This anecdote appears also at *Moralia* 185E and 541E. However, the comparison is not very appropriate, since in fact plane trees, common in Greece, are much more useful for the *shade* which they provide in summer, and are pruned at the approach of winter. There is probably an allusion here, in the word κολούειν ("prune"), to the Athenian procedure of ostracism (see 21.7, 22.4 and notes).

18.5 **the man from Seriphos:** This is the only anecdote in the chapter which has any connection with the preceding narrative. It is found in its original form in Herodotus (8.125). Themistocles, on his return to Athens after his triumphant visit to Sparta, is abused by an *Athenian* named Timodemus, from the deme of Aphidna, who attacks him on the grounds that his honours were not earned by his own merits, but by the fame of his city, Athens. Themistocles replies, "It is true that I should never have received these honours if I had come from somewhere insignificant like Belbina" (a rocky islet, a few miles south of Sunium, but politically independent from Athens), "but *you* could never be honoured (at Sparta, like me), *even though you are an Athenian* (like me)".

Plutarch's version of the anecdote (cf. *Moralia* 185C) is first found in Plato *Republic* 329E, where the original version has been adapted by Plato to fit the case of Cephalus, who answers the taunt, that he can bear old age easily only because he is very rich, by claiming that some men would not be able to bear it easily even if they were rich. Hence, in this version, Themistocles replies to the man of Seriphos that *he* would never have become famous *even if he were an Athenian* (i.e. from a famous city). Through the influence of Ammonius (see 32.6 and note) Plutarch was even more familiar with Plato than he was with Herodotus (cf. Frost [1980], 49–50 – Plutarch cites Plato over 600 times), and so it is Plato's rather less pointed version which he reproduces here.

Seriphos, an island in the western Cyclades, supposedly colonised originally by Athenians, was proverbial for its insignificance (cf. Ar.

Acharnians 542). It sent one ship, a penteconter, to Salamis (Hdt. 8.48), but its name was not included on the Serpent Column.

18.6 **another member of the board of generals:** This anecdote is found elsewhere in Plutarch, at *Moralia* 270B–C and 320E–F, passages which specify, more plausibly, that this general was one who "came after" Themistocles. It is at least correct in positing a *board* of generals at Athens (in fact ten in number, elected annually), in which no one *strategos* had overriding powers (see 6.1 note). The Festival Day (ἑορτή) was a day of intense public activity, the Day After (ἐπίβδα) was one for recovering from these activities.

18.6 **if I had not come then:** i.e. at the time of Salamis.

18.7 **said jokingly of his son ... that he was the most powerful person in Greece:** For this anecdote cf. *Cato Maior* 8.4–5, *Moralia* 185D. The story might be thought to provide evidence that Greek wives were rather more than mere doormats. However, it involves a flagrant anachronism. It would not have occurred to anyone to speak of the Athenians as "giving orders to" or "ruling" the Greeks until at least the reduction of Naxos in c. 469, by which time Themistocles had lost his political power and no longer even lived in Athens (see 25.2 note). A more plausible version of the story, which does not include the notion of the Athenians "ruling the Greeks", is found at *Moralia* 1C.

18.8 **putting an estate up for sale:** Again, this is an anecdote found elsewhere in Plutarch (*Moralia* 185E, fr. 50 [Loeb]). It could, however, be attached to anyone, at any time, and so cannot be used as evidence that land was legally alienable in Athens and Attica in the early fifth century (on this point see N.G.L. Hammond, *JHS* 81 [1961], 83–8).

18.9 **two suitors for his daughter's hand:** Cf. *Moralia* 185E. Themistocles had no fewer than five daughters (32.2–3). However, in an apparently earlier version of this story (Diodorus 10.32), Themistocles' comment is *advice* given to a rich man, who asked him where he could find a rich son-in-law. Themistocles advised him to marry her to (his great rival) Cimon (see 20.4 note), who was, at the time, impoverished and in jail because of his inability to pay the fine imposed on his father Miltiades (Diodorus 10.30). Plutarch, who seems to be running out of steam at this point, has made the story more personal, but less punchy.

18.9 **So he showed in his sayings the sort of man he was:** So, too, a hotch-potch of a chapter comes to a rather lame end (see ch. 18 introductory note). An exciting second half is about to begin.

Chapter 19

Plutarch resumes the Themistocles story (from the end of chapter 17) nearly a year on. In this chapter he gives an account of Themistocles' role in the rebuilding of

Athens' city walls (and the associated deception of the Spartans) in winter 479/8, and his subsequent fortification of the Piraeus harbour, two famous achievements which greatly contributed to the post-war growth of Athenian power, and which Thucydides, probably Plutarch's ultimate source here, discusses in some detail (1.89.3–93.8). However, Plutarch's attitude towards these achievements is not particularly approving. For him they foreshadow, in their more narrow focus, the self-centred actions which will bring about Themistocles' downfall (see chs. 20–22 introductory note).

Our sources say nothing about any role played by Themistocles in the events of 479, and it seems that Plutarch could find nothing in his far more numerous sources either. Themistocles is not mentioned at all by Herodotus after 8.125, and the impression he gives is that "the" Athenian commanders in 479 were Aristides (by land) and Xanthippus (by sea). Nor was Themistocles chosen as one of the high-level delegation sent to Sparta on Aristides' proposal in summer 479 to plead for military support (*Aristides* 10.10).

It has been suggested that Themistocles was not even elected to the board of generals in spring 479. Indeed, Diodorus (11.27.3) alleges that the assembly actually deposed him as *strategos* for having accepted the Spartan gifts, and gave his office to Xanthippus. However, this sounds suspiciously like an attempt by Diodorus' source, Ephorus, to explain Herodotus' silence about Themistocles in 479. There is no other evidence for any animosity between Athens and Sparta as yet, nor is it likely that the jealousy of his fellow citizens had already, within a few weeks of Salamis, become great enough for them to take such serious action against him. Furthermore, Themistocles was back playing a leading role in the winter of 479/8, when he led the delegation to Sparta which deceived them about the rebuilding of Athens' walls, and organised the renewed construction and fortification of the Piraeus (see above).

Almost certainly Themistocles *was* one of the *strategoi* during the 479 campaign, and may well have participated in the battle of Mycale. But Herodotus' informants (on the basis of what evidence we do not know) did not wish to give Themistocles any credit for, or role in, the Greek success there, and they presented Xanthippus as "the" Athenian commander at Mycale, and in the subsequent actions at Sestos and the Hellespont (8.131, 9.114, 120).

19.1 he bribed the ephors ... or so Theopompus records: Theopompus of Chios was a pupil of Isocrates and a contemporary of Ephorus. He wrote two historical works in the later fourth century, the *Hellenica* and the *Philippica*, the latter containing a digression *On Demagogues*, in which he seems to have made much of alleged acts of bribery of and by Athenian politicians (see 25.3 note, Frost [1980], 24–25, Connor [1968], 6). This digression was doubtless where Plutarch found the detail he records here.

The historical problem here is whether Theopompus had any credible evidence for his alternative version, which is at variance with that of "most authorities", i.e. Thucydides (1.89.3–92), followed closely by

Diodorus/Ephorus (11.39–40) and Nepos (*Them.* 6–7). It has been suggested (Frost [1980], 173) that a passage in Andocides' *On The Peace* (392/1 B.C.) indicates that there was an early, alternative, tradition to the effect that Themistocles bribed the Spartan ephors. But the passage cited (chs. 37–8) does not support this interpretation. Andocides describes how the Athenians built up their fifth century empire, employing "persuasion, deception, bribery and force", and he supplies a historical example of each method. The rebuilding of the walls, he claims, was achieved by a deception of the Peloponnesians, and then bribery ensured that the Spartans did not subsequently punish the Athenians for what they had done. Andocides is very vague on the chronology, though he appears to envisage two separate stages in Athens' dealings with the Spartans. However, there is no other evidence for Athenian bribery of Spartan officials in the 470's. The first attested example of this did not occur till much later – Pericles' successful bribery of their king, Pleistoanax, when he invaded Attica in 446 (Thuc. 1.114, 5.16, *Pericles* 22.2). This invasion could perhaps have been represented as an attack on Athens in revenge for the building of the Long Walls (not the city walls) in the 450's (Thuc. 1.107.1), and it may be that Andocides, whose account of earlier Athenian history is very confused and inaccurate throughout *On the Peace*, is alluding to this most famous example of Athens' successful bribery of Sparta. In any case, it is clear that the Andocides passage provides no support for the hypothesis that there was an early tradition, which Theopompus followed, that Themistocles really bribed the ephors not to oppose the Athenian wall building at the time of his embassy to Sparta in 478.

We do not know where Theopompus got his version from, but it is not inconceivable that he simply made it up (see 25.3, 31.3 notes).

19.2 **having ensured that his name ... was put down for the embassy:** Plutarch does not supply us, either here or in the *Aristides*, with the names of the other envoys (nor does Nepos in his *Themistocles* or *Aristides*), and the impression he gives is that Themistocles alone was responsible for this act of gross deception of Athens' recent ally. Thucydides, however, tells us (1.91.3) that Themistocles was joined at Sparta by his fellow envoys, Habronichus (who had been a liaison officer with Leonidas at Thermopylae [Hdt. 8.21]) and, interestingly, Aristides. This information is confirmed by *Ath. Pol.* 23.4.

It is very significant that Themistocles and Habronichus were prepared to sacrifice their special status and political backing at Sparta, in order to protect what they saw as Athens' essential national interests. This must have been the decisive turning point for personal relations between Sparta and Themistocles (see 20.4 note), and the reason why the Spartans began to cultivate and support Cimon (*not* Aristides, who must also have compromised himself in their eyes).

19.2 Polyarchus ... from Aegina: This detail does not appear in Thucydides' account, and we do not hear of such a person elsewhere. It is tempting (*pace* Frost [1980], 174, and Flacelière [1972], 75) to accept Schaefer's emendation Πολυκρίτου. Polycritus was the name of a well-attested Aeginetan opponent of Themistocles (cf. Hdt. 8.92).

19.3 the Spartans ... concealed their anger: Plutarch follows Thucydides (1.92) here. It is hard to believe the Spartans seriously thought that there was any realistic possibility that the Athenians would voluntarily refrain from rebuilding their city walls, but they must have been furious about Themistocles' calculated betrayal of their trust, after the exceptional honours they had given him only the year before (17.3 note). His precautions against being detained there were probably well justified.

19.3 he started to develop the Piraeus ... wished to join the entire city to the sea: Thucydides says (1.93.3) that Themistocles persuaded the Athenians to complete the building programme at the Piraeus which had been begun in his year of office as archon (i.e. 493/2; see 3.1 note), "since he considered that by becoming a seafaring people their power would increase greatly, and thus he laid the foundations of their empire."

In the later fifth century a theory developed which postulated an inherent connection between naval power and radical (and, to its proponents, undesirable) democracy, since the triremes' crews, who were paid by the state, came mainly from the Thetes, men belonging to the poorest but most numerous Athenian property-class. This view can be clearly seen in the pamphlet, entitled *The Constitution of the Athenians*, of the so-called "Old Oligarch" (pseudo-Xenophon), written probably in the 420's, and it pervaded anti-democratic thinking and writing from then on. For such critics, Themistocles was the man most responsible. He did not just lay the foundations for the fifth century Athenian empire (as Thucydides claimed), but foresaw and intended the increased political power of the Athenian *demos*, which for them meant the Thetes. This they portrayed as a sort of dictatorship of the proletariat (see 19.5 note).

This kind of source material was, of couse, available to Plutarch, and he sometimes utilises or adapts it (see 3.3, 4.4 and notes). On occasions he can take a robust attitude towards it (see 4.6 note). However, here, in sections 3–6, he reproduces it rather uncritically, probably because he wishes his readers now to start thinking of the other, darker, side of Themistocles, which will come to the fore in the narrative of chs. 20–22 (see ch. 19 introductory note).

19.3 the ancient kings of Athens: It was commonly, and probably correctly, believed that Athens had originally been ruled by kings (cf. Hdt. 8.44, Thuc. 2.15.1, *Ath. Pol.* fr. 1, 41.2). However, the idea that Athens' early kings, several hundred years before the time of Themistocles, had been concerned to divert the people away from a maritime way of life, because, it is implied, they feared its subversive political consequences, i.e. extreme democracy, is an absurd anachronism.

19.4 **Athena ... when Poseidon was contending with her ... the sacred olive tree:** The earliest reference in surviving literature to the famous legend of the contest between Athena and Poseidon, god of the sea, for patron authority over Athens and Attica occurs at Herodotus 8.55. The fullest account is to be found in the late second century B.C. writer, Apollodorus (3.14.1). The judges were the other gods, and the decisive witness was Cecrops, the legendary first king of Athens. The story of the contest was depicted in reliefs sculptured on the west gable of the Parthenon c. 440, at a period when Athens was both a maritime power and a radical democracy, and so it was obviously not at that time thought to have any ideological connotations. The interpretation put on it in this account, whereby Athena's victory with the olive tree signified a commitment to a thoroughgoing agricultural society, was a product of later oligarchic ingenuity.

Athena's sacred olive tree (like Poseidon's salt water spring) was situated within the pre-Persian War Erechtheum (cf.10.1 note).

19.4 **"knead the Piraeus onto the city", as Aristophanes the comic poet puts it:** The Athenian Aristophanes (c.450–c.385) was the most famous, and probably greatest, writer of Old Comedy. Eleven of his plays survive. Plutarch's point (derived from his oligarchic source) is that Themistocles, by developing the Piraeus, created an unnatural relationship between the city and the harbour, in which "the tail wagged the dog", the Piraeus became more important than the city itself. This goes well beyond the view of Thucydides (1.93.5), that Themistocles considered the Piraeus would be more valuable than the city *in the event of another invasion.* The expressions which Plutarch uses here, "he wished to *join* the entire city to the sea", "he *fastened* the city on to the Piraeus, and the land on to the sea", seem to contain an allusion to the Long Walls, which provided a physical link between the city and the Piraeus. However, the Long Walls were not built until the 450's (Thuc. 1.107.1, 4) and later (Andoc. 3.7), a development which had nothing to do with Themistocles.

Plutarch's quotation comes from Aristophanes *Knights* (424 B.C.), line 815. His deliberate reversal of the original expression seems to be his own contribution to the oligarchic material he is transmitting in this chapter. Aristophanes' line probably suggested itself to him because it comes in a scene where the villain, Paphlagon (= Cleon), has dared to compare himself with the great Themistocles (812–3, 818). The reply, from his adversary, the Sausage-Seller, is actually greatly to Themistocles' credit, and provides an interesting sidelight on public perceptions of Themistocles in 424.

Plutarch, however, misunderstands the original, where προσέμαξεν does not mean "kneaded Piraeus *onto* (the city)" but "kneaded Piraeus (into a loaf) *in addition* (for the city to eat)", i.e. as well as "filling up her cup", by rebuilding the city walls. The two most famous post-war achievements of Themistocles are referred to in *Knights* 814–15 by way of a consumption metaphor. Thus Plutarch's ingenuity here is misconceived. See my article, "History as Lunch: Aristophanes *Knights* 810–19", in *CQ* 46.2 (1996), 561–64.

19.5 **he increased the strength of the common people ... filled them with boldness ... political power fell into the hands of oarsmen:** See 19.3 note. The theory which portrayed Themistocles as the ideologically motivated founder of extreme democracy, *via* naval power and maritime empire, which supposedly must lead to it, did not correspond with the empirical evidence. The Athenian empire certainly developed out of the Delian League, founded in 478/7, but none of our sources specifically associates Themistocles with the League's foundation. The Athenian *strategoi*, who commanded the fleet and directed its offensives, continued to be chosen down to the time of the Peloponnesian War from the ranks of wealthy aristocratic families, and the most successful naval imperialist in the 470's and 460's was Themistocles' biggest rival, the "conservative" Cimon. Nor is there any evidence that the sailors, who were mostly, though not exclusively (cf. 4.4 note; Thuc. 3.18.4), drawn from the poorest citizen property-class, the Thetes, ever voted in the Athenian assembly as a self-conscious block, or supported a policy of class conflict.

Nevertheless, Themistocles *was* a political populist, who used his appeal to the "common people" to defeat his opponents of the day, and secure the adoption of his policies by the assembly. This was a key aspect of his success, as Plutarch rightly emphasises (see 5.6–7, 22.2 and notes).

19.6 **the speaker's platform on the Pnyx ... was later turned round:** Sessions of the Athenian assembly were normally held (after Ephialtes' reforms in 462/1) on the Pnyx hill, to the south-west of the *agora*. Archaeological evidence confirms the tradition that the auditorium and the speaker's platform (*bema*) facing it were turned around towards the end of the fifth century, so that the speakers now faced north-east (i.e. inland), and the audience south-west (see M. Hansen, *The Athenian Assembly* [Oxford, 1987], 12–13). However, this reconstruction does not seem to have been completed until after the restoration of democracy in late 403. The re-orientation and turning round of the speaker's platform was probably not, *pace* Plutarch, a symbolic gesture on the part of the oligarchic government of the Thirty, since it is unlikely that these hardliners had any use for a place of assembly at all (so Frost [1980], 178). In any case, since the platform was sited *below* the level of most of the seated audience, a speaker standing on it after the reconstruction could not see the *agora* or anything else inland beyond them, whereas they could perhaps catch a glimpse of the sea beyond him.

The "symbolic" interpretation presented here was probably just another piece of later anti-democratic ingenuity.

19.6 maritime empire ... begetter of democracy: See 19.3 note.

19.6 those who worked on the land were less hostile to an oligarchy: This was a view characteristic of anti-democrats (cf. the "Old Oligarch", *Constitution of the Athenians*, 2.14). However, since the majority of Athenian citizens were farmers (Thuc. 2.16.1), it was, at the least, a serious over-simplification.

Chapters 20–22

In these important chapters Plutarch's narrative registers a significant turning point in Themistocles' fortunes. After his career and reputation have deservedly risen to dizzying heights, he now starts to act in a way which causes him to lose his popularity, with Sparta, with the other allies, and with his fellow Athenians, so that, finally, he is ostracised.

20.1–2 Greek fleet ... at Pagasae ... burn ... in its dockyard: This story occurs also in *Aristides*, 22.2, where the location is not specified. It is, however, almost certainly a fiction, derived from the "Aristides the Just" tradition, in which Aristides is always presented as a defender of what is morally right as against what is expedient (cf. e.g. *Aristides* 6.1, 25.6).

Another, probably earlier, version of the story is to be found in Cicero, *De Officiis* 3.49, and Valerius Maximus, 6.5 ext. 2. In this the ships involved are the Spartan fleet, stationed in their dockyard at Gytheum. But such a project, which would certainly have provoked outrage, and probably swift retaliation, on the part of the other erstwhile allies, would not have secured any great advantages for Athens at this period, since the Spartan fleet was a comparatively insignificant force (they had just 16 ships at Salamis; cf. Hdt. 8.43). It is highly unlikely that Themistocles ever came up with such a provocative and counterproductive scheme.

Presumably because of this implausibility in the original version, Plutarch, or his source, has turned the intended target into the united fleet of the Hellenic League, and placed the project in the context of an attested allied expedition to Thessaly. Pagasae is the port of Pherae, in southern Thessaly. This expedition, doubtless intended to punish the Thessalian medisers (cf. Hdt. 7.132), was commanded by the Spartan king, Leotychidas, and took place in 478, or possibly 477 (cf. Hdt. 6.72, *Malice* 859D, Pausanias 3.7.9–10).

However, Plutarch has ignored the crucial fact that, following the usual Greek practice (cf. Hdt. 8.124, 9.121), the various naval contingents would have sailed home to their respective cities to spend the winter there. They would not have remained at Pagasae.

This particular story may go back to the period of the so-called First Peloponnesian War, when an Athenian fleet under Tolmides burned the

Spartan dockyard at Gytheum, c. 455 (Thuc. 1.108.5). It is possible that this action was presented at the time as something which Themistocles had once advised.

20.3 **At a meeting of the Amphictyonic delegates the Spartans put forward a proposal ... views of the delegates:** The Amphictyonic Council administered the affairs of the temple of Apollo at Delphi, and was composed of representatives from 12 Greek peoples. It was actually the officials called ἱερομνήμονες who voted. The πυλάγοροι acted as their advisers (Dem. 18.148–49).

Plutarch is our only source for this story, which might therefore have to be viewed with suspicion, especially since this Council does not seem to have been seriously exploited for political purposes until the mid-fourth century B.C. However, the story does have a certain plausibility. The figure given, in Themistocles' reported argument, of 31 cities, corresponds precisely with the number of cities whose names are inscribed on the Serpent Column (12.8 note), and the proposal fits well with what we know from elsewhere of Sparta's policy in the period (see Flacelière [1972], 78).

Before the war the Greek allies swore an oath to "tithe" (δεκατεῦσαι) to Apollo at Delphi those states which voluntarily medised (Hdt. 7.132). This word (*pace* Frost [1980], 179), means something far more serious than merely "fine". How and Wells (1912, vol. II, 178), are surely right in taking the word to imply the capture by force of these cities, the confiscation of all their goods, the enslavement of their people, and the sending of one tenth of the overall booty as a dedicatory offering to Apollo.

The Spartan proposal after the victory at Mycale in autumn 479, that the Ionians should be resettled in mainland Greece on territory from which the medising peoples had been evicted (Hdt. 9.106), certainly implies that, at that time, they still assumed that the threat of 481 would be carried out. This particular proposal was successfully opposed by the Athenians, and in fact nothing was subsequently done about the oath promising to tithe the medisers. It would have involved immense efforts and considerable loss of life, and threatened states could always argue that they had only medised under compulsion. The political will on the part of the other allies was simply not there.

It is possible that the Spartans then demanded as a *quid pro quo* (perhaps at the meeting in spring 478) that the medising states should at least be expelled from the Amphictyonic Council. This body, presumably at the instigation of the Spartans, had already taken action against the traitor of Thermopylae, Ephialtes of Malis, by putting a price on his head, and, significantly, his killer was subsequently honoured at Sparta (Hdt. 7.213). Themistocles may well have opposed such a proposal as impractical, thus securing the good will and gratitude of the threatened states. He went to live in Argos after his ostracism in 470 (see 23.1 note).

20.3 **Thessalians ... Argives ... Thebans:** The Thessalians argued that, apart from the Aleuadae clan, they had only medised under compulsion (Hdt. 7.172), and Leotychidas' punitive expedition to Thessaly seems to have been abandoned without having done any very serious damage (Hdt. 6.72, *Malice* 859D). The Argives took no part in the war on either side (Hdt. 7.148–152, 8.73). In the event, the invaders did not penetrate the Peloponnese. This enabled the Argives subsequently to claim that they had not actually medised. The Thebans, who had certainly medised (Hdt. 7.131, 233), did suffer limited reprisals after Plataea (Hdt. 9.86–88), but even they were able to claim subsequently that it had all been the work of a small clique, unrepresentative of the city as a whole (Thuc. 3.62.3–4).

20.4 **As a result they started to promote the career of Cimon:** There can be no doubt that the Philaid Cimon, the son of Miltiades (see 3.4, 5.4, and notes), a man who had visited Sparta on a high-level embassy in summer 479 (*Aristides* 10.10), did enjoy Spartan patronage and political support (which he fully reciprocated) from early in his political career (*Cimon* 16.1–3), or that Cimon was the main political rival of Themistocles in Athens in the later 470's (*Them.* 24.6, *Arist.* 25.7, *Cimon* 9.1), and was regarded as Aristides' successor in that role (*Cimon* 5.4).

But, even if we accept the historicity of Plutarch's story of Themistocles' opposition to Sparta at the Amphictyonic Council, it is unlikely that *this* was the principal reason for Sparta's change of attitude towards him. He had already put himself beyond the pale with the Spartans through his deceptive embassy in winter 479/8 (see 19.2 note), and this speech, if it occurred, was merely adding insult to injury.

21.1 **obnoxious to the allies as well ... trying to extort money from them:** Having shown how Themistocles offended Athens' most important ally in the war, Sparta (through his narrow and aggressive nationalism, and lack of patriotic Hellenic zeal), Plutarch now proceeds to explain how he offended Athens' other allies (through his greed). However, in his account Plutarch confuses two different sets of allies, from two different periods. Herodotus tells us (8.111–12) that after Salamis, i.e. in late 480, the Greek fleet attacked Andros, and sent financial demands to Carystus in Euboea, Paros, and other islands. As usual, Herodotus' account has a strongly anti-Themistocles slant (the money is demanded by and for Themistocles personally; the other commanders know nothing of his proceedings), but at least Themistocles' targets are clearly presented by Herodotus as Greek states which had medised in the war (i.e. not allies), and thus, in the immediate aftermath of Salamis, fair game for financial exactions on the part of the victors. In 21.1–2 Plutarch is obviously following Herodotus' account (he actually cites him by name), but he mistakenly refers to these islands as *"allies"*, and he appears to date Themistocles' activities to the period after the foundation of the Delian League in 478/7, when many of the Aegean islands *were* allies of Athens, but in a new military organisation. He thus makes Themistocles guilty of piracy, as well as greed and extortion.

21.2 **Persuasion and Force ... Poverty and Scarcity:** In addition to his chronological confusion, Plutarch, who is clearly quoting Herodotus from memory here, rather than working from a text (cf. 12.4, 12.8, 14.4 notes), misquotes his source on the names of these deities. Herodotus (8.111) actually has "Persuasion and Necessity (Πειθώ τε καὶ 'Αναγκαίην)" and "Poverty and Helplessness (Πενίην τε καὶ 'Αμηχανίην)".

21.3 **Timocreon, the lyric poet of Rhodes:** Timocreon came from Ialysus (21.4), one of the three cities on the island of Rhodes (the others being Lindus and Cameirus). He is called "the Rhodian" in a mock-epitaph, probably composed by Simonides:– "Here I lie, Timocreon of Rhodes, having drunk much, eaten much, and much abused my fellow men" (fr. 110, quoted by Athenaeus, 10.415f).

He was an athlete and boxer, as well as a poet and (alleged) glutton. According to the Suda, s.v. Τιμοκρέων, he was a personal enemy of Simonides, as well as of Themistocles, and this seems to be confirmed both by the unflattering mock-epitaph and by Timocreon's abusive reply to its "Ceian nonsense" (fr. 10 = *AP* 13.31), which itself parodies a couplet of Simonides (fr. 111).

Diodorus (11.3.8) says there were 40 ships in Xerxes' navy from the Rhodian cities, Cos, and the Dorians of Caria. Herodotus says nothing of any Rhodian participation, though it is likely *prima facie* that there was some. It is true that they would not have been regarded by the nationalist Greeks as "medisers" *en bloc*, since, like the Ionians, they were serving under compulsion. Nevertheless, after the liberation of Ionia, doubtless many personal scores were settled locally under cover of legislation against "collaborators", and Timocreon's personal enemies were obviously able to suggest he had been too close to the Persians, and to get him exiled. The story of the late fifth century B.C. sophist, Thrasymachus of Chalcedon, quoted by Athenaeus (10.415f), that Timocreon went to the court of the Persian King and was invited to dinner, where he behaved badly, perhaps derives from allegations made by his enemies at his trial.

21.3 **attacks Themistocles rather bitterly in a song:** When was this poem written? A date soon after 479 is suggested by the complimentary references to the four great heroes, two from each of the leading allied states, of the military campaigns of that year; Pausanias and Aristides at Plataea, Leotychidas and Xanthippus at Mycale. It must certainly have been written before Pausanias and Leotychidas became publicly discredited figures.

Pausanias was recalled to Sparta, after Ionian complaints had been made against him, in late 478. He was acquitted on the main charges, but not sent out again in spring 477. Leotychidas was accused of receiving bribes when in command of an expedition to Thessaly (Hdt. 6.72). Herodotus does not date this campaign, but a punitive expedition against Thessalian medisers was most likely to have been mounted as soon as it was practicable to do so, i.e. in 478 (see 20.1–2 note).

The approving reference to Aristides is probably due to his leadership at Plataea (Hdt. 9.28), rather than his role in the formation of the Delian League in winter 478/7 (*Ath. Pol.* 23.4–5), and Timocreon's poem is best dated to 478, when Plataea and Mycale, and their heroes, were still the most recent "great events" in Greek minds. In the summer of 478 Aristides led the Athenian contingent which went with Pausanias to Cyprus and to attack Byzantium, but he took only 30 ships (Thuc. 1.94.1). It is likely that, at the same time, Themistocles led another squadron which consolidated the liberation of Rhodes and other eastern Aegean islands. Timocreon's poem certainly implies that Themistocles visited Rhodes personally (see next note).

For Timocreon and Themistocles see Meiggs (1972), 414–15, N. Robertson, "Timocreon and Themistocles", *AJP* 101 (1980), 61–78.

21.3 **in return for a bribe Themistocles secured the restoration home of other exiles, but abandoned him:** Timocreon's grouse was not that Themistocles had had him exiled in the first place, but that, after he had been exiled on a charge of Medism, Themistocles had refused to secure his restoration (οὐ κατᾶγεν εἰς πατρίδα), though he *had* done this for others.

Does this imply that, after the liberation of the Ionian Greeks, some sort of supra-national tribunal was set up (on which Themistocles sat), with authority to adjudicate on cases of alleged collaboration in the various cities? Plutarch's expression at 21.7, "(it is said that) Themistocles participated in the vote of condemnation (συγκαταψηφισαμένου)" has been thought to indicate that there was a tradition to that effect, which he is following. But the comment is probably no more than an explanatory gloss based on Timocreon's own quoted words, without independent authority, and the expression itself just a mistaken inference.

Timocreon's poem suggests that, to start with, he had been prosecuted by his political enemies and condemned in a local court at Ialysus. What action could Themistocles have subsequently taken? Probably it was then a matter, not so much of international tribunals, as of the political pressure on local courts and authorities which could be applied by a visit of a Greek (i.e. mostly Athenian) fleet. This would have been able to enforce the expulsion of "medisers", and perhaps secure the return of unfairly expelled "loyalists". However, Timocreon's claim on Themistocles seems to have been based on a tie of hospitality, rather than on the injustice of the charge, and, given that the return of Greek exiles tended to cause troublesome property problems (see Frost [1980], 183), that tie might well have not seemed enough to Themistocles to justify putting pressure on the Ialysians to overturn a previous judicial verdict. Timocreon's allegation, that Themistocles had pocketed a bribe of three talents from Timocreon's enemies to take no action to restore him, has to be taken with a large pinch of salt. Such personal slanders, easy to make, difficult to disprove, were a stock-in-trade of Greek political invective (cf. e.g. Thuc. 3.38.2, 40.1, 42.3, Ar. *Knights* 438–45, 472–3, 834–5).

21.4 He speaks as follows: The metre of these eleven lines is dactylo-epitrite, a type of verse in which dactyls (– ∪ ∪) and cretics (– ∪ –) predominate.

21.4 Leto: The dialect of the Rhodian cities was Dorian, thus Timocreon writes Λατώ, the Dorian form of the name of Apollo's mother. Presumably she had, like her son, a hatred of liars (cf. *Homeric Hymns* 3.83–8 for her solemn oath to Delos). There may be an added sting in the reference to Leto in that her daughter, Artemis, was particularly cultivated by Themistocles (see 22.2 note).

21.4 Themistocles, that liar, criminal and traitor: This is the earliest appearance in surviving literature of alleged character defects which later became standard in the anti-Themistocles tradition. He is stigmatised by the aggrieved Timocreon as greedy for money, a liar, and a crook. However, the word προδόταν has a purely personal reference here ("traitor to me"), and does not imply "betrayer of his country". All the evidence suggests that it was not until the end of the 470's, or even later, that Themistocles was alleged to have had any treasonable dealings with Persia (see 22.4, 23.1–6 notes).

21.4 for a dirty bribe: This is a translation of (ἀργυρίοισι) κοβαλικοῖσι, "knavish", which is Diehl's emendation of the unmetrical reading σκυβαλικοῖσι, "shitty", found in the manuscript tradition represented by U and A. S has the nonsensical κυμβαλικοῖσι

21.4 when he gave a banquet at the Isthmus: This appears to refer to a real historical occasion. If so, when was it? It can hardly have been the Isthmian festival of 480, which was the occasion of the judgment by the Greek commanders for the prize of valour (Hdt. 8.123; see 17.1–2 note), since the sequence of topics in Timocreon's poem implies that Themistocles' inadequate banquet was given *after* the exile of Timocreon and Themistocles' subsequent refusal to engineer his return, events which could not have occurred until late 479 at the earliest (see 21.3 note). Thus the Isthmian festival referred to is probably that of 478.

21.5 after Themistocles' flight and condemnation: Plutarch is referring, not to Themistocles' ostracism, but to his subsequent trial and condemnation *in absentia* for treason, probably in 468 (23.1, 25.2 notes). Timocreon may have been allowed to return to Ialysus by then. He certainly survived to enjoy his revenge.

21.7 **not the only one with a docked tail ... other foxes like me:** The fox was proverbially crafty. But this one has lost its tail in a trap, like the one in the fable of Aesop (no. 41 in the Budé edition by E. Chambry [1960]). The words κολούω/κόλουσις were often used metaphorically to refer to a curtailment of political rights through ostracism or exile (see 18.4 note, 22.4, *Aristides* 7.2), and that is clearly what κόλουρις here implies.

22.1 **his fellow citizens ... remind the assembly ... he became annoying:** Finally, and most decisively for his political demise (see chs. 20–22 introductory note), Themistocles offended his fellow citizens at Athens (through his boastfulness and egocentricity).

22.1 **"How can you grow tired ..." :** Plutarch quotes this impatient remark, with the addition of ὦ μακάριοι ("you lucky people"), several times elsewhere (*Moralia* 185E, 541D, 800B, 812B).

22.2 **He upset the common people also:** For Plutarch the key element in Themistocles' political success was his ability to appeal to, and command the support of, the common people, οἱ πολλοί (see 5.6–7 and note). For him to lose that support was therefore fatal to his career.

22.2 **the temple of ... Artemis ... "Best Counsellor":** For this temple cf. *Malice* 869D. The physical trappings of Greek religion afforded considerable scope for political self-advertisement (see 1.4). Themistocles seems to have felt a particular affinity with Artemis, possibly as a result of the naval success at Artemisium (8.4–6). Artemis was worshipped at a shrine in the Lycomid deme Phlya (Paus. 1.31.4), and, when Themistocles' sons returned to Athens, they dedicated a statue of Artemis Leucophryne on the Acropolis (Paus. 1.26.4). The location of this temple has almost certainly been identified (cf. J. Threpsiades and E. Vanderpool, *Arch. Delt.* 19 [1964], 26–36), despite the scepticism of P. Amandry (*Charisterion eis A. Orlandon* 4 [Athens, 1967], 265–79).

22.2 **his own house in Melite:** Melite was a city deme, situated just west of the Acropolis and *agora*. It belonged to the tribe Cecropis, which was also the tribe to which the deme Phlya, with its Lycomid family estate, belonged (see 1.4 note). This was doubtless Themistocles' "town house", situated in a much more convenient location for an active politician than Phrearrhioi (see 1.1 note).

22.3 **a bust of Themistocles stood ... right down to my time, and it shows that:** This is a clear example of personal autopsy on Plutarch's part (cf. 8.3–4 and note). His use of the imperfect tense, ἔκειτο does not imply that the bust had been removed before the time at which he was writing; only that it was there when he visited the shrine. The word εἰκονιον literally means "likeness", and can denote a painting or a full statue, but here it more likely means a head-and-shoulders bust (see 5.7 note), like the one found at Ostia in 1939 – a second century A.D. Roman copy, probably of a Greek original. See Podlecki (1975), *frontispiece* and plate 1, and his excellent discussion of this bust, 143–46.

22.4 they employed the procedure of ostracism against him: The *fact* of Themistocles' ostracism is well attested, e.g. by Thucydides 1.135.3, Plato *Gorgias* 516D, Diodorus 11.55.1, and Nepos *Them.* 8.1–2.

The *date* is more problematic. The Themistocles ostraca themselves, though numerous (Mabel Lang [1990], 102, reports a total of 2279), are no help on this question, since they are not dated, and, in any case, come from many different *ostrakophoriai.* Of the literary sources only Diodorus (11.54.1) provides us with a fixed date – the archonship of Praxiergus, i.e. 471/0. The ostracism procedure involved two stages:– (a) a decision by the assembly on whether or not to hold an ostracism vote, *ostrakophoria*, which was taken in the sixth prytany (out of ten) of the official year (*Ath. Pol.* 43.5), and (b) the *ostrakophoria* itself, held in the eighth prytany (Philochorus, *FGH* 328 F30). The year began in midsummer. Thus Diodorus dates Themistocles' ostracism to late March/early April 470. However, Diodorus goes on to relate all the events of the rest of Themistocles' life, down to his death at Magnesia (in reality at least ten years later), under the same year-heading (11.55–59), and this obviously cannot be right. Nevertheless he may be correct on his date for Themistocles' ostracism, since the *first* item of a series which he mentions under a year-heading is most often the one which belongs to that year, and Themistocles' ostracism seems to be the first event concerning him in this section (though there is some confusion in 11.54.2–55.1). Diodorus does at least apologise at the end of his account of events for 471/0 (11.59.4) for his "lengthy digression" about Themistocles' life.

Frost (1980), 188–91, following R. Lenardon, 'The Chronology of Themistocles' Ostracism and Exile', *Historia* 8 (1959), 23–48, adopts an "early" chronology for the events of Themistocles' life from his ostracism onwards, and suggests c. 472 for the ostracism and c. 471 for his exile. Such an early date cannot be disproved, since we have so little firm evidence for anything in Themistocles' life in the 470's, but it does create problems when we try to reconstruct the chronology of his later activities (see 25.2 note).

Frost argues that the date 471/0 was traditional for Themistocles' *condemnation*, and may have got into the tradition from Craterus' collection of decrees (see 6.4, 23.1 notes), which preserved the date of the decree recording his exile. However, the dates of successful ostracisms also seem to have been officially recorded, to judge from *Ath. Pol.* 22.4–7, a passage which gives precise archon dates for four different ostracisms in the 480's.

It is possible that some later sources confused the ostracism and the later exile. There may be a reflection of this in Diodorus' account, where the ostracism is *preceded* by a charge of treason, on which Themistocles is acquitted (see 23.6 note), and then followed by the threat of a second such charge, as a result of which he flees to the north-west. However, there is no suggestion of this in the accounts of Thucydides, Plato and Nepos, all of whom are explicit that Themistocles was first ostracised, then prosecuted (for the first and only time), and, as a result, exiled.

On balance, I feel it is preferable to follow the one source (Diodorus) who does provide us with a definite date for the ostracism, since this is a date which fits perfectly well with what little we know of Themistocles' life in the 470's, and which provides a better chronology for subsequent events (see 25.2 note).

What was the *reason* for Themistocles' ostracism at the end of the 470's? Plutarch attributes it to his boastful remarks and offensive behaviour, which aroused the resentment of the common people (22.2 and note), and this explanation, though probably no more than an assumption which fits his thesis in chs. 20–22, may well be right. Others have suggested it must have been the result of a policy clash, in which he lost out to his political opponents. However, we have virtually no evidence for Athenian politics during the 470's, and we should not necessarily assume that there must have been a major, defining clash over foreign policy between Themistocles and, say, Cimon, which had a decisive effect on Themistocles' popularity. It is true that our sources do not mention Themistocles as being personally involved in the formation of the Delian League in 478/7. But there is no reason to think that Themistocles did not support this naval-based alliance. After all he played a key role in the fortification and development of the Piraeus harbour, surely an essential element in the strategic planning of the alliance.

The inscribed tablet set up by Themistocles to commemorate his success as the choregus for Phrynichus' play in 476 (see 5.5 and note) suggests a still confident and high-profile public figure, rather than someone under pressure. It is probable that the first dent in his popularity was not made until Cimon's success at Scyros, when the supposed bones of Theseus were discovered, and brought back in triumph to Athens (Thuc. 1.98.2, *Theseus* 36.1–2, *Cimon* 8.5–6). Every last drop of propaganda was milked by Cimon and his supporters from this episode, which cannot be certainly dated, but probably occurred in 475.

A passage in Aeschylus' *Persians*, which clearly refers to Themistocles, even though he is not named (355–62), may imply that by spring 472, the date of the play, Themistocles was coming under some pressure politically. Hence the Athenian audience is reminded that at Salamis, less than eight years earlier, it was indeed Themistocles who had saved them all.

Themistocles' biggest problem was that he had many bitter and implacable political enemies at Athens, in particular Cimon and the Alcmaeonids, now in close alliance (cf. *Cimon* 4.9). As the public memory of Salamis faded, they were able to exploit the fact that the most glamorous and most obviously successful elements of Athenian policy in the 470's, namely the formation under Athenian auspices of the Delian League, and a series of booty-acquiring expeditions against Aegean medisers and Persian-held bases (all of which might well have been supported by Themistocles) had, unluckily for him, been personally hijacked by his political rivals, Aristides and Cimon.

There is no evidence that Themistocles' unpopularity at Athens in the later 470's resulted from his anti-Spartan "programme" (if he had one), or that his ostracism was a matter of policy differences at all. In the end, it may have been mostly a matter of electoral organisation by his enemies (at last getting their act, and their supporters' votes, together), added to the resentment felt, as Plutarch suggests, by a growing number of Athenians against his counter-productive harking back to Salamis, which can be seen, for example, in the names he gave two of his daughters, Mnesiptolema ("memorial of the war") and Nicomache ("victory in battle"); see 32.2 and note.

22.5 For ostracism was not a punishment: Plutarch is consistent in his explanation of the purpose of ostracism, i.e. that it was designed to allow the people to humble and cut down to size the high and mighty, and thus purge from the Athenian body politic the spirit of resentment and envy. He expresses this view also at *Aristides* 7.2, *Nicias* 11.1, and *Alcibiades* 13.4. It is a view which is to be found in Aristotle (e.g. *Politics* 1284a, 1302b, and 1308b), and it seems to have been the view of Nepos' source: *tamen non effugit civium suorum invidiam*, "nevertheless he did not escape the envy of his fellow-citizens" (*Them.* 8.1). Diodorus, in a passage which almost certainly goes back to Ephorus (11.55.1–3), offers the same explanation, in very similar language to that used by Plutarch here. It seems very probable that Ephorus was Plutarch's ultimate source for his view of ostracism (so Jacoby, *FGH* 111b, Suppl.ii, n. 12, *ad* 328 F30).

A slightly different explanation, which associated ostracism, at least in its earliest deployments, specifically with a desire to prevent tyranny, or remove would-be tyrants and their friends from Athens (it only later being employed for a wider purpose), is to be found in *Ath. Pol.* 22.4–6, and Philochorus, *FGH* 328 F30, probably because these writers believed that the procedure was instituted by Cleisthenes soon after the fall of the Pisistratid tyranny.

All our sources agree that ostracism was not a punishment for a specific crime, and did not involve loss of citizenship or confiscation of property. Where they differ over a number of procedural details Plutarch's version seems to be preferable, e.g. the period of absence/exile imposed on an *ostracisé* was ten years (*Aristides* 7.2, Nicias 11.1), not five (Diodorus 11.55.2), or ten later reduced to five (Philochorus, *FGH* 328 F30); the requirement that there should be 6000 votes for an ostracism to be valid was a requirement for the total number of votes cast (*Aristides* 7.5), not for the highest individual total (Philochorus).

Chapters 23–25

Plutarch continues the narrative of Themistocles' post-war troubles, his ostracism being followed by a charge of treason, and he goes on to explain how and why Themistocles eventually fled to Asia and sought sanctuary with the Persian King. However, the tone is more sympathetic than in chs. 19–22; we get the impression that Themistocles was not to blame for what happened from now on.

23.1 he ... was living in Argos: The tradition is unanimous that, on being ostracised, Themistocles went to live in Argos (Thuc. 1.135.3, Diodorus 11.55.3, Nepos *Them.* 8.1), where he must have had friends at least from the time of his support for Argos at the Amphictyonic Council debate (see 20.3 and note), if not before. Plutarch's narrative implies that Themistocles was staying there just to sit out his ostracism. Thucydides, however, supplies the interesting, if rather cryptic, detail that "he used to travel about in the rest of the Peloponnese". If so, it is hard to believe that this was mere tourism on Themistocles' part, and, given the fact, agreed by all our sources, that the Spartans subsequently took the initiative in denouncing Themistocles at Athens for allegedly being involved in the treasonable activities of Pausanias, it seems reasonable to conclude that Themistocles had been engaging in political activities in the Peloponnese which were not to the Spartans' liking. Quite possibly he had been encouraging the formation of democratic governments, and anti-Spartan alliances, from his base in democratic Argos (see W.G. Forrest, "Themistocles and Argos", *CQ* 10 [1960], 221–41).

23.1 the man who brought the indictment ... was Leobotes, the son of Alcmaeon: Plutarch almost certainly got this name from Craterus' collection of decrees (*FGH* 342 F11; see 6.4 note). The name of Leobotes' father strongly suggests someone connected with the Alcmaeonid *genos*, though not a member of the main branch of the family, whose deme was Alopece (of the tribe Antiochis), not Agryle ('Αγραυλῆθεν is a misspelling by Plutarch; cf. *Alcibiades* 22.5). Leobotes was the name of an Agiad king in Sparta (Hdt. 1.65, 7.204), but it is otherwise unattested in Athens or Attica. For this man it was surely programmatic, advertising a family link or interest (cf. 32.2 note). This family may have been Spartan *proxenoi*, "public friends", at Athens (cf. P.J. Bicknell, "Leobotes Alkmeonos and Alkmeon Aristonymou", *Studies in Athenian Politics and Genealogy*, *Historia* Supplement 19 [1972], 58).

Plutarch also names Leobotes as the prosecutor of Themistocles at *Moralia* 605E; but there is an apparent discrepancy at *Aristides* 25.10, where he says that Themistocles' accusers were *Alcmaeon* and Cimon. And at *Moralia* 805C he gives the role to Alcmaeon alone. Frost (1980), 193, attributes this to a "simple error of memory" on Plutarch's part. Sansone (1989), 201, following J.F. Barrett, "The Downfall of Themistocles", *GRBS* 18 (1977), 291–305, attempts (using Diodorus 11.54–55), to explain "the problem" by postulating two prosecutions of, or attempts to prosecute Themistocles, one by Alcmaeon, and one by his son, Leobotes (cf. 23.6 note).

But there is no problem, nor is Plutarch this time guilty of an error of memory. In this passage he is quoting from an official decree, preserved by Craterus in his collection, which gave the name, patronymic, and demotic of the man who brought the formal prosecution against Themistocles. By contrast, at *Aristides* 25.10 the words ἐλαυνόντων καὶ κατηγορούντων refer *not* to formal court proceedings, but to speeches by Alcmaeon and Cimon *attacking Themistocles in the assembly* and other public places. The implied context seems to be the time of his ostracism rather than his trial (Aristides,we are told, was ostracised at the instigation of Themistocles, but he did not harbour grudges when he had the opportunity to do the same thing to Themistocles). As with the English word "accuse", this wider, non-technical sense of κατηγορέω/κατηγορία is common in Greek, and is found several times later in this very chapter. Similarly, at *Moralia* 805C Plutarch uses the verb προσμάχεσθαι of Alcmaeon's dealings with Themistocles. But, obviously, "fight against" need not have the specific, narrow, sense of "prosecute in court".

The notion of Diodorus, which presumably derives from Ephorus, that there were *two* attempts to prosecute Themistocles for treason, is not supported by any other source, and is almost certainly unhistorical (see 23.6 note).

23.1 indictment for treason: In his account (1.135.2–3) Thucydides does not say explicitly that treason (προδοσία) was the charge brought against Themistocles, though his reference there to the "medism" of Pausanias suggests that it was, and a subsequent comment very strongly implies it: "at his request his relatives brought his bones back and buried them in Attica secretly, for it was not lawful to bury there one who had been exiled for treason" (1.138.6; see 32.4 note). That treason was the charge is stated explicitly by Diodorus (11.54.5, 55.4) and by Nepos (*Them.* 8.3).

All the sources agree that Themistocles did not return to stand trial. He must therefore, like Hipparchus, son of Charmus (Lycurgus *Against Leocrates* 117–18), and Alcibiades (Thuc. 6.61.7), have been tried and condemned in his absence (it was technically an ἐρήμη δίκη). Nepos is explicit, *hoc crimine absens proditionis damnatus est*, "he was condemned in his absence on this charge of treason". Plutarch is silent on this point here, but probably intends us to assume a parallel with Camillus, who was so condemned (see *Camillus* 13.1).

What was the sentence imposed on Themistocles? A formal sentence of exile (φυγή) seems to be implied by the words used by Thucydides 1.138.6 (see above), and by Ar. *Knights* 819, ἐκεῖνος ... φεύγει τὴν γῆν, and "exile" is alleged by Socrates to have been the penalty imposed on Themistocles (Plato *Gorgias* 516D). The most explicit testimony to this effect comes from the early third century B.C. writer, Idomeneus of Lampsacus, quoted in a scholion to Ar. *Wasps* 947: "the Athenians sentenced him and his family to eternal exile for betraying Greece, and his property was confiscated" (*FGH* 338 F1).

However, though the penalty imposed on Themistocles obviously necessitated exile (cf. *Aristides* 26.3), for both himself and his sons (Pausanias 1.1.2), and confiscation of his property, the official sentence was perhaps not formally one of φυγή. It is interesting that none of the sources refers to or suggests a sentence of death, though we might surely have expected that, given the serious nature of the charge. The explanation may be that, on being convicted, Themistocles was officially declared to be an ἄτιμος ("outlaw"), which, in the early fifth century, meant not that he merely lost some or all of his political rights, but that he lost his personal rights too, and so could be robbed, injured, or even killed with impunity by any of his fellow citizens (see 6.4 note). With such a sentence there was no need to specify a penalty of death or, indeed, exile. Later in the fifth century, when *atimia*, outlawry, had been "tamed", and limited to loss of political rights, it was necessary to spell out that those found guilty of treason were to be executed, their property confiscated and their descendants disfranchised. This happened in the case of Archeptolemus and Antiphon in 410 (the decree is quoted, probably from Craterus, at *Moralia* 834A–B). A sentence of "untamed" *atimia* would also explain why Themistocles was so alarmed when his ship passed close to the Athenian fleet besieging Naxos (25.2 note). Capture risked execution, either on the spot or back in Athens.

Themistocles' trial *in absentia* probably went ahead immediately after he had been formally given sanctuary by Admetus, king of the Molossians (24.2 and note), since there would then no longer have been any prospect that the pursuing posse of Athenians and Spartans were going to bring him back.

In the 450's a very different political climate prevailed at Athens, following the disgrace and ostracism of Cimon, and Ephialtes' reform of the Areopagus (see 31.4 note). In these changed circumstances Themistocles' sons were officially recalled to Athens, probably not long after his death (cf. Pausanias 1.1.2, 26.4, Plato *Meno* 93D). Their rights of citizenship were restored, and they seem to have been able to regain at least some of their property (see 25.3, 32.1 notes; Davies [1971], 6669 VI, 218).

For the location of Themistocles' trial see 23.6 note, and for the chronology of the events of this period of his life see 25.2 note.

23.2–3 Pausanias ... invited him ... Themistocles ... rejected the ... partnership: Plutarch's sources for the medism of Pausanias and the alleged connection of Themistocles appear to be Thucydides (1.128–134) and Ephorus (there is a very close similarity of language between *Malice* 855F and Diodorus 11.54.4). Thucydides himself seems to have put his story of Pausanias' treason together partly from what he was officially told at Sparta, and partly on the basis of the "evidence" brought by the Spartans to Athens, after Pausanias' death, to incriminate Themistocles. The inadequacies and inconsistencies in Thucydides' account have often been pointed out (e.g. by Mabel Lang, "Scapegoat Pausanias", *CJ* 63 [1967], 79–85, and P.J. Rhodes, "Thucydides on Pausanias and Themistocles", *Historia* 19 [1970], 387–400). As for the alleged connection of Themistocles with Pausanias, the evidence against him could have been fabricated with impunity by the Spartans, and probably was, given that the prime witness was now very conveniently dead.

Thucydides (1.135.2–3) does not supply any details of the evidence brought against Themistocles. Ephorus, however, did, and they appear in Diodorus (11.54.2–5). The allegation was that Pausanias had communicated by letter with, and perhaps visited, his "friend" Themistocles (while Themistocles was in Argos), disclosed his treasonable plans, and invited Themistocles to join in the enterprise. The Spartans were able to produce a copy of Pausanias' letter, though they do not seem to have had any documentary evidence of a reply from Themistocles incriminating himself. So their accusation was that, although Themistocles had rejected Pausanias' proposal, he had not disclosed the treasonable plan to the authorities, as he should have.

23.4 he defended himself in a letter ... allegations ... levelled against him previously: The phrase ταῖς προτέραις κατηγορίαις means "by making use of the allegations made against him previously", and the argument refers back to the time of his ostracism. The word κατηγορία is here used in its non-technical sense (see 23.1 note). Themistocles' argument supposedly was: "my political enemies attacked me for being by nature too high and mighty, a man who always wants to be in charge, and is never prepared to accept anyone else's authority. That was how they succeeded in getting me ostracised. Therefore, for them *now* to allege that I have been willing to hand Greece and myself over to the absolute authority of the Persian king is a complete contradiction of the picture of me which they got you to accept then".

However, this story of a *letter* of self-defence, for which Plutarch is our only authority, is probably unhistorical. Apart from the practical problems it poses (where, when, and by whom was this letter read out?), Themistocles' argument, as recorded by Plutarch, is very weak. In reply the prosecution could immediately draw attention to the examples of the ex-tyrant Hippias, and the ex-Spartan king Demaratus, powerful individuals who nevertheless medised. Frost (1980), 196, is probably right in suggesting that the "letter" was concocted by the rhetorical schools (perhaps in the first century A.D.), which had been unable to resist compiling an *Apologia Themistoclis*, "Defence of Themistocles".

23.6 **the people were convinced by his accusers:** Plutarch is using the word κατηγορέω in its wider sense here (cf. 23.4 note), and referring to Themistocles' political enemies who supported the Spartans by attacking him publicly in the assembly. It was clearly a vote of the assembly that he should be brought back from Argos and put on trial.

23.6 **to stand trial before a Panhellenic court:** Literally, "before the Greeks". However, there is no mention of such a court in the account of Thucydides 1.135.2–3, where the Athenians agree to the Spartan envoys' request that Themistocles should be punished "in the same way as" Pausanias, i.e. by execution, though Pausanias was not actually put on trial at all. They send off a posse of men, together with some Spartans, to find him and bring him back (presumably to Athens). At 1.138.6 Thucydides adds that Themistocles' relatives say that his bones were brought back from Magnesia secretly, "since it was against the [Athenian] law to bury anyone convicted of treason in Attica". The implication here clearly is that Themistocles had been convicted in an *Athenian* court. Nor is there any mention of a Panhellenic court in Nepos' account (*Them.* 8.1–5).

Plutarch has taken this detail, which doubtless appealed to his own Hellenic sensibilities, from a tradition which he or his source found in Ephorus. Diodorus (11.55.4–5) refers to a Spartan *proposal* (made to the Athenians) that Themistocles should be put on trial "before the common Council of the Greeks" (ἐπὶ τοῦ κοινοῦ συνεδρίου τῶν Ἑλλήνων). But what exactly was this Panhellenic *synhedrion*, which is not heard of anywhere else? At Diodorus 11.55.5–7 Themistocles is made to equate it with the (biased) body which made the awards for valour after Salamis in late 480, and gave first prize to Aegina, not Athens. However, in Herodotus (8.121–3) that body seems to have been (though Herodotus is not entirely clear on the point) simply an *ad hoc* meeting of the various Greek naval commanders, similar to the one which denied Themistocles the individual prize, and there is certainly no suggestion in Herodotus that the decision was made by any supra-national judicial tribunal.

There are other problems about Diodorus' account. He is silent about what happened to the Panhellenic synhedrion proposal after Themistocles fled from Argos and escaped arrest. Did the *synhedrion* meet and condemn him in absentia, or was the proposal abandoned? If so, was the matter then left to an Athenian court? In Diodorus' account there is no mention of any condemnation of Themistocles at all, by any court. In fact he tells us that

Themistocles had been *acquitted*, at an earlier trial for treason at Athens, *before* his ostracism (11.54.2–5). This seems very unlikely. There is no suggestion of any such pre-ostracism trial in any of our other sources (see 22.4 note).

It is probable that the rather muddled and confused account of Diodorus has been much influenced by, and ultimately goes back through Ephorus to, a strongly pro-Themistocles version of events, which was first put into circulation by his sons and their families, on their return to Athens in the 450's (see 23.1 note). Plutarch has for the most part followed Thucydides for the essential elements of his story, but he has taken this last detail, of a Panhellenic court, from Ephorus, and, by turning a Spartan proposal into an Athenian decision, has involved himself in a semi-contradiction with what he has said earlier in the chapter. There, by giving the name, patronymic and demotic of Themistocles' Athenian prosecutor, Leobotes (official details most probably taken from Craterus' collection of decrees), he has strongly implied that the trial was held at Athens.

On the reasonable assumption that Themistocles was tried once only, in his absence, on a charge of treason, and in Athens, the question arises, in which court was his case heard? The usual procedure for bringing charges of treason was known as εἰσαγγελία, impeachment, and, according to Craterus (*FGH* 342 F11), the prosecution of Themistocles *was* formally an *eisangelia.* In accordance with a provision of Solon (*Ath. Pol.* 8.4) the body which had jurisdiction to hear charges of treason, brought by this procedure, was the Council of the Areopagus (see 10.6 note), and the Areopagus almost certainly still retained this jurisdiction, exclusively, in the early fifth century (see Wallace [1985, 1989], 74–6). If the Areopagus was the body which condemned Themistocles, then that would surely have provided an added incentive for Ephialtes and his supporters (the "political heirs" of Themistocles) to attack it and severely reduce its powers, as they did a few years later, in 462/1 (*Ath. Pol.* 25.1–2, Rhodes [1981], 317). It would also, perhaps, have provided a starting point for the tradition of *earlier* rivalry between Themistocles and the Areopagus (see 10.6 note).

24.1 he ... went across to Corcyra ... public benefactor ... arbitrator ... dispute with the Corinthians: Plutarch follows Thucydides (1.136.1) closely in the first sentence, but, because Thucydides does not explain the circumstances of Themistocles' *euergesia* to the island state of Corcyra, he has gone to another source for the details. That source, it seems, was Theophrastus, in his work Περὶ Καίρων (*On Periods*), a passage of which is quoted by a grammarian, and preserved in a third century A.D. papyrus, *P. Oxy.* vii, 1012C (for text and discussion see L. Piccirilli, "Temistocle evergetes dei Corciresi", *ASNP* 3 [1973], 317–55, and his *Arbitrati interstatali greci* [Pisa, 1973], 61–6).

However, Theophrastus, who was Aristotle's successor in the late fourth century B.C. as head of the Lyceum, cannot (*pace* Frost [1980], 201), whatever his other merits, be regarded as an authoritative historian (see 25.1 note). Prominent individuals did sometimes act as agreed arbitrators in disputes between states, especially in the archaic period. For example, Periander of Corinth arbitrated in the dispute between Athens and Mytilene over Sigeum in c. 590, giving a decision favourable to Athens (Hdt. 5.95). But there are serious doubts about this particular alleged arbitration. Its date must be sometime before 480, as the Corinthians would subsequently have been very unlikely to accept as an arbitrator a man who had so fiercely and personally attacked their commander Adeimantus on the eve of Salamis (Hdt. 8.59–61). But why should Themistocles have been chosen at all then? Before 480 he was hardly an internationally famous name, and, traditionally, Aristides was the Athenian of the time with a great reputation for justice. Furthermore, the alleged judgment, by which Leucas, an island off Acarnania, became a joint colony of Corinth and Corcyra, is hard to square with such historical facts as we know regarding Leucas in the fifth century. The sources are unanimous in naming Corinth alone as its mother city (Hdt. 8.45, Thuc. 1.90.2, Scylax 34, Strabo 10.2.8, Nicolaus of Damascus, *FGH* 90 F57); the Leucadians seem to be functioning as a fully independent state at the time of Salamis – they sent three ships (Hdt. 8.45); and forty five years later the Corcyraeans, after their victory over the Corinthian fleet at Leucimme in 435, proceeded to attack Leucas on the grounds that it was an ex-colony and ally of Corinth (Thuc. 1.30.2–4).

Either Plutarch is mistaken in saying that Themistocles "settled the quarrel", or, more likely, this story of a supposed arbitration by Themistocles, favourable to the Corcyraeans, is fictitious. It was invented by Theophrastus or his source, in order to explain what Thucydides does not explain, by expanding on the Herodotean tradition of Themistocles' toughness towards the Corinthians.

An alternative explanation is offered in a scholion on Thucydides 1.136.1, that Themistocles had saved the Corcyraeans from being punished by the Greek allies for not having taken part in the war against Xerxes. This can hardly be right as it stands, since the Corcyraeans, though their promised fleet had not ventured round the Peloponnese into the Aegean (Hdt. 7.168), had certainly not "medised", and thus would not have been liable to punitive action. It may be that, in accordance with his post-war policy of no reprisals (see 20.3 note), Themistocles had interceded to stop a proposal to debar them from some religious festival. There is a hint in Herodotus (7.168) that the Corcyraeans were criticised in some public forum. However, we simply do not know why Themistocles was honoured as a benefactor at Corcyra, if indeed he was.

24.2 From there he fled to Epirus: Plutarch forgets to say, or perhaps tactfully chooses not to record, that the Corcyraeans, when confronted by the demands of Athens and Sparta, refused to protect Themistocles and give him asylum. That is why he was forced to cross to Epirus, on the mainland of north-west Greece, opposite Corcyra.

24.2 taking refuge with Admetus: The story of Themistocles' supplication of Admetus is told at some length by Thucydides (1.136–137.1). Plutarch seems to be following and embroidering Thucydides' account. Diodorus (11.56.1–3) and Nepos (*Them.* 8.3–5) also tell the story, but make it less dramatic, by portraying Admetus as an old friend of Themistocles. There are other variations of detail. In Nepos, Admetus' child is a daughter (Plutarch follows Thucydides), and Plutarch refers to a version which made Admetus himself suggest the form of supplication to Themistocles. The story perhaps originated with Themistocles himself, via his sons on their return to Athens (see 23.1 note).

It has been pointed out (e.g. by Gomme [1945], 439, Frost [1980], 204) that Thucydides does not state that Themistocles *threatened* Admetus' infant son in any way (nor does Plutarch here) – this is something stated only by the author of the late and spurious *Letters of Themistocles*, 5.745 (for these see Podlecki [1975], 129–33). Indeed, the essence of supplication for Greeks was the *complete submission* of oneself before the person supplicated. So why *did* Themistocles, according to the story, take the child in his arms?

The question is complicated by the apparent similarity of this episode to the legendary tale about Telephus and Agamemnon's child, Orestes, which was the subject of two fifth century tragedies, both now lost, by Aeschylus and Euripides. Louis Séchan has argued (*Études sur la tragédie grècque dans ses rapports avec la céramique* [Paris, 1926], 123–27) that Aeschylus' play commemorated the Themistocles story, and that in it Telephus held Orestes without threatening to kill him, but that in Euripides' play, written later, there was a more melodramatic version, in which the threat was made. It does seem from the parody in Ar. *Acharnians* 326ff. that this is how Euripides portrayed the scene in his *Telephus* (cf. Handley and Rea, *BICS* Suppl. 5 [1957], 36–7), but we cannot be absolutely certain about how Aeschylus presented it, still less that he intended it to have a perceived connection with the Themistocles supplication story. After all, the situations of Telephus and Themistocles were rather different.

It is probably better to consider the Themistocles supplication story independently from speculative reconstructions of Aeschylus' and Euripides' Telephus plays. It is significant that Plutarch says that this was considered to be the most powerful form of supplication by the (remote and feudal) Molossians, and that it was a "peculiar and extraordinary" method (ἰδιόν τινα καὶ παρηλλαγμένον τρόπον). The implication is that it was not what would be considered normal by more civilised Greek standards. So, assuming the story is not just a fabrication, it seems that we are being presented with a more superstitious, and possibly non-Greek, ritual of supplication, in which the total subjection of the suppliant is *further* reinforced by the close physical presence of the most precious person or object within the household of the person supplicated. This person/object is to be regarded, *not* as someone/something that is under threat from the suppliant, but as an actual or assumed supporter of, interceder on behalf of, the suppliant. Thus Admetus' infant son, though mute, is deemed to *support the plea* of Themistocles. Admetus' wife, Phthia, does not herself make a plea on behalf of Themistocles, as we might initally expect, given her sympathy, but she does (in Thucydides' version) arrange for Themistocles to be "supported" by someone deemed to be even more important to Admetus than she is, i.e. their infant son.

24.2 **asked the Athenians for some favour ... humiliatingly rebuffed:** This comes from Thucydides' version (1.136.4). We do not know what Admetus' request had been for, and the detail may well be an unhistorical embellishment, to give the story added drama, and emphasize the contrast between the responses of Corcyra and Admetus.

24.5 **Some say that it was Phthia:** e.g. Thucydides (1.136.3).

24.5–6 **obliged him to refuse to surrender the man to his pursuers ... wife and children ... sent to join him:** Plutarch is surely right in the assumption he seems to make at this point in the narrative, that, once Themistocles as a suppliant had been vouchsafed Admetus' support, his safety was assured for the foreseeable future. Diodorus (11.56.1–2) and Nepos (*Them.* 8.5) implausibly make Admetus give Themistocles a solemn guarantee, and then send him away.

24.6 **His wife and children were smuggled out of Athens ... by Epicrates. He was subsequently prosecuted for this by Cimon ... as Stesimbrotus records:** For Stesimbrotus see 2.5, 4.5 and notes. He was a highly unreliable historical source, as Plutarch himself demonstrates at 2.5. However, Plutarch's attempt here to show that Stesimbrotus contradicts himself in the two cited stories is itself not very convincing. The fact that Themistocles' (presumably second) wife (see 32.2 note) went to join him in Epirus would not have created an impossible obstacle to a subsequent proposal to marry Hieron's daughter. He could have divorced his Athenian wife if necessary.

In itself the Epicrates story is plausible enough. Epicrates of Acharnae is not mentioned elsewhere, but two men with the same name and demotic, probably his descendants, are attested by inscriptions of the late fourth century (IGii2 1492B.110–11, 306/5 B.C., and IGii2 505.5, 302/1 B.C.). A vindictive prosecution of a friend and accomplice of Themistocles by Cimon, now riding the crest of the wave at Athens, would certainly fit the politics of the 460's.

However, the charge brought against Epicrates can hardly have been that he had smuggled Themistocles' wife and children out of Athens, since Themistocles' sons, at least, had almost certainly been included in the penalty of outlawry imposed on him (see 23.1, 32.3 notes), thus necessitating their own exile. If Epicrates was prosecuted, it must surely have been for smuggling away some of Themistocles' *property and possessions*, which were liable to confiscation (see 25.3 and note).

24.7 **he says that he sailed to Sicily and asked the tyrant Hieron for ... his daughter in marriage:** It is unlikely that Themistocles ever went to Sicily. No source, apart from the unreliable Stesimbrotus, says that he did, and the wild promises supposedly made by Themistocles to Hieron in this story read suspiciously like those allegedly made by Pausanias in a (probably forged) letter to Xerxes (Thuc. 1.128.7; see 23.2–3 note).

But the story which Plutarch produces from Theophrastus at 25.1 to disprove Stesimbrotus' account, by demonstrating that there was in fact strong antipathy between Themistocles and Hieron, is itself equally suspect, and should probably be rejected as an unhistorical doublet (see next note).

The author of the *Letters* (see 24.2 note) speaks of an intention on Themistocles' part, after being refused sanctuary by the Corcyraeans, to seek help from the tyrant of Syracuse; but, just before Themistocles set sail for Sicily, a message arrived to say that he had died. So Themistocles abandoned the plan, and went to Admetus instead (20.758). However, in this account the tyrant of Syracuse is called Gelon, and that cannot be right, since Gelon had died in c. 478 (Diodorus 11.38.3), some ten years earlier.

Nevertheless, despite this error, and the poor authority of the sources which refer to a contact with Sicily, it is an attractive hypothesis that Themistocles had been in communication with the ruler of Syracuse (Hieron, not Gelon). After all, there is a serious problem about Themistocles' flight from Argos, which is otherwise hard to resolve. *Why* did he flee to north-west Greece? He cannot have felt confident that Corcyra would provide him with a permanent refuge, against the double pressure of Athens and Sparta. Equally, he cannot have been planning at this stage to turn to the Persian King. If he had, he would surely have gone there more directly, and not taken such a circuitous route, which involved him in a total change of direction, and a long and dangerous journey overland back to the Aegean, and then across it to Asia.

Yet everything we know about Themistocles suggests that, when he voluntarily left Argos (there is no suggestion in the sources that he was abruptly expelled), he would not have been reduced to an unplanned, random dash for safety. He *must* have had a contingency plan. The powerful Greek city of Syracuse, with its large fleet (200 ships in 480, according to Herodotus, 7.158), well beyond the reach of Athens or Sparta, would surely have seemed to Themistocles an ideal place of refuge and base for his restless energies. Hieron welcomed distinguished Greek visitors and immigrants. Themistocles' friend, the poet Simonides (see 1.4, 5.6, 15.4 and notes), spent some time at Hieron's court in Syracuse, and died there (cf. Xen. *Hieron, passim*, Aristotle *Rhet.* 2.1391a8, Athenaeus 14.656d, Suda s.v. Σιμωνίδης [3rd notice]).

That Themistocles was interested in the Greek West at this period of his life is very strongly implied by the significant names he chose for two younger daughters, Italia and Sybaris (32.2; note also his reported remark to Eurybiades at Hdt. 8.67). It is more than likely that he had at least been in contact with Hieron, and that Syracuse was his intended final destination when he left Argos for Corcyra, which was the obvious point of departure for a journey to Italy or Sicily. He had to divert from Corcyra to the mainland, but he remained for some time in the area of Greece most convenient for a departure to Sicily.

Why then did Themistocles in the end not go to Syracuse after all? I would suggest that his plan had to be aborted, not because Gelon died, but because his brother and successor, Hieron, died, in c. 467 (Diodorus 11.66.4). Hence Themistocles was forced to remain in Epirus for longer than he had originally intended.

The issues of chronology involved in the reconstruction of Themistocles' activities during this period are discussed below (see 25.2 note on **Naxos**).

25.1 **Theophrastus in his work *On Kingship* records ... Hieron ... Olympia:** This story can hardly be historical. Why should Themistocles have violently attacked Hieron in a speech at the Olympic Games (presumably those of 476; see 17.4 and note)? Themistocles' record seems to have been one of opposition to post-war witch-hunts (cf. 20.3, 24.1 notes). The Deinomenid tyrants of Syracuse, Gelon and Hieron, had themselves suffered external attack, by the Carthaginians, and received no help from the eastern Greeks, and, although the Syracusans had not joined in the resistance to Xerxes' invasion (Hdt. 7.153–67), they had certainly not medised. They had as much nationalist credibility as most other Greek states in the 470's.

It looks as though Theophrastus has badly mixed up his Sicilian tyrants (so Frost [1980], 206, following A. Schaeffer, *Philologus* 18 [1862], 187–90). He was actually thinking of the fourth century tyrant of Syracuse, Dionysius I, who was the object of an inflammatory speech, written by Lysias, and delivered at the Olympic Games, probably of 388 (Lysias 33, Dionysius of Halicarnassus, *On Lysias* 29–30, Diodorus 14.105). Thus what we have here is an unhistorical doublet.

That being so, serious questions have to be asked about the worth of Theophrastus as a historical source (see 24.1 note), despite Plutarch's commendation of him at *Alc.* 10.4 as "a listener and reseacher to compare favourably with any philosopher". After all, he was writing no more than 80 years or so after Lysias' Olympic speech.

25.2 **Naxos, which at that time was being besieged by the Athenians:** The precise date of the Athenian siege of Naxos, the first occasion on which an allied state within the Delian League was reduced to subject status (Thuc. 1.98.4), is uncertain, but it can hardly have been later than 468 (see Gomme [1945], 397–98, 408). Thus, if Themistocles did not leave Epirus until sometime after 467 (as I have suggested above at 24.7 note), this detail cannot be right. But Plutarch, as he tells us explicitly, is following the account of Thucydides (1.137.1–3), and there too the location of Themistocles' narrow escape is said to be Naxos, as it is also in Nepos (*Them.* 8.6). Diodorus omits the incident entirely (11.56.3–4).

However, one manuscript of Plutarch, the normally reliable Seitenstettensis (S), has a different reading, Θάσον (Thasos) for Νάξον (Naxos). The Athenian siege of Thasos started about three years after the reduction of Naxos and lasted for two years (Thuc. 1.100.2 –101.3), i.e., probably, 465–3. If it was the Athenian fleet besieging Thasos in 465 which Themistocles narrowly avoided, that would certainly fit better chronologically with what follows in Thucydides' account. On landing on the Asiatic coast, at Ephesus, Themistocles travelled some way inland, and communicated by letter with the Persian king Artaxerxes, son of Xerxes (Plutarch follows this tradition; see 27.1 and note). Thucydides says that Artaxerxes "had recently come to the throne", and Persian records indicate that Artaxerxes succeeded his father in late 465 or early 464 (see 27.1 note).

The clear implication of Thucydides' account is that Themistocles got in touch with Artaxerxes as soon as he could after arriving in Asia, and it is very difficult to believe (*pace* Frost [1980], 211) that Themistocles could have lingered anonymously at Ephesus, or elsewhere in Ionia, for some three to four years, apparently waiting hopefully for Xerxes to die and his more sympathetic son to succeed. He was, after all, in a very vulnerable situation, as, probably, an *atimos* (23.1 note), who could be arrested and taken back to Athens, and perhaps even be killed on the spot, stranded as he was in a region which must have been frequently visited by the Athenian fleet and Athenian officials and merchants.

On the other hand it is improbable that the reading of a single manuscript of Plutarch, which is also different from that of all the manuscripts of Thucydides and Nepos, preserves a genuinely independent historical tradition. It is much more likely to be a copyist's mistake, or a deliberate correction by someone who realised the chronological problems involved here.

There are also meteorological and geographical difficulties about the reading Θάσον. The prevailing wind in the Aegean in summer blows from the north. Hence a ship on a voyage from Pydna, on the Thermaic gulf, to

Ephesus, more than half way down the Aegean coastline of Asia, would not be blown by a gale off course to Thasos, an island in the extreme north Aegean, just off the mainland of Thrace. It is possible, though unlikely, that the voyage was undertaken during the winter, when southerly gales do occur in the Aegean, but then we might have expected the captain of the merchant ship simply to go on to seek shelter at a harbour on the Thracian coast, a mere couple of miles away from Thasos.

However, Naxos does not make much better sense from this point of view either. It seems too far south; there are several more likely island harbours for a storm-driven ship to find shelter in, situated closer to the direct route between Pydna and Ephesus.

It is thus most likely that what we have here, in the "narrow-escape" incident, is an unhistorical story, a fabrication, which probably originated with Themistocles himself, embroidering the tale of his adventures to an eager audience in Magnesia (cf. 24.2), and which was passed on by his sons and grandchildren (see ch. 30 introductory note, 31.1, 31.5, 32.4 notes), after their return to Athens (so, rightly, P.J. Rhodes, "Thucydides on Pausanias and Themistocles", *Historia* 19 [1970], 395–400). Thus the supposed Naxos/ Thasos incident cannot be used to help determine the chronology of this period of Themistocles' life, between his ostracism and his meeting with Artaxerxes.

There are problems with both an "early" and a "late" chronology, but, on balance, it is, I think, preferable to assume that Themistocles spent two to three years with Admetus in Epirus (Plutarch at 24.5–6 seems to imply that his stay there became more than a temporary sojourn), rather than three years in dangerous limbo in Ionia. Thus the most likely chronology is:– ostracism in spring 470; flight from Argos to Corcyra 468; trial and condemnation at Athens *in absentia* in late 468 or early 467; stay in Epirus 468–465; crossing to Ephesus via Pydna (when he had heard that his old adversary Xerxes was dying or dead) 465; letter sent to Artaxerxes in early 464; first meeting with him in early 463 (cf. Thuc. 1.137.4).

25.2 **he became alarmed:** Plutarch follows Thucydides (1.137.2), who says that Themistocles was frightened (δείσας). But why should he have been, if he had merely been sentenced to exile from Athens and Attica? The suggestion that something even more unpleasant than being an exile will happen to Themistocles, if the Athenian forces find him, is plain (see 26.1 note). This detail seems to provide further confirmation that Themistocles now was officially an Athenian *atimos* (see 23.1 note), who could be arrested and killed with impunity.

25.2 **revealed his identity to the captain and the helmsman:** Both Plutarch and Nepos (*Them.* 8.6) follow Thucydides (1.137.2) on this detail, that Themistocles was originally travelling incognito.

25.2 to the effect that he would denounce them to the Athenians: Thucydides (1.137.2) refers both to threats made by Themistocles, that he would accuse the captain of knowingly carrying him for a bribe, and to his promise of a financial reward – a promise which he fulfilled later, when money reached him at Ephesus. Plutarch here mentions only the threats (and entreaties), Nepos (*Them.* 8.6) only the promise and delivery of a reward. But Plutarch still has the account of Thucydides in his mind, hence in 25.3 there is a rather abrupt switch in the narrative, with a remark about the transfer of some of Themistocles' possessions and resources to Asia.

25.2 he forced them to sail by the island and make the coast of Asia: The story as told by Thucydides (1.137.2) – followed virtually word for word by Nepos (*Them.* 8.7) – is actually more dramatic. The ship rode out the storm for a day and a night at anchor (presumably behind a sheltering headland), at a short distance from the Athenian fleet. Plutarch may be following a different source here, but, more likely, his memory of Thucydides' story is slightly defective, and he does not have the text in front of him (cf. 12.8, 14.4, 21.2 notes).

25.3 the total value of that which was openly declared and confiscated by the Athenian treasury: For public confiscation of Themistocles' property as a part of the sentence imposed on him see 23.1, 24.6 notes. The state sold it off in lots, through officials called πωληταί (*Ath. Pol.* 47.2, 52.1). Presumably Themistocles, having decided not to return to face a trial, had been able to arrange for a transfer of cash and some assets into the hands of friends and relatives, such as his father-in-law (see 32.1 note), before the estate was confiscated. His son Cleophantus, after his return to Athens, seems to have regained possession of at least some of the family estate (cf. Plato *Meno* 93D, Davies [1971], 6669 VI, 218).

25.3 one hundred talents ... eighty ... three: Details of the sale of Themistocles' assets were probably officially recorded on a *stele*, as was done in 414 with the confiscated property of those convicted of involvement in the mutilation of the Hermae (ML, no. 79, pp. 240–47 = Fornara, no. 147, pp. 170–75). So reliable figures were available. The figures given here, however, are almost certainly pure fantasy. They are way beyond what the scanty evidence suggests the estates of even the wealthiest individual Athenian citizens were worth in the fifth century. Even in the fourth, when values were probably higher, an estate worth just three talents represented a fair sized fortune, and any valued at four (or above) rendered its owner liable to the liturgies which were thought of as a mark of the very wealthiest citizens (see Davies [1971], xx–xxiv).

It appears that the figures of one hundred (for which Plutarch cites Theopompus as his authority) and three, given here, derive ultimately from a pamphlet written by Critias, the extreme oligarch of the late fifth century, who was one of the "Thirty Tyrants". The pamphlet is referred to and cited by Aelian, *VH* 10.17. It is also clear from Aelian's citation that this was a work of propaganda, not factual record, "exposing" the corrupt activities of populist politicians like Themistocles and Cleon, by contrasting the supposed size of their fortunes at the beginning and end of their careers (in the same passage, Cleon is alleged to have gone from being in debt to start with to having fifty talents worth of property at his death). The work would have possessed an obvious attraction for Theopompus, with his fondness for bribery stories (see 19.1 note).

It is not clear where Theophrastus' equally unlikely figure of eighty came from. His authority as a historical source is slight (see 25.1 note).

Chapters 26–29

These four chapters constitute a unified, largely self-contained, narrative, telling the dramatic story of the salvation of Themistocles, an exile and a hunted man in Asia, thanks to the unexpected goodwill of the Persian King. This is the so-called "Themistocles Romance". It is a strong possibility that Plutarch was, to a large extent, following a single source for this account (adding the occasional "scholarly" comment), and that his source was Phanias of Lesbos, whom he twice refers to by name, at 27.8 and 29.11 (see L. Bodin, *REG* 28 [1915], 251–81, Frost [1980], 209–11). For Phanias see 1.2 note.

26.1 **When he landed at Cyme:** According to Thucydides (1.137.2), followed by Nepos (*Them.* 8.7), Themistocles' port of arrival in Asia was Ephesus, much further to the south. It is thus evident that Plutarch, who was following Thucydides at 25.2, has now switched to a different authority. This may have been Ephorus, who came from Cyme, though Diodorus, who generally follows Ephorus, does not specify the place where Themistocles landed (11.56.4–5). In view of what follows, it is more likely that Plutarch took the detail from Phanias, who, as an Aeolian himself, doubtless preferred an Aeolian locale.

26.1 **Ergoteles and Pythodorus and their associates:** These two characters are not heard of elsewhere in the surviving literature. The use of the plural definite article plus περί before a name may be periphrastic, the equivalent of the name alone, as it certainly seems to be at 7.5 (see note). However, here the context seems to imply a group of bounty hunters, and I have translated accordingly.

26.1 **a price of two hundred talents ... set on his head by the King:** There is nothing of this in any of our other sources, and almost certainly it is a historical fiction, invented to provide a unifying motif for the Themistocles Romance (cf. 29.3). The drama is much increased by the fact that, as long as Themistocles is in Asia, it is vital that he should remain anonymous until he can get to speak to the King in person (cf. 26.2, 4–6, 27.7). But there had been no reason to expect that Themistocles would turn up, alone and vulnerable, in this part of the world, and hence no reason for Artaxerxes or his father to think that putting a price on his head would have any point.

Themistocles surely had much more to fear on the Asiatic coast from Athens and Athens' allies, since he was probably an *atimos* (see 23.1, 25.2 notes), who could be arrested and handed over to the Athenian authorities, or even killed on the spot. That is the reason he lost no time in travelling inland, away from the area of Athenian influence, and why, in his letter to Artaxerxes, he described himself as "pursued by the Greeks" (Thuc. 1.137.3–4).

26.1 **his host Nicogenes:** Like Ergoteles and Pythodorus, Nicogenes is not heard of elsewhere. In this version Themistocles' host is a wealthy and well connected Greek. In Thucydides (1.137.3), more plausibly, he is an unnamed Persian, whom he met at Ephesus, and who then escorted him "inland" (i.e. presumably, to Sardis), from where he writes a letter to the King in his own name. In Diodorus (11.56.4–5) his host (place unspecified) is an old friend, a wealthy Greek called Lysitheides, who also happens to be a friend of the Persian King, and he personally conducts Themistocles to the King.

26.1 **the authorities to the east:** i.e. the King of Persia and his advisers.

26.2 **"To night entrust voice ...":** The Greek forms a single line of verse, a trochaic tetrameter (catalectic): – ∪ – –/ – ∪ – –/ – ∪ – –/ – ∪ – . The point of the utterance is that Themistocles will find good counsel in the night to come, through the dream he is going to have; and Olbius' ecstatic trance itself guarantees that the dream-omen will be one which genuinely comes from the gods.

26.3 **a snake ... turned into an eagle:** The motif of a conflict between an eagle and a snake (in which the snake usually has the better of it) seems to have been common in omens and prophecies (e.g. *Iliad* 12.260–7, Ar. *Knights* 197–201, *Wasps* 15–19). Here the snake represents death, whereas the eagle, into which it turns, is a symbol of salvation, because a golden eagle was the emblem of the Persian King (Xen. *Anab.* 1.10.12, *Cyr.* 7.1.3).

In the Themistocles Romance it is only at this point in his flight that Themistocles decides to approach the King directly. However, this version is a contradiction of Thucydides (1.137.1), and it is, surely, most unlikely that Themistocles had left Admetus in Epirus and travelled across the Aegean to Asia without knowing what he was going to do next (see 28.5 and note).

26.3 **herald's staff made of gold:** The herald's staff represents the peace which follows a period of hostilities or perils. It is golden, thus indicating Themistocles' future prosperity.

26.4 **who had devised the following plan:** Themistocles' journey into the interior of Asia, hidden in a palanquin which supposedly contained a woman, is an element of the story which is also found in the Ephorus/Diodorus version

(11.56.7–8), though there the danger to Themistocles comes simply because of who he is and what he has done, and not from any supposed price on his head.

26.4 **barbarian nations ... cruel and harsh ... jealous attitude towards their women:** Plutarch's assumption that, in contrast to the world of the *barbaroi*, Greek society was comparatively liberal in terms of male attitudes towards, and treatment of, women, is worth noting.

26.5 **female slaves and concubines:** A παλλακή ("concubine") was a free woman who lived with a man in a regular relationship (hence more than a "mistress"), but was not married to him, either because she was not a citizen or because the man was married already (cf. Ar. *Wasps* 1352–3, Menander, *The Samian Woman* 35–41).

26.6 **young Greek woman:** γύναιον may be a contemptuous diminutive here (= "weak woman", i.e. too frail to expose to the elements). In Diodorus' account (11.56.7) the supposed concubine is being conducted to the King himself (cf. Xen. *Cyr.* 6.4.11 for the royal palanquin).

26.6 **one of the King's courtiers:** The Greek literally means "one of those at the King's doors". For this idiomatic expression cf. Xen. *Anab.* 1.9.3. Contrast 29.1, where the phrase simply denotes guards at the palace gates.

27.1 **Thucydides and Charon of Lampsacus ... Xerxes' son:** Thucydides (1.137.3) tells us that Themistocles communicated with Xerxes' son, Artaxerxes, "who had recently become King (νεωστί βασιλεύοντα)". This can be dated according to Persian records to late 465 or early 464 (see M.E. White, "Some Agiad dates: Pausanias and his sons", *JHS* 84 [1964], p. 142 and note 13). Charon of Lampsacus, apparently an earlier contemporary of Herodotus (*Malice* 859B, Dionysius of Halicarnassus, *On Thucydides* 5) wrote a *Persika* and a *Hellenika* (both now lost), and came from a city which subsequently had some sort of connection with Themistocles and his son, Cleophantus (see 29.11 note). Plutarch shows good historical sense in preferring the authority of the two fifth century sources.

Nepos (*Them.* 9.1) also refers to the source conflict on this point, and, like Plutarch, expresses a preference for the version of Thucydides, though for different reasons:– "I know that many have written that Themistocles crossed to Asia when Xerxes was King. But I prefer to believe Thucydides, because, of those who have left a history of that period, he was the closest in time (to Themistocles), and came from the same city".

27.1 **Ephorus, Dinon, Clitarchus, Heraclides, and many others:** These writers all belong to the fourth century. Heraclides, like Ephorus (whose version is followed by Diodorus, 11.56.5, 58.2–3), came from Cyme; Dinon, whose son was Clitarchus, from Colophon. The temptation to exploit the melodramatic possibilities of a meeting between Themistocles and his old adversary Xerxes was inevitably too strong for most historians to resist.

27.2 corresponds better with the chronological data: Plutarch seems to be referring to Greek chronological tables like those mentioned at *Solon* 27.1, rather than to Persian records. Systematic lists of dates were first drawn up by Eratosthenes (see 27.8 note).

27.2 these are not firmly in accordance with one another: The translation follows the reading συνταττομένοις, which is found in the UA group of manuscripts. S has the nominative συντεταγμένος, which is ungrammatical, and gives an unwanted perfect tense, as does Ziegler's correction, συντεταγμένοις.

27.2 Artabanus the Chiliarch: The Chiliarch, literally "commander of a thousand men", seems to have combined two functions, Chief Chamberlain, who admits to the King, and Commander of the Royal Bodyguard (cf. Nepos, *Conon* 3.2; Cook [1983], 143–44). This man is presumably the Artabanus, captain of the royal bodyguard, who (according to a story whose details are themselves rather suspicious) murdered Xerxes and attempted to kill Artaxerxes, but was himself killed in the attempt (Ctesias 60–61, Diodorus 11.69.1–6). In other words, Plutarch has immediately reverted to a source (Phanias, cited at 27.8), who followed the tradition which he has just rejected, that Xerxes was still alive, and that it was Xerxes whom Themistocles met (i.e. before Artabanus' fatal plot). At 29.2 the Chiliarch's name is given as Roxanes, who was, perhaps, Artaxerxes' Chiliarch.

27.4 prostrate oneself before him as an image of the god: Bodily prostration (προσκύνησις) before the King is the second linking motif of the Themistocles Romance in chs. 26–29 (it recurs at 28.1 and 29.3). It serves to illustrate Themistocles' supreme adaptability, through his willingness to perform an action deeply repugnant to Greek sentiment, in contrast to, e.g., the Spartans, Sperchias and Bulis, in the 470's (Hdt. 7.136), and Conon in 395 (Nepos, *Conon* 3.3).

For the Greeks prostration implied worship of a divinity (Xen. *Anab.* 3.2.13). For the Persians it did not. It was merely a formal recognition of a social superior (Hdt. 1.134; cf. R. Lane Fox, *Alexander the Great* [London, 1973], 320–22). The gesture actually performed seems to have varied from a bow and a blown kiss (cf. Cook [1983], 138, and plate 9, facing p. 36) to full bodily prostration (Hdt. 7.136). The King was not regarded by the Persians as a god, though he did rule by grace of the supreme god, Ahura Mazda (cf. Cook [1983], 67–9, 147–50).

27.6 through my efforts more men than do so now: See 28.6, 31.4 notes. Plutarch is much more specific about what Themistocles promised to do for the King at *Cimon* 18.6. So is Thucydides ("the hope he held out that he would make Greece subject to him", 1.138.2), followed as usual by Nepos (*Them.* 10.2).

27.8 the story ... told to us ... by Phanias: See chs. 26–29 introductory note.

27.8 Eratosthenes in his book *On Wealth* adds the detail ... woman of Eretria: Eratosthenes of Cyrene, c. 275–194 B.C., a noted polymath, succeeded Apollonius of Rhodes as the head of the Library of Alexandria. He compiled the first systematic tables of dates for Greek history and literature. This comparatively trivial detail may have come from a collection of examples illustrating Themistocles' ability to exploit women's influence with powerful men (see 31.2 and note). After the capture of Eretria by Darius' forces in 490 (see 11.6 note) much of its population had been deported to Susa (Hdt. 6.101, 119, *AP* 7.259).

28.2 I ... am Themistocles the Athenian: Thucydides (1.137.3–4) says that Themistocles, having travelled inland after his arrival at Ephesus, sent Artaxerxes a letter. He actually quotes part of the text of the letter *verbatim*, and summarises the rest of it. Nepos (*Them.* 9 2–4) also refers to this letter, and quotes the text in full, in words which show he is closely following the account of Thucydides.

Plutarch also follows Thucydides closely, though he has expanded the text, and turned the letter into a speech delivered by Themistocles in person before the King. This more dramatic version doubtless goes back to Phanias (see chs. 26–29 introductory note). Surprisingly perhaps, Diodorus, having brought Themistocles before the King, supplies no details of his speech (11.56.8).

28.2 now an exile pursued by the Greeks: See 25.2, 26.1 notes.

28.2 since I prevented the Greeks from pursuing them: This is a reference to the second message, supposedly sent by Themistocles to Xerxes after Salamis (see 16.2–5 and notes). It seems to have been customary for anyone seeking a favour from the King to claim that they had done him or his house some service previously (e.g. Pausanias at Thuc. 1.128.7). Thus Themistocles now claims that his message warning Xerxes to retreat back across the Hellespont bridge as quickly as possible, which Plutarch presents at 16.4–6 as a patriotically motivated stratagem, had been a genuine attempt to help the Persians.

28.5 the oracle given by Zeus at Dodona ... "namesake of the god": Plutarch seems to assume his readers will be familiar with this story, though he has not mentioned it earlier in his narrative, and it does not appear elsewhere in the surviving literature. Dodona, the site of an ancient and influential oracle of Zeus Naios, was close to Admetus' court in Epirus. Themistocles' visit to Dodona is likely to have occurred during the period of his sojourn there (see 24.2–5 and notes).

Both the god and the King enjoyed the appellation μέγας, "great", (cf. Pindar *O.* 7.34, Hdt. 1.188).

28.6 struck with admiration at his bold and spirited approach: Plutarch takes this comment virtually *verbatim* from Thucydides (1.138.1). Similarly Nepos

(*Them.* 10.1): *Huius rex animi magnitudinem admirans...* "the king, admiring his brave spirit..."

28.6 he prayed the god Arimanius: In the Zoroastrian religion of the Persians the god Ahriman, who personified the principle of evil, was set against Ormuzd, who represented the good (cf. *Moralia* 370 A–C). The invocation of deities to harm one's enemies, however, was characteristically Greek.

28.6 "I have Themistocles the Athenian." : Why *was* Artaxerxes willing to give Themistocles sanctuary and financial support (as, historically, we have to accept that he was)? It was almost certainly not a matter of gratitude for alleged benefits in the past (see 28.2 note), or any very great belief in his apparently lavish promises of services to come (see 27.6 note), though, naturally, he would have realised that Themistocles might be useful in the future.

The immediate reason most probably was, as Frost suggests (1980, 217), the considerable propaganda value which the defection of Themistocles represented, at a time when Persian prestige in the eastern Mediterranean was low, as a result of their crushing defeat at the battle of Eurymedon in c. 468 (Thuc. 1.100.1, *Cimon* 12–13). That this was the primary consideration is clearly implied by Artaxerxes' joyful night-time utterance, quoted here by Plutarch in Greek – though, presumably, expressed originally in Persian!

29.2 Roxanes the Chiliarch: See 27.2 note. Here the Chiliarch is seen in his other role, as the Commander of the Royal Bodyguard.

29.3 when he had come face to face with the King ... prostrated himself again: This *second* meeting with the King (and a second act of prostration), on the following day, is a detail which probably comes directly from Phanias' Themistocles Romance. It may have been an "improvement" of the version of Ephorus. Diodorus (11.56.8) records an initial meeting between the King and Themistocles' friend Lysitheides, acting as an intermediary, which is then followed by a meeting of the King and Themistocles face to face.

29.4 human speech was like embroidered tapestries: This became a famous comparison, cf. *Moralia* 185E.

29.5 Themistocles asked for a year ... learnt Persian ... audiences ... all by himself: This story goes back to and expands on the account of Thucydides, who makes Themistocles' request for a year's grace, before coming to see Artaxerxes, a part of his letter. Having been granted it, he learnt "as much as he could" of the Persian language and customs (1.137.4, 138.1–2). Nepos (*Them.* 9.5) follows Thucydides in reporting that the request was part of the letter Themistocles sent, but adds that he learnt Persian so thoroughly that "it is said that he conversed with the King much more ably (*commodius*) than those who were native Persians could" (*Them.* 10.1) – an exaggeration which is perhaps a misunderstanding of the source which Plutarch follows in more detail.

29.6 **the marks of honour he received ... other foreigners:** Thucydides merely says that Themistocles became more influential with the King than any previous *Greek* had been, and he does not go into details (1.138.2).

29.6 **doctrines of the Magi:** The Magi were originally a local tribe of Media (Hdt. 1.101), but they had developed a specialised religious function. When a Persian wished to sacrifice, he had to employ a Magus (Hdt. 1.132). There were Magi, employed for this purpose, in Xerxes' expedition (Hdt. 7.43), and, by incantations, they "put a spell on" the wind at Sepias (Hdt. 7.191). See Cook (1983), 154–55.

29.7 **Demaratus the Spartan:** This story provides a further illustration of Themistocles' exceptional influence with the King. The Spartan king Demaratus had been deposed in 491, and subsequently defected to the court of Darius (Hdt. 6.65–70). He had presumably participated, together with the Athenian ex-tyrant Hippias, in Datis' punitive expedition against Eretria and Athens in 490 (Hdt. 6.102, 107). He was certainly with Xerxes' forces at Thermopylae in 480, and later when they occupied Attica (Hdt. 7.101–4, 209, 234–7, 8.65). He was the senior member of a significant group of Greek exiles at the Persian court, which included Gongylus of Eretria, and the Athenians Hipparchus, son of Charmus, and Dicaeus (Thuc. 1.128.6, Xen. *Hell.* 3.1.6, *Ath. Pol.* 22.4, Lycurgus *Ag. Leoc*. 117, Hdt. 8.65).

However, such a presumptuous request seems very out of character from a man who had succeeded in staying in favour at the Persian court for some 25 years, and who is portrayed by Herodotus as careful not to offend Xerxes in 480. As Frost (1980, 219) points out, 219, this anecdote could be attached at will to any Greek exile at the King's court. Plutarch gives no indication of his source for the story, but it is attributed to the unreliable third century B.C. writer Phylarchus (see 32.4 and note) by two lexicographers (Suda, Photius, s.v.τιάρα).

On the other hand, there is no reason to doubt that Demaratus was still alive and influential at the Persian court in the mid 460's (according to Xen. *Hell.* 3.1.6 two of his descendants were still ruling territory in Asia in the 390's), and it is possible that Themistocles used Demaratus' good offices in securing the King's goodwill at the time of his request for sanctuary, i.e. that the intercession had actually been the other way round from the way it is presented in this story.

29.7 **wearing ... the tiara as the Persian kings do:** i.e. in an upright position. For the "top hat" (τιάρα or κίταρις) as a privilege of headwear restricted to the Persian kings cf. Ar. *Birds* 486–7, Xen. *Anab.* 2.5.23.

29.10 **"My children, we would be ruined now ...":** This remark is frequently quoted by Plutarch (e.g. *Moralia* 185F, 328E, 602A). The previous "ruin" was his condemnation and flight from Greece. The implication is that, if that had not occurred, and the family had remained in Athens, they would by now have been impoverished, and Themistocles' achievements forgotten.

29.11 for his bread, wine, and fish: The tripartite division of bread, wine, and ὄψον (which by the fifth century B.C. usually denoted "cooked fish" or "fish paste") was a standard method of characterising a "full" Greek meal (cf. *Odyssey* 3.479–80, Plato *Gorgias* 518C), with the most important item, bread (the "staff of life"), usually coming first in the list of three.

This conceit, applied to the King's gift of cities to Themistocles, became a very popular detail in the later Themistocles tradition. It goes back at least to the account of Thucydides (1.138.5). I have argued (*CQ* 44.2 [1994], 536–39) that it should be interpreted purely metaphorically. For his financial support Themistocles was given the tax revenues which came from these three cities, which would normally have gone to the King; and the most important of the three cities was Magnesia, which, we are told, brought him in 50 talents per year (Thuc. 1.138.5; see 31.3 and notes).

29.11 Magnesia, Lampsacus, and Myus: The city of Magnesia was situated well away from the Aegean coast, several miles up the river Maeander, and for this reason remained under Persian control in the later 460's. It clearly became Themistocles' headquarters. He had his family house there, received its tax revenues, issued a personal coinage there, died and was buried in a fine tomb there (see 31.3–6, 32.4 and notes; Thuc. 1.138.5).

Myus, however, was on the estuary of the Maeander, only a little way up the coast from Miletus, and thus by this period probably vulnerable to pressure from the Athenian fleet. It was assessed as a tribute-paying member of the Delian League in 454/3, the date of the first Tribute List (*ATL* iii [1950], p. 24, no. 100). Was it still under Persian control in 463, and, if not, how could the King "give" it to Themistocles? Gomme (1945), 292, has plausibly suggested that the gift of Myus was simply empty show, it being a place over which the King claimed, but did not actually exercise, control. It was certainly a subject-ally of Athens in 428/7 (Thuc. 3.19.1, his only mention of Myus).

Lampsacus was in an altogether different area, strategically situated on the Asiatic coast at the northern end of the Hellespont. It too features in the first Tribute List of 454/3. However, the suggestion that it also must have been a gift in name only, since Lampsacus was already a member of the Delian League, is much less plausible. An inscription of c. 200 B.C. from Lampsacus attests an annual festival there in honour of Themistocles, and refers to benefits enjoyed by his son Cleophantus and his descendants (Hill^2, p. 324, B122, Meiggs [1972], 53–54; the inscription, now lost, was originally published by H.G. Lolling in 1881). Thus the connection between Themistocles and Lampsacus must have been more than a merely nominal one.

The evidence seems to indicate that Lampsacus was still not a member of the Delian League in 463, and it may be that Artaxerxes gave it to Themistocles because its Persian-supported dynasty of Greek tyrants, going back to at least 520 B.C. (Hdt. 4.138, Thuc. 6.59.3), had recently died out. Even if Themistocles did not actually exercise political control of the city in person, there is no reason to doubt that he and his son Cleophantus received some or all of its tax revenues, or that they visited it on occasions.

It seems likely that, after Themistocles' death, when his sons were rehabilitated and returned to Athens, probably in the early 450's (see 23.1, 32.1 notes), Cleophantus renounced his claim to these revenues (so Davies [1971], 218, citing *Letter* 20.761, where the renunciation is attributed to Themistocles himself). Cleophantus' claim was surely more than just a doubtful one. He may even have persuaded the Lampsacenes to "liberate" themselves by joining the Delian League, with a tribute assessment (12 talents) which no doubt compared favourably with what they had previously been paying to the King and/or his father.

29.11 Neanthes of Cyzicus ... Phanias ... Percote and Palaiscepsis: For Neanthes see 1.2 and note. He seems to have been fond of supplying such extra topographical tit-bits.

Percote and Palaiscepsis were small towns in the Troad near Lampsacus. The temptation to expand on the original conceit proved irresistible. Thus Athenaeus (1.29f) not only includes Percote and Palaiscepsis in his list, without specifying, as Plutarch does, that they were additions by later writers, but adds a sixth gift, Gambreion, "for Themistocles' Persian clothes."

Chapter 30

This chapter has a thematic connection with the Themistocles Romance of chs. 26–29, but it also forms a self-contained unit, telling the foundation legend of Themistocles' temple of Cybele Dindymene at Magnesia. It is possible that the story came originally from the temple itself, but more likely that it too was disseminated by Themistocles' sons on their return to Athens (see 23.1, 24.2, 25.2 notes). In 400 B.C. the site of Magnesia was relocated to a more defensible position by the Spartan general Thibron (Diodorus 14.36.4), and the temple of Cybele built by Themistocles was abandoned (Strabo 14.1.40).

There seems to have been some rivalry at Magnesia between the cult of the Anatolian Great Mother, Cybele or Cybebe, and that of Artemis. At Leucophrys, near Magnesia, there was a very holy shrine of Artemis (Xen. *Hell.* 3.2.19). When Themistocles' sons returned to Athens they dedicated a statue of Artemis Leucophryne on the Acropolis (Pausanias 1.26.4), perhaps to "redress the balance" (see 22.2 note). The Artemis cult was the one which became most prominent at Magnesia after the relocation of the city.

30.1 **to the Aegean coast ... Greek affairs:** i.e. to take up his position of authority in Magnesia (see 31.3 note).

30.1 **Epixyes ... the governor:** Epixyes is an otherwise unknown satrap (governor). His plot is motivated by jealousy (see 29.5, chs. 31–32 introductory note).

30.1 **Upper Phrygia:** A region of central Anatolia, so called to distinguish it from Hellespontine Phrygia (see 6.4 note), further to the north-west.

30.1 **Pisidians:** Pisidia was a mountainous region south of Upper Phrygia, inhabited by warlike and fiercely independent tribesmen.

30.1 **Lions Head:** Leontocephalum lay to the east of Sardis, on the main road leading to it through Upper Phrygia (Appian *Mithr.* 19).

30.2 **The Mother of the Gods:** The Great Mother, Μήτηρ, was an Anatolian divinity called Cybele or Cybebe (Hdt. 5.102), whose chief sanctuary was at Pessinus in eastern Phrygia. By the later fifth century her cult had been firmly established within Greece (cf. Soph. *Phil.* 391–402), and she was sometimes identified with Rhea, mother of the Olympian gods. See E.O. James, *The Cult of the Mother Goddess* (London, 1959), 141–43, 161–174, Burkert (1985), 177–79.

30.2 **not to fall into the clutches of a lion:** Representations in art of Cybele invariably portray her in the company of a lion or lions (see e.g. E. Will, "Aspects du culte et de la légende de la Grande Mère dans le monde grec", *Eléments orientaux dans la réligion grècque* [Paris, 1960], 98–102). Thus her warning reference to a lion is appropriate. However, in the story as presented here, the lion seems to function primarily as a symbol of danger, rather than as an associate of Cybele.

30.3 **Mnesiptolema to be my maidservant:** See 30.6 and 32.2 note. She was a daughter of Themistocles by his second wife, born probably in the mid-470's (see 22.4 note [end]), who subsequently married her half-brother, Archeptolis. The shrines of female deities were normally administered by women.

30.5 **The moon did not allow them to see clearly:** This is what saved Themistocles' life. Had he been staying in the village, a better-lit and more familiar place, the assassins would have had no difficulty in locating his sleeping quarters.

30.6 **Cybele Dindymene:** This was a local cult title of the Great Mother (cf. Hdt. 1.80.1). Mount Dindymon lay to the north-east of Sardis.

Chapters 31 and 32

These chapters constitute the concluding section of the *Life*. The anecdote in chapter 31 about Themistocles and the Athenian statue in the temple of Cybele at Sardis (1–3) has a pivotal function. It refers both backwards and forwards in the narrative. It links thematically with the story of satrapal jealousy and Cybele's epiphany just related in chapter 30, and it explains why Themistocles, in Plutarch's view, subsequently restricted himself to a quiet life at his residence in Magnesia, the city which was to be the scene of his death. It also introduces the theme of the exiled Themistocles' continuing concern for his homeland, a motif which recurs more strongly at 31.5, in the account of the circumstances of, and reasons for, Themistocles' death by suicide (31.4–7).

In chapter 32 Plutarch first records the names of all Themistocles' children, both male and female, and several sons-in-law (sections 1–3). He moves on to a discussion of the two tombs of Themistocles, in Magnesia and the Piraeus (sections 4–6), and ends on an unexpected, but very effective, personal note.

31.1 When he had arrived at Sardis: That is, on his return journey from Artaxerxes' court at Susa, bound for Magnesia (see 30.1, 31.3 notes).

31.1 viewing in his spare time the architecture: As Frost (1980, 225) points out, if this story is historical, Themistocles would surely have been visiting the temple of the Mother in Sardis in order to express heartfelt thanks for his recent narrow escape from death, not in the course of the sort of leisurely tourism which appealed to Plutarch.

31.1 in the temple of the Mother: See 30.2 note. This temple of Cybele at Sardis had been burnt down by the Athenians and Ionians in 498 (Hdt. 5.101–2). In revenge Xerxes, after capturing Athens in 480, looted the temple of Athena on the Acropolis (Hdt. 8.53), and sent its statues as reparations to the rebuilt temple of Cybele.

31.1 the so-called "Water carrier" ... a bronze female figure, two cubits tall: The female ὑδροφόρος is a familiar type in Greek sculpture (see e.g. *Hesperia* 22 [1953], plate 19). Used as a standard of measure, a πῆχυς ("cubit") was the length of a forearm.

31.1 when he was superintendent of the water supply at Athens: Athens did have a water supply problem (see Mabel Lang, *Waterworks in the Athenian Agora* [Agora Excavations, Picture Book no. 11, 1968]). At the time of the plague in 430 drinking water was still being kept in storage tanks in the Piraeus, "for there were no wells there as yet" (Thuc. 2.48.2). In the later fourth century there was an elected official, τῶν κρηνῶν ἐπιμελητής, "curator of the wells" (*Ath. Pol.* 43.1), attested by inscriptions (*IG* ii2 215, *IG* ii2 338), and κρηνῶν ἐπιμεληταί are referred to by Plato (*Laws* 6.758E) and Aristotle (*Politics* 6.1321 b26) as officials needed by a city.

However, we do not know if this office at Athens went back as far as the early fifth century. There is certainly no literary or epigraphic evidence for it, and it is more likely that, at that period, such matters simply came within the general competence of the nine archons.

31.1 because he wanted to demonstrate to the Athenians ... how much ... power he enjoyed: As Frost (1980, 225) argues, this seems a most unlikely motive, given his recent narrow escape from death through the miraculous intervention of Cybele, and his as yet rather precarious position in Asia. The whole story probably came from his relatives on their return to Athens (see 23.1 [end], 24.2, 25.2 notes, ch. 30 introductory note), and formed part of their campaign to rehabilitate Themistocles in Athenian public opinion and memory (see 31.5 note).

31.1 **the governor of Lydia:** Sardis was the headquarters of the satrap of Lydia.

31.2 **Themistocles... had recourse to the harem:** The motif of Themistocles' use of women to gain personal and political favours recurs here (see 27.8 note).

31.3 **he did not travel, as Theopompus says:** The Greek is ambiguous here, but I take it that Plutarch is denying a statement of Theopompus, to the effect that Themistocles *did* "travel all over Asia" (there is a similar expression at 19.4, where Plutarch denies a comment in Aristophanes). For Theopompus see 19.1 note. It would be interesting to know more about what he had to say on this point (cf. Connor [1968], 22). Themistocles and his family certainly had some connection with Lampsacus, and probably visited it (see 29.11 note).

31.3 **substantial gifts:** A handsome income of 50 talents per year, according to Thucydides, (1.138.5).

31.3 **receiving honours equal to ... the highest Persian nobility:** This may be a reference to his issuing of a personal coinage from Magnesia (for an example see Hill[2] , C 10(a), p. 332 = Podlecki [1975], plate 3a, facing p. 176).

31.3 **the king paid no attention ... to Greek affairs:** There is no doubt that Themistocles had his family residence in Magnesia, where he clearly enjoyed a comfortable lifestyle (see 29.11 note), but it is hard to believe that, in return for the asylum, wealth, and power bestowed on him by the King, Themistocles was not expected to do anything at all for several years. Even if Artaxerxes had to deal with a revolt in Bactria soon after his accession (cf. Ctesias 62, Diodorus 11.69.2), that would in no way have entailed a total suspension of all activities on his empire's western frontier. It is likely that there was some *quid pro quo* arrangement with Themistocles, which required him to try to destabilise and subvert the loyalties of Delian League cities on the Aegean coast. Hence the choice of Magnesia as Themistocles' headquarters, conveniently situated close to Miletus and a stategically important area of Ionia.

31.4 **Athenian assistance in the revolt of Egypt:** The emphasis on Egypt at the beginning of this sentence suggests that Plutarch (or, more likely, his source) had in mind the first, and more serious, revolt in Egypt, led by Inaros against Artaxerxes, which lasted six years, and began in c. 460. The Athenians and their allies intervened in support of the rebels, diverting an expeditionary force of no less than 200 ships, which had originally been sent to fight against the Persians in Cyprus (Thuc. 1.104.1–2, 109, 110). An inscription at Athens, listing and commemorating the casualties suffered by the Erechtheid tribe in one campaigning year, "in Cyprus, Egypt and Phoenicia", probably refers to the first year of this expedition (ML, no. 33, pp. 73–6 = Fornara, no. 78, pp. 77–9).

The connection between the start of this campaign and Themistocles' suicide, which is postulated by Plutarch in this chapter (31.4–5; cf. Thucydides 1.138.4, Diodorus 11.58.2–3), thus seems to provide us with a date for Themistocles' death of 460 or 459. If we accept Plutarch's figure of 65 years for the length of his life (see 31.6 and note) we get overall dates of c. 525/524 – 460/459 for Themistocles' life. This chronology fits well enough with the few datable details of his life which we are given by our sources. Thus he would have been 32 at the time of his archonship in 493/2 (see 3.1 note), and 35 when commanding his tribal regiment at Marathon in 490 (*Aristides* 5.3). It would mean that he lived at Magnesia for about four years after his favourable reception by Artaxerxes, time enough for him to have become well established there (see 29.11 note).

The problem, however, is that Plutarch states that Cimon was "in control of the high seas" at the same time as the revolt. But, Cimon had been ostracised, probably in 461, and was thus living in less than glorious exile at the time of the first Egyptian revolt and the supporting Athenian expedition (Thucydides makes no mention of any participation in it by Cimon). His ostracism (for which see *Cimon* 17.2, 5–6, Plato *Gorgias* 516D) was the result of a strong swing in public opinion at Athens, which followed the humiliating rebuff by the Spartans of the expeditionary force which the Athenians sent to help against the helots at Ithome, and was almost certainly effected at the same time as Ephialtes' radical reform of the Areopagus, dated to the archon year 462/1 by *Ath. Pol.* 25.2 (cf. 23.6 note [end]).

There was another big expedition to Cyprus by the Athenians and their allies, about ten years later. This one *was* commanded by Cimon, now returned after his period of exile. This also consisted of 200 ships, and of these 60 were detached and sent to Egypt to help Amyrtaeus, a survivor of the 460–454 campaign, who was still holding out in the Nile delta (Thuc. 1.112.1–4). Cimon went with the main force to Cyprus and died there, at the siege of Citium (Thuc. 1.112.4). The implication of Thucydides' brief narrative is that this Cyprus campaign, and the associated sideshow in Egypt, lasted for just one campaigning season (though Diodorus, 12.3.1– 4.4, assigns it to two archon years, 450/49 and 449/8).

That Plutarch in this chapter is actually thinking of this later expedition, and thus implicitly dating the death of Themistocles to 450 or 449, is suggested by his account of it in *Cimon* 18–19, where (unlike Thucydides) he strongly emphasises Cimon's personal success (cf. also Diodorus 12.3.1– 4.4), and is more explicit that it was this expedition with which Themistocles' suicide was connected (*Cimon* 18.5–6). Thus Plutarch's implied dates for Themistocles' life would seem to be c. 515/514 – 450/449 (see R. Flacelière,

"Sur quelques points obscurs de la vie de Thémistocle", *REA* 55 [1953], 15–19).

However, such a chronology can hardly be right in fact. It would mean that Themistocles was only 22 at the time of his archonship, and that he spent no less than 15 years in Asia, not dying or committing suicide until hostilities on a major scale had been going on between Athens and the King for over ten years – surely very unlikely.

There is a strong possibility that Plutarch has erroneously conflated into one expedition the two different mid-fifth century campaigns in Cyprus and Egypt. The first expedition, though it reached Cyprus and Cilicia, does not seem, to judge from Thucydides' account, to have stayed there very long, and subsequently it was totally and heavily occupied in Egypt for six years. Conversely, the later expedition was concerned primarily with Cyprus. Thucydides' account of it suggests the activities in Egypt were very much subordinate to the main strategy, and Diodorus does not mention Egypt at all in his account of this later campaign. Plutarch's prominent mention of Egypt at the beginning of 31.4 suggests that his ultimate source for the date of the death of Themistocles was actually referring to, and connecting it with, the first Athenian expedition, for which help for the revolt in Egypt became the overriding priority. This would also have been the first occasion on which Themistocles' relationship with Artaxerxes was, or could be thought to have been, plunged into crisis. His narrative, however, has also been influenced by another, and strongly pro-Cimon, tradition (to be seen more clearly in his *Life of Cimon*), which glossed over Cimon's ostracism, magnified his personal success in the Cyprus campaign, brought him to Egypt as well as Cyprus (*Cimon* 18.6–7 even adds a visit to the oracle of Ammon), gave him a heroic death from a wound, rather than as a result of illness (*Cimon* 19.1), and made Themistocles' despairing suicide (see 31.5 note) the result of his jealousy of Cimon's unbroken success (*Cimon* 18.6). The chronological obscurity of this chapter is probably the result of an attempt (either by Plutarch or his immediate source) to combine these two divergent traditions.

31.4 to make good his promises, by applying himself ... to the Greek problem: See 27.6 note. For obvious narrative reasons Plutarch plays down, and is vague about the nature of, these promises in the *Themistocles* (a brief allusion only at 27.6; contrast his treatment at *Cimon* 18.5–6). Themistocles had presumably promised *something*, but it is unlikely that he had gone as far as the other sources suggest. He was a supreme realist, who must have known there was no prospect at that time of bringing about the subjection of the whole of Greece to Persia, nor would Artaxerxes have believed any such vaunting. See 31.3 note for a consideration of what he could reasonably have been expected to achieve at Magnesia.

31.5 **conducting the war:** It is rather improbable that Themistocles, a 65 year old Greek, would have been asked to play an active military role in command of the Persian army which was being sent to Egypt to deal with the nationalist revolt and the Athenian intervention in support of it. As we would expect, the commander was in fact a Persian, Megabyzus (Thuc. 1.109.3–4).

31.5 **to put a fitting end to his life. :** Thucydides (1.138.4) refers to the suicide tradition, but rejects it. He says Themistocles died a natural death, through illness. Nepos (*Them.* 10.4) again chooses to follow Thucydides (see 27.1 note).

It seems very likely that the tradition of Themistocles' death by suicide originated with the sons and family of Themistocles, who, on their return to Athens (see 23.1 note [end]), put it about in public speeches and private conversations, in an attempt to rehabilitate his memory. This original version stressed his honourable and patriotic motivation, and it is this version which, naturally, is highlighted by Plutarch here. Themistocles killed himself in a heroic fashion, to avoid having to take up arms against his fellow countrymen. At some stage an even more pro-Themistocles version got into circulation. According to this, as reported by Diodorus (11.58.2–3), the King invited Themistocles to take command of a second expedition against Greece. Themistocles agreed to do so, but only on condition that the King promised not to send the expedition without him. Having secured this guarantee, Themistocles committed suicide, thus forcing the King to abandon his plan. So Themistocles actually saved Greece a second time!

Themistocles' political enemies at Athens (see 22.4, 23.1 notes) seem to have countered the favourable family tradition, not by arguing that in fact he had just died as a result of an illness, but by accepting the suicide story but assigning to it a discreditable motive:– Themistocles committed suicide *out of despair* at his inability to make good the treasonable promises he had made to the King, and/or *through jealousy* at the military successes of his rival, their hero Cimon (see 31.4 note [end]). This version is referred to by Plutarch here, but only as a less likely possibility (ἴσως μέν). However, it is the only one recorded by him at *Cimon* 18.5–6, and the discreditable motive is the only one mentioned by Thucydides at 1.138.4.

Thus "death by suicide" became an agreed tradition in both the pro- and anti-Themistocles camps. Its general acceptance was helped by the fact that, in the absence of autopsies in the ancient world, it was always possible to suggest that the sudden or unexpected death of a famous man, which was not obviously due to violence or an accident, was the result of poison.

On the factual issue, Thucydides is probably correct. Themistocles was still no doubt a wily political operator. It was perhaps at his suggestion that the Persian Megabazus was sent to bribe the Spartans to invade Attica during the period of the Egyptian campaign (Thuc. 1.109.2–3). However, at 65, he was surely too old to play an active military role (see 31.4 note), and thus, since the prospect did not arise, he could not have been terminally worried about not being up to it. Conversely, the fact that the Persian authorities were happy to see Themistocles' honours at Magnesia continue long after his death (see 32.4 and note; Thuc. 1.138.5, Diodorus 11.58.1, Nepos *Them.* 10.3) strongly suggests that, in their eyes, there had been nothing strikingly anti-Persian about his death either. Thus neither of the postulated motives for his supposed suicide is very plausible. It seems most likely that Themistocles died a natural death, as Thucydides claims, through an "illness", whose effect was perhaps unusually rapid, maybe a sudden massive heart attack or stroke. See my article, "The Death of Themistocles", in *Greece and Rome* xlii, 2 (1995), 159–67.

31.6 **he drank bull's blood:** Bull's blood is actually harmless to drink, but the Greeks seem to have firmly believed it was "poisonous" because it congeals quickly, and thus was thought to produce a lethal choking effect in the stomach and throat if swallowed (Aristotle *Hist. Anim.* 3.19, Pliny *NH* 11.222). It is significant that this was supposedly the method of death chosen by the Egyptian king Psammenitus (Psamtik the Third), the son of Amasis, after his failed revolt against the Persian king Cambyses in c. 525 (Hdt. 3.15). It thus had strong connotations of heroic, anti-Persian defiance.

This particularly lurid (and obviously popular) version of Themistocles' death (found also in Diodorus, 11.58.3) was not (*pace* Atticus in Cicero's *Brutus*, 42–3) a fiction made up by later sensationalising Greek historians, such as Clitarchus and Stratocles. It was current as early as 424 (cf. Ar. *Knights* 83–4).

31.6 **He died... at the age of sixty five:** We do not know from what source Plutarch got this figure, let alone how reliable it is. Though unattested elsewhere, it may be correct. He had access to a direct family tradition (see 32.1, 32.6 notes).

32.1 **Themistocles left three sons ... excellent horseman:** The Greek word ἀπέλιπε ("left") implies both "alive" and "legally his". In fact he had five sons in all, apparently all by his first wife Archippe. Of these the eldest, Neocles (it was a common practice to call one's first son after one's father), died in boyhood from a septic horse-bite. It is worth noting this family interest in horse breeding (Cleophantus is described as an excellent horseman at Plato *Meno* 93D–E), which was an expensive pastime affordable only by the wealthy, landed gentry. Themistocles' second son, Diocles, was legally adopted by his maternal grandfather Lysander, presumably because Lysander had no sons of his own. Having changed his *genos*, he therefore did not have to go into exile with his father and younger brothers. He was enrolled in his grandfather's deme, Alopece, which, ironically, was the deme of Themistocles' bitterest enemies, the Alcmaeonids.

Themistocles' three other sons went into exile along with him (see 23.1 note), but Cleophantus certainly (cf. Plato *Meno* 93D), and Polyeuctus almost certainly (cf. Pausanias 1.1.2, 1.26.4) returned to Athens, probably in the early 450's (see Davies [1971], 218), where their rights of citizenship were restored, and they seem to have regained some of their property. Archeptolis may also have returned, but more likely he remained in Magnesia, taking charge of the family property there, since he married his half-sister Mnesiptolema, who was the priestess of the Magnesian temple of Cybele Dindymene (30.2,6, 32.2 and notes).

Much of Plutarch's information about Themistocles' family may have come from the friend of his student days, a direct descendant of the great man (see 32.6 and note).

32.2 **He had several daughters ... born to his second wife:** Themistocles' second wife is not named by our sources. By her he apparently had five daughters – an interesting symmetry! He must have married his first wife, Archippe, before 490, since some of his sons were old enough to have a tutor (παιδαγωγός) in 480 (see 12.4, Hdt. 8.65). Probably Archippe died. Given the strength of the anti-Themistocles tradition, we should have expected a mention of marital discord and a divorce to appear in our sources, if any such potentially discrediting event had occurred.

Themistocles married his second wife probably in the 470's, and certainly before his ostracism, since the names Mnesiptolema ("memorial of the war") and Nicomache ("victory in battle") imply a period when the choice of such significant, self-advertising names was still expected to have populist appeal. She therefore must be the wife referred to at 24.6, who left Athens to join him in exile in Epirus. There is no reason to think she was not Athenian. No doubt she also joined him subsequently in Magnesia, where their youngest daughter was born, as her name, Asia, clearly indicates. Italia and Sybaris were probably born while the family was in Epirus, when Themistocles still had hopes of a new life and career in the Greek West, before the death of Hieron of Syracuse (see 24.7 note).

32.2 **Mnesiptolema ... married to Archeptolis, her half-brother by a different mother:** Marriages between children of the same father (ὁμοπάτριοι) were allowed at Athens. Those between children of the same mother (ὁμομήτριοι) were not (cf. A.R W. Harrison, *The Law of Athens 1* [1968], p. 22, note 3). The marriages of Archeptolis and Mnesiptolema, and Phrasicles and Nicomache (see 32.3), were doubtless arranged in order to keep the estate within the family rather than allow it to be diminished through dowries. For Mnesiptolema see 30.3 note. For the Greeks priesthood was not a distinct, full-time vocation, and it was not uncommon for priests and priestesses to be married (cf. Burkert [1985], 95–8).

32.2 Nicodemus the Athenian: Νικόδημος is the reading of S. The other manuscripts have Νικομήδης (Nicomedes). There is similar manuscript confusion at *Ath. Pol.* 22.7 over the name of the man who was archon in 483/2, the year of Themistocles' Naval Bill (see 4.1–3 and notes). These may be the same man, but there is too much uncertainty over the form of the names to allow us to make the identification with any confidence.

32.3 his nephew Phrasicles: The word ἀδελφιδοῦς usually means "brother's son". It is interesting to discover that the great Themistocles probably had a brother (apparently not exiled along with him, since Phrasicles, his son, had clearly been resident in Athens before "sailing", as we are told, to marry Nicomache), who has remained totally unknown to history.

32.3 given ... by her brothers: The marriage of Phrasicles and Nicomache seems to have occurred almost immediately after Themistocles' death, and some time before his sons were formally recalled to Athens. Plutarch's account implies that Phrasicles, his wife, and the young Asia returned to Athens straight after the marriage. It does not seem that Themistocles' daughters were ever legally barred from Athens and Attica.

A man called Phrasicles (D.H. *AR* 10.1.1, *Moralia* 835C), or Phrasiclides (Diodorus 11.77.1) was archon eponymous at Athens in 460/59. He may well have been the nephew and son-in-law of Themistocles mentioned here (so E. Badian, "Archons and *Strategoi*", *Antichthon* 5 [1971], 34). If so, his influence must surely have been significant in getting Themistocles' sons recalled soon afterwards.

32.4 The Magnesians have a splendid tomb of Themistocles in their market place: Thucydides refers to a monument (μνημεῖον) to Themistocles in the *agora* at Magnesia (1.138.5). Diodorus (11.58.1) also refers to a monument, "which remains to this day". It seems that this tomb was surmounted by a statue of Themistocles (Nepos *Them.* 10.3) in a heroic pose, which is depicted on a Magnesian coin of the Antonine period (see Hill², C 10(b), p. 332 = Podlecki [1975], plate 3c, facing p. 176). The site of Magnesia was moved for greater security by the Spartan general Thibron in 400 B.C. (Diodorus 14.36.4), but no doubt the monument was moved with it. For an individual to be buried, not just within the walls, but in the heart of the city, was an exceptional honour (cf. Thuc. 5.11.1, *Theseus* 36.4, Cicero *ad Fam.* 4.12.3).

32.4 As for his actual remains ... Andocides ... in his Address to his Comrades: Thucydides (1.138.6), cited and followed by Nepos (*Them.* 10.5), makes it clear that Themistocles, as someone who had been convicted of treason (see 23.1 note; he was probably an *atimos*), could not legally be buried in Attica (cf. Xen. *Hell.* 1.7.22). His exile continued even after his death. In the same passage Thucydides reports that there was a current story, which came directly from Themistocles' relatives (φασὶ ... οἱ προσήκοντες) to the effect that, at his request, his bones had been brought back from Magnesia, and secretly buried in Attica. Presumably the location was still a secret at the time Thucydides was writing, since, otherwise, he could have checked the site personally and confirmed the story. Plutarch does not refer explicitly to this tradition, but he does have it in his mind in this section of the narrative.

Andocides' *Address to his Comrades*, a work (now lost) probably written shortly before 415, was, on Plutarch's testimony, an inflammatory oligarchic pamphlet, which apparently played up the supposed fickleness and ingratitude of the Athenian *demos* towards its former leaders and saviours. Though Plutarch here rejects Andocides' account, it is not completely clear whether he is rejecting just the added detail that the Athenians desecrated Themistocles' remains, or the whole tradition that his remains were surreptitiously removed from Magnesia (see 32.5 note). Andocides' claim may have had some historical basis. Possibly, when the rumours of a transfer and secret burial of Themistocles' remains by his relatives first circulated in Athens, a grave (unmarked) was dug up by some zealots, and the bones in it scattered, in the belief that they were those of "the traitor" Themistocles. For such desecration cf. Thuc.1.126.12 (Alcmaeonids), Lycurgus *Ag. Leocr.* 113–15 (Phrynichus).

A scholion (provenance unknown) on Ar. *Knights* 84 refers to an undercover removal from Magnesia of Themistocles' bones by "the Athenians", who had been told by Apollo, when they were suffering from a plague (presumably the Great Plague which affected Athens in two outbreaks between 430 and 426; see Thuc. 2.47–54, 3.87), to bring home the bones of Themistocles. This story implies that the return of his remains was the result of an official decision rather than an illicit family enterprise. However, if that were the case, Thucydides would surely have mentioned it at 1.138.6, and in the reference to Themistocles at Ar. *Knights* 819 (φεύγει τὴν γῆν) the present tense seems to imply that he was still officially an exile in 424.

Although Themistocles' *atimia* was probably never formally repealed, it does seem that he had been rehabilitated in practice by the end of the fifth century. This was certainly the tradition current in Pausanias' day (1.1.2), and the lines of Plato the comic poet, written not later than the early fourth century (see 32.6 and note), strongly suggest that by then the "tomb of Themistocles" in the Piraeus was well known, and at least tolerated by the state, if not officially sanctioned.

32.4 **Phylarchus too:** Phylarchus of Athens was a third century B.C. historian, with marked rhetorical and dramatising tendencies (see 29.7 note; *Moralia* 345C). Plutarch rejects as a fiction his story involving Themistocles' sons (without, however, telling us what it was), because of the names Phylarchus gives them. Neocles died in childhood, and so cannot have been involved in an incident occurring after his father's death, and Demopolis was not a name which Plutarch could find attested anywhere in his other sources for a son of Themistocles.

Frost (1980), 234 (cf. "Phylarchus, fragment 76", *AJP* 83 [1962], 419–22), suggests that Phylarchus' story was the same as the one recorded by the Suda, s.v. Θεμιστοκλέους παῖδες, which refers to Neocles and Demopolis competing incognito at some funeral games at Athens. But then, having won, they were recognised, and were in danger of being stoned to death by Themistocles' enemies on the grounds that they were exiles. However, it is not clear what connection this story as it stands has with Themistocles' *remains and tomb*, which constitute the linking motif throughout sections 4–6 of this chapter. Possibly Phylarchus' story also included some sort of dramatic public debate at Athens about the fate of the supposed bones or tomb of Themistocles.

32.4 **virtually erects a theatrical machine within his history, as though it were a tragedy:** For this comparison (which Plutarch seems fond of) see 10.1 and note.

32.5 **Diodorus the Topographer in his work *On Tombs*... as an inference ... the tomb of Themistocles:** Diodorus was a third century B.C. antiquarian writer who also wrote a work *On the Demes* (cf. Whitehead [1986], 53–4 and note 68). He is cited as an apparently reliable authority by Plutarch at *Cimon* 16.1. The "inference" of Diodorus was that the Piraeus tomb was that of Themistocles. Thus the tomb must still have been unlabelled at the time he was writing. As a resident of Athens, who must have visited the site, he could have read the epitaph, if there had been one inscribed, thus "knowing for sure" that it was the tomb of Themistocles. His inference was presumably based on local tradition, as well as the words of Plato the comic writer. Nepos (*Them.* 10.3) refers to two surviving monuments of Themistocles, the statue in Magnesia (see 32.4 note) and *sepulcrum prope oppidum in quo est sepultus*, "a tomb near the town, in which he is buried". This is ambiguous, but he is probably referring to the Piraeus tomb (cf. Nepos *Miltiades* 4.2 for *oppidum* = Athens).

By the time of Pausanias, c.170 A.D., the Piraeus tomb was clearly labelled as that of Themistocles (1.1.2), doubtless because by then it had become a tourist attraction.

32.5 **near the great harbour of the Piraeus a sort of elbow juts out from the promontory facing Alcimus:** This is the only mention of Alcimus in ancient literature, though now "Alcimus" is the name given to a small promontory on the Acte peninsula, i.e. on the southern side of the entrance to the main ("great") harbour. If we assume that Plutarch is quoting Diodorus accurately, and translate κατά as "opposite", "facing" (surely the natural sense here), this would mean that Diodorus located the tomb on the northern side of the entrance to the harbour, just west of Eetioneia.

However, this does not appear to be the correct location (see P. Wallace, "The Tomb of Themistocles in the Piraeus", *Hesperia* 41 [1972], 451–62).

The mistake is probably that of Plutarch, quoting slightly inaccurately, rather than Diodorus'. The remains of what is almost certainly the tomb referred to by Diodorus, situated on a site on the *southern side* of the entrance to the main harbour, in what is now an area of officially restricted access, have been described by Wallace. There is a square foundation of ashlar masonry, approached by a walkway to the south east corner. It contains a now mostly submerged stone sarcophagus in the south west corner. However, much of the tomb, including an inscription which gets the name of Themistocles' father wrong (reading NIKOKLEOS instead of NEOKLEOS), is the product of later reconstruction.

Possibly because of what his student friend (32.6 and note) had told him, Plutarch seems distinctly hesitant about accepting the identity of the Piraeus tomb as being that of Themistocles. Surprisingly, perhaps (cf. 8.3, 22.3 and notes), he does not appear to have visited the site himself. Nevertheless, it does not seem unreasonable to suppose, if we accept that Plato's lines do refer to Diodorus' Piraeus tomb, that, in popular belief at least, this was "the tomb of Themistocles" at the end of the fifth century. Whether it really did contain the remains of the great man is another, and unanswerable, question.

32.6 **Plato the comic poet:** A rival and almost exact contemporary of Aristophanes. The lines are iambic trimeters.

32.6 **on a lovely site:** It was also a most appropriate one for the man who founded Athenian naval power, and made Piraeus what it still is today, *the* harbour of Athens (see 4.4, 19.3–5 and notes, Thuc. 1.93.4–8).

32.6 **every trireme race:** ἅμιλλ(α) refers to trireme racing (cf.Thuc. 6.3.2). At the Piraeus the race seems to have been between the great harbour and that of Munychia (*IG*ii2 1006, 29–30). There was also a trireme race at Sunium (Lysias 21.5).

32.6 **a Themistocles of Athens who became my ... friend:** After quoting Plato's fine valedictory tribute, Plutarch closes his *Life of Themistocles* with an attractive finishing touch of his own. We learn that, more than 500 years after the death of the great Themistocles, his memory was still kept tangibly alive in Magnesia, and that a direct descendant of his, also called Themistocles, had been a personal friend of the biographer at the time when he was a young student in Athens (cf. *Moralia* 626 E–F).

The "honours" referred to here presumably took the form of a hereditary pension.

32.6 **school of Ammonius the philosopher:** Ammonius came originally from Egypt. He was a Platonist, whose school at Athens Plutarch attended in the late 60's A.D., when he was about twenty years old. After becoming a citizen, Ammonius played a prominent role in Athenian public life, holding the prestigious post of hoplite general three times. He appears on numerous occasions in Plutarch's works (cf. *Moralia* 385Bff, 645Dff, 720Cff, 736Dff);

see C.P. Jones, "The Teacher of Plutarch", *HSCP* 71 (1966), 205–15. Like Plutarch (after he was granted honorary Athenian citizenship), and his pupil Themistocles, Ammonius belonged to the tribe Leontis, that of the great Themistocles (see 1.1 and note).

Index of persons and places

The page numbers listed are those of the Introduction and Commentary sections. Themistocles, Athens, Attica, Persia, Greece, and simple author references are not included.

Persons

Acestorides 5, 104
Adeimantus of Corinth 88, 98, 139
Admetus 135, 140-1, 145, 148, 151
Aeacus 110
Aeschylus 5, 78, 100, 102, 106-10, 131, 140
Aesop 128
Ahura Mazda 150
Alcibiades 134
Alcmaeon 133-4
Alcmaeonids 72, 74, 84, 96-7, 102, 131, 133, 162, 165
Ameinias 108, 114
Ammonius 1, 116, 167-8
Anaxagoras 73
Andocides 6, 98, 118-9, 164-5
Antiphates 116
Apollo 93, 110-1, 114, 124, 128, 165
Archeptolis 156, 163
Archippe, wife of T. 162-3
Architeles 89
Ariamenes 108
Arimanius 152
Aristides 4-5, 75-6, 81-4, 95-7, 103-4, 110, 112, 118-9, 123, 126-7, 132, 134, 139
Ariston 5, 76
Aristophanes 5, 121, 158, 167
Aristotle 5, 71, 94-5, 110, 138
Arnaces 113
Artabanus 150
Artaxerxes 144-5, 148-50, 152, 155, 157-60
Artayctes 105-6
Artemis 90, 128-9, 155
Artemisia 108-9
Arthmius of Zeleia 85
Asia, daughter of T. 163-4
Athena 120-1, 157
Athenaeus 70, 155
Autobulus 1
Camillus 2, 68-9, 84, 86, 134
Cecrops 121
Charon of Lampsacus 6, 149
Cheileos 86
Cimon 5, 70, 73, 76, 80, 85, 102, 111, 117, 119, 122, 125, 131-5, 141, 159-61
Cleidemus 5, 94-5
Cleisthenes 69-70, 94, 132
Cleophantus 80, 146, 149, 154-5, 162-3
Clitarchus 6, 149, 162
Craterus 85, 130, 133-5, 138
Critias 146
Cybele 101, 155-8, 163
Darius 78, 85, 108, 151, 153
Demaratus 97, 109, 136, 153
Dicaeus 109, 153
Dinon 6, 149
Diocles 162
Diodorus Siculus 5, 6, 100, 102, 108, 113-4, 118, 130, 132, 134, 137, 147, 151, 160-1
Diodorus the topographer 6, 166-7
Dionysius of Syracuse 143
Dionysus 81, 106, 109
Diphilides 80
Ephialtes 135, 138, 159
Ephorus 5-6, 102, 118, 132, 135-8, 149, 152
Epicles 80
Epicrates 141-2
Epicydes 84

Epixyes 156
Eratosthenes 6, 150-1
Erechtheus/Erichthonius 92-3
Ergoteles 147-8
Euphrantides 106
Euripides 140
Eurybiades 74, 88-9, 98-9, 112, 143
Euterpe 71
Gelon 88, 142-3
Habrotonon 70, 72
Hadrian 2
Heracles 72, 104
Heraclides 6, 149
Herodotus 4-6, 69-71, 74, 77-8, 84, 87-8, 92-4, 98, 100, 102, 104-5, 108-15, 125
Hieron 141-3, 163
Hipparchus, son of Charmus 97, 134, 153
Hippias 97, 136, 153
Iacchus 109-10
Idomeneus of Lampsacus 135
Ion of Chios 73, 106
Italia, daughter of T. 143, 163
Lamprias 1
Leobotes 133, 138
Leonidas 89, 91, 119
Leontis tribe 69-70, 168
Leotychidas 123, 126
Leto 128
Lycomedes 110
Lycomidae/Lycomids 69, 72, 110-1, 129
Lysitheides 148, 152
Magi 153
Mardonius 79
Megabyzus 161
Megacles 96
Melissus 73-4
Miltiades 76, 79-80, 117, 125
Mnesiphilus 74, 98
Mnesiptolema 132, 156, 163
Neanthes 5, 71, 155
Neocles, father of T. 68-70, 72
Neocles, son of T. 80, 162, 165-6
Nepos, Cornelius 2, 6, 69 71, 100, 149, 152, 161, 166
Nicagoras 94
Nicodemus 164
Nicogenes 148
Nicomache 132, 163-4
Panaetius 104
Pausanias the Spartan regent 85, 90, 126-7, 133-7, 142
Pausanias the traveller 165-6
Pelagon 88
Periander 139
Pericles 6, 70, 72-3, 77, 95, 119
Phanias 5, 70-1, 89, 105-6, 147, 150-2, 155
Phanodemus 5, 104
Philaids 76, 80-1, 110, 125
Philoctetes 90
Phrasicles 163-4
Phrynichus the politician 165
Phrynichus the tragedian 81, 131
Phthia 141
Phylarchus 6, 153, 165-6
Pindar 5, 90
Pisistratids 132
Plato the comic poet 6, 165-7
Plato the philosopher 5, 75, 79, 116
Polyarchus/Polycritus 119
Polyeuctus 163
Poseidon 114, 120-1
Psammenitus 162
Pythodorus 147-8
Roxanes 150, 152
Sandauce 105
Sicinnus 100-2, 113
Simonides 5, 72, 82, 90, 111, 126, 142
Solon 2, 74, 83, 138
Sophanes/Socles 108
Stesileos 76
Stesimbrotus 5, 73, 79, 141-2
Sybaris, daughter of T. 143, 163
Themistocles, descendant of T. 167-8
Theophrastus 5, 71, 138-9, 142-3, 147

Theopompus 5, 118-9, 146-7, 158
Theseus 2, 94, 131
Thucydides 5-6, 120, 149, 159, 165
Timocreon 5, 80, 126-8
Trajan 2, 115
Xanthippus 95-6, 118, 126
Xerxes 75, 78-9, 84, 100-2, 104-6, 108-9, 111-2, 144-5, 149-51, 153, 157
Zeus 151

Places

Acarnania 71, 139
Acharnae 141
Acropolis (of Athens) 68, 82, 85, 92, 95, 106, 155, 157
Aegina/Aeginetans 76, 78, 86, 93, 96, 99, 103, 110, 114, 119, 137
Aeolis/Aeolian 147
Alcimus 166
Alexandria 151
Alopece 133, 162
Amphicytonic Council 123-5, 133
Andros 112, 125
Areopagus 94-5, 135, 138, 159
Argos/Argolid/Argives 80, 94, 124-5, 133, 136-7, 142-3, 145
Artemisium 87-91, 99, 101, 107, 110
Asia 142, 144, 146-9, 153, 158
Boeotia/Boeotians 1, 78, 90-2
Byzantium 127
Caria 71
Ceos 76, 82
Ceramicus 68, 74
Chaeronea 1
Chalcis/Chalcidians 78, 87-8, 107
Chersonese 79
Cilicia 160
Corcyra 138-43, 145
Corinth/Corinthians 78, 82, 90, 138-9
Cyme 147, 149
Cynosarges 71-2
Cynosura 104-5
Cyprus 127, 158-60
Deceleia 108
Delos/Delian League 85, 89, 122, 125, 127, 131, 144, 154-5, 158
Delphi 2, 90, 104, 114, 124
Dodona 151
Egypt/Egyptian 102, 158-62, 167
Eleusis 104, 109
Ephesus 144-8, 151
Epirus 139-41, 144-5, 148, 151, 163
Eresus 71
Eretria 99, 151, 153
Euboea 87-8, 90, 125
Euripus 88, 91
Halicarnassus/ian 70-1, 109
Hellespont 84, 86, 112, 118, 151, 154
Hermione 80
Hestiaea 90
Ialysus 126-8
Ionia/Ionians 91, 124, 126-7, 144-5, 157-8
Isthmus 91-2, 98-9, 114, 128
Lampsacus 149, 154-5, 158
Laureum 77
Leucas 139
Lydia 158
Maeander 154
Magnesia 87, 130, 137, 145, 154-60, 162-5, 167
Marathon 76, 78-9, 83-4, 99, 159
Megara/Megarians 99
Melite 70, 129
Miletus 154, 158
Mycale 118, 124, 126-7
Myus 154
Naxos 117, 135, 144-5
Olizon 90
Olympia/Olympic Festival/Games 80, 115, 143
Pagasae 123
Pallene 108

Paros 76, 79
Peloponnese/Peloponnesians 91, 98, 112, 119, 133, 139
Phalerum 100
Phlya 72, 110, 129
Phocis/Phocians 91
Phoenicia/Phoenicians 91, 108, 158
Phrearrhioi 69, 70, 72, 74, 81, 110, 129
Phrygia 85, 101, 156
Piraeus 117-8, 120-1, 131, 157, 165-7
Pisidia 156
Plataea 79-80, 126-7
Pnyx 122
Psyttaleia 103, 105
Pydna 144-5
Rhodes 126
Salamis 5, 71, 74, 78-81, 84, 88-9, 92-6, 98-100, 102-3, 105-7, 109-10, 112, 114, 115-7, 125, 131-2, 139, 151
Sardis 84, 148, 156-8
Sciathos 88
Scyros 131
Seriphos 116
Sestos 118
Sicily 142-3
Siris 98
Sparta/Spartans 86, 88, 91, 98, 101, 111, 114-20, 123-6, 133, 136-7, 139, 153, 155, 159, 161
Susa 84, 151, 157
Syracuse 88, 142-3, 163
Tempe 84, 86-7, 96
Tenedos/Tenos 104
Thasos 144-5
Thebes/Thebans 91, 124-5
Thermopylae 87, 89-92, 96, 124, 153
Thespiae 102
Thessaly 86-7, 124, 126
Thrace/Thracian 70, 145
Thriasian Plain 109
Troezen 80, 87, 93-4, 103